STRATEGIC CONFLICT

Strategic Conflict offers a research-based, accessible analysis of how people can manage conflict productively. Moving beyond the basics of conflict, it examines interpersonal situations in which conflict occurs and promotes strategic communicative responses based on the latest theoretical research. Daniel J. Canary and Sandra Lakey add personal observations and samples of actual interaction to provide concrete illustrations of the research findings. This comprehensive volume provides students with the tools to understand conflict in real-world contexts.

Daniel J. Canary is Professor in the Hugh Downs School of Human Communication at Arizona State University and has previously taught at Penn State University, Ohio University, Cal State Fullerton, and Florida Tech. His research interests include conflict communication, conversational argument, relational maintenance behaviors, and sex differences and similarities in communication.

Sandra Lakey is Associate Professor of Communication and Composition and head of the Communication and Literature Department at Pennsylvania College of Technology. She previously taught at Lycoming College and C. S. Mott Community College. Her research interests include conflict communication, communication competence, and classroom communication.

Routledge Communication Series
Jennings Bryant/Dolf Zillmann, Series Editors

Selected titles include:

- Frey: *Group Communication in Context: Studies of Bona Fide Groups, Second Edition*
- Bucy/Holbert: *The Sourcebook for Political Communication Research*
- Heath/Bryant: *Human Communication Theory and Research, Second Edition*
- Stacks/Salwen: *An Integrated Approach to Communication Theory and Research, Second Edition*
- Rubin et al.: *Communication Research Measures II*
- Frey/Cissna: *Routledge Handbook of Applied Communication Research*
- Hollingshead/Poole: *Research Methods for Studying Groups and Teams*

STRATEGIC CONFLICT

*Daniel J. Canary and
Sandra Lakey*

*With contributions by
Jennifer Marmo*

Routledge
Taylor & Francis Group

NEW YORK AND LONDON

First published 2013
by Routledge
711 Third Avenue, New York, NY 10017

Simultaneously published in the UK
by Routledge
2 Park Square, Milton Park, Abingdon, Oxon OX14 4RN

Routledge is an imprint of the Taylor & Francis Group, an informa business

Library of Congress Cataloging in Publication Data
    Strategic conflict / Daniel J. Canary and Sandra Lakey.
    p. cm.
    1. Interpersonal conflict. 2. Interpersonal communication.
    3. Conflict management. I. Canary, Daniel J. II. Lakey, Sandra.
    BF637.I48S77 2012
    303.6'9—dc23
    2011044906

ISBN: 978–0–8058–5063–5 (hbk)
ISBN: 978–0–8058–5064–2 (pbk)
ISBN: 978–0–203–14874–7 (ebk)

Typeset in Bembo
by Swales & Willis Ltd, Exeter, Devon

Printed and bound in the United States of America by Walsworth Publishing Company, Marceline, MO.

This book is dedicated to Donald and Nancy Canary
for their constant love and positive example,
and to Isaiah, Kylar, and Orion Potter,
for whom the journey has just begun.

CONTENTS

PREFACE

Conflict is inevitable in ongoing interpersonal relationships. The presence of conflict is not in itself a problem; the problem in many relationships is that the two people involved handle the conflict badly, often behaving mindlessly, without thinking about their choices or the consequences. This book focuses on how readers can apply research-based conclusions and suggestions to become more strategic in conflict interactions. For us, this book represents our own steps toward applying theoretic and empirical knowledge. The research on conflict management is vast and nuanced, so we do not claim inclusiveness in our presentation of the literature. Rather we claim representativeness as we offer implications regarding what sound strategic conflict behavior looks like.

It should come as no surprise that some conclusions and suggestions are repeated. The reader might become immune to the advice of employing cooperative and direct tactics. What is revealing perhaps is that this repetition occurs because similar conclusions and suggestions evolve from alternative areas of study. Given the breadth of the research, then, this convergence leads to greater validity for the suggestions offered.

As always, however, each reader must decide what is best for him or her. The empirical research draws inferences from samples that are more or less representative of their larger populations. Accordingly, our conclusions and suggestions often represent averages of individuals. Readers must ascertain whether the average applies to them. The research indicates that it often does.

Instructors who use this book should find the suggestions and conclusions helpful when students want to know the relevance of the theoretic knowledge for them. Instructors can indicate that the conclusions and findings represent the average and ask whether students find similar or even alternative advice from different sources—including personal experience. Indeed, some instructors might want to test our conclusions and suggestions by asking whether they apply to them and to their students. We imagine that even though many students will agree with the ideas presented here, answers will vary in some cases.

Two features of this book are designed to make the theory and research come alive. The first is our use of actual interaction. Actual interactions portray how communication unfolds in time in realistic ways. Authors might be good at creating dialogue to make their points, but what people really say provides immediate recognition of voice that people can only create themselves during an interaction. The second feature is the student stories. These stories, selected from sections of an upper-division conflict communication class at Arizona State University, provide a real life connection that cannot be replicated in hypothetical scenarios.

This book was written for use at the undergraduate level as well as the beginning graduate level. The content reflects a synthesis of issues and findings, of theory and application, that is useful on both levels. The book is geared to educate through theory and research as well as to make practical suggestions because people need to understand why ideas work in order to make the best choices about how to use the ideas and information. Although many of the findings refer to what people tend to do, we believe that all students will appreciate a book that goes beyond a report of the literature to one that is applied in nature.

Several people made this book possible. They contributed in ways that helped our initial idea become a reality. First, we thank Jennifer Marmo for her help, and for the excellent job she did while taking courses in the ASU PhD program. Also, seven students contributed their personal stories. These people are Jennifer Allen, Richard Bosco, Lindsey Bridges, Ben Brosseau, Benjamin Kearl, Danielle Pascu, and Tawine Tomlinson. We appreciate their willingness to have their personal stories published.

Friends and family members merit our thanks. Our spouses—Heather Canary and Richard Lakey—often provided the motivation we needed to research and write. Michael Cody deserves mention as we referenced his thinking in the 'Power' chapter. Likewise, Bill Cupach and Brian Spitzberg deserve mention for their ideas regarding the competent communication of conflict messages.

We also are grateful for the people at Routledge/Taylor & Francis who helped us. Our editor, Linda Bathgate, was the first person to believe in this project. And over several years, her encouragements were both patient and persuasive. Next, Kayley Hoffman was helpful in directing us through the final stages of preparation, and Emma Håkonsen oversaw the production. Richard Willis (at Swales & Willis Ltd.) worked with us on finishing the book. We thank him for his careful and timely responses to copy edit queries and page proofs.

Conflict in interpersonal relationships will not disappear—even if people follow all of these suggestions. Rather, people will be better prepared to handle conflict when it occurs. Readers should become more strategic in their conflict communication. We hope people will use the theory, conclusions, and suggestions presented here to help them strategically navigate their conflicts so they can reach productive outcomes that protect and even strengthen their relationships.

Daniel Canary
Sandra Lakey

1

THE NEED FOR STRATEGIC CONFLICT

Strategic conflict refers to managing conflict events by mindfully using thoughts and communication to obtain what you want. *Strategies* refer to various approaches for taking action, and *tactics* institute strategies through specific behaviors (Newton & Burgoon, 1990a). *Conflict* has been defined in numerous ways (Putnam, 2006). Definitions of conflict vary in whether specific behaviors define conflict (or not) and whether conflict is a type of a particular situation episode (or not) (Canary, Cupach, & Messman, 1995). We define *conflict* as any incompatibility that can be expressed between people. This definition coincides with Deutsch's (1973) classic definition, and it allows us to discuss conflict processes that psychologists, communication researchers, and scholars in related disciplines have investigated.

Over 50 years of research has examined how conflict management behaviors both affect a variety of outcomes and are affected by various factors (Oetzel & Ting-Toomey, 2006). *We use this research to support the conclusions and related conflict strategies in this book.* We do not present a list of strategies based primarily on our personal experiences, stories of other people's experiences, or hypothetical scenarios. We prefer to rely on data of the highest quality.

In addition, we present examples of actual conflict interaction and selected student stories. Examples of actual interaction bring to life how people use strategies and tactics. Some of these examples are comical and some are sad. They all illustrate research findings. Moreover, stories from students provide examples that generate discussion questions for the reader to ponder.

Ultimately, you must judge whether our conclusions and implied strategies work for you. Although research suggests that our conclusions and strategies apply to many people in different situations, you must determine if they apply to you in your situations. The only way to know is for you to think through the conclusions and strategies in this book. And no doubt, you will arrive at other conclusions and implications for your strategic conflict.

We begin this chapter with a set of reasons why you should learn strategic conflict. Next we argue that mindful attention to conflict events will enable you to engage in strategic conflict. Being clueless helps no one. Third, we present the conceptual model that guides most of our ideas (Canary & Lakey, 2006). Finally, we offer three scope conditions that help us focus on strategic conflict in interpersonal settings. At this point, the reader might wonder why we are excited about the ideas contained in this book.

Why Strategic Conflict?

First, how people manage conflict strategically leads to positive versus negative consequences (Deutsch, 1973). Putnam (2006, p. 9) listed several positive and negative outcomes. On the positive side, conflict can protect against stagnation, stimulate curiosity about a topic, provide an outlet for frustration, lead to change, and promote cohesiveness between and among group members (Putnam, 2006). On the negative side, conflict can lead to dissatisfying relationships, rigid patterns of behavior, decreases in message exchanges, and stand-offs (Putnam, 2006). As we document, the key to outcomes rests on how people use strategic conflict.

Second, and related to the first point, the use of conflict strategies and tactics largely determines the quality of your work associations, social ties, and the quality of your close relationships (Canary et al., 1995). Burpee and Langer (2005) exemplify results regarding the connection of conflict management and relational quality:

> When characterized by stubbornness, defensiveness, and withdrawal, conflicts become detrimental to the relationship because *these elements remove the possibility* for cooperation and constructive interaction. When couples handle conflict together with the mutual intent to repair emotional damage, however, each spouse is likely to leave the conflict feeling better. (emphasis ours)

Next, how people manage interpersonal conflicts at work or at play tends to affect their physical health. As we elaborate in a later chapter, researchers now point to poor conflict management as a major cause of problems in the cardiovascular, endocrine, and immunological systems (Kiecolt-Glaser & Newton, 2001). For instance, the use of hostile conflict has been found to predict heart disease, high blood pressure, heart attacks, strokes, decreased ability to fight colds, sexual dysfunction, and so on (e.g., Metz & Epstein, 2002; Suarez, 2004). In his lab at the Duke Medical Center, North Carolina, Dr. Suarez researches why certain heart attacks occur. Suarez shows that physical and family genetic history can explain approximately 50% of heart failures. Suarez has suggested that social interaction factors (esp. conflict) can explain the remaining 50% of the reasons for heart attack and stroke causes.

Finally, a cynic might argue that learning strategic conflict is self-serving and ignores ethical considerations. However, *strategic conflict requires the consideration of ethical behavior* (for elaboration, see Cupach, Canary, & Spitzberg, 2010). The ethical position in this book is clearly instrumental. Attempts to achieve one's desired goals succeed most when they follow the principles of one's interaction partner. People in modern societies engage in interdependent thoughts and actions. Such interdependence indicates that you can obtain what you want a vast majority of the time simply by using civil communicative behavior. Being strategic, then, requires that people adjust their thoughts and actions to meet the standards of what is considered civil and ethical.

By extension, other people are similar in one respect: they are instrumental in achieving their desired goals through strategic conflict. Individuals who coerce or manipulate to get their way are often bullies and liars. These people fail to use three important facets of being a strategic communicator in the twenty-first century—*knowledge, motivation, and skill* (Spitzberg & Cupach, 1984). That is, you should know various thoughts and messages that lead to your benefit, be motivated enough to act on your knowledge, and apply your thoughts and tactics to manage your interactions—especially interpersonal conflicts. Of course, atypical situations can call for atypical actions. Strategic conflict, however, is about how a vast majority of people, most of the time, and in typical situations rely on their intelligence and communication competence in ethical ways. If the reader hoped to find a book on how to manipulate people, he or she must continue to search.

Parties in conflict each have the right to pursue happiness. The problem is that people's visions of happiness often collide. Mindful thoughts and message behaviors provide the primary means for people to obtain their valued goals. And research on conflict has demonstrated that one's effectiveness in obtaining goals positively connects to appropriateness—that is, meeting the other person's expectations for behavior during conflict (Spitzberg, Canary, & Cupach, 1994). Importantly as well, people are judged as more competent during conflict the more they consider the other person's goals at stake (Lakey & Canary, 2002).

Obtaining Goals

In general terms, people pursue three goals through interaction: instrumental, relational, and self-presentation (Cody, Canary, & Smith, 1994). *Instrumental goals* involve getting resources or favors from another person. *Relational goals* concern how close and how equal you want to be with the other person. *Self-presentation goals* refer to how you manage your public identity, that is, how you want to be seen by other people. Most often, one goal is more salient (primary) and other goals are less salient (secondary). Later, we elaborate the nature of valued goals and how one achieves them.

For now, we simply indicate that people's goals drive their thoughts, emotions, and actions. People think about how they can improve their resources, relationships, and public identities. The value you place on your desired goals becomes quite important when you believe someone is interfering with you. For instance, imagine you need to submit a proposal a week late. You must get an extension from your supervisor. Your instrumental goal then involves getting the extension; your relational goal might involve an indication that you know she has higher status; and your self-presentation goal could involve being seen as reliable and, perhaps, likeable. So you say something like, "I know the proposal is due tomorrow, but I need to ask a big favor. I need more time to do research, because I want to verify some facts. If you would please give me another week, I won't disappoint you." The reader can see the three goals in operation. And you could consider how your knowledge of these three goals might operate in your own interactions.

The reader might believe that he or she cannot study strategic conflict or cannot learn new communication strategies. You might already be adept at communicating with others. Still, you can polish your skills. In an intensive review, Kellermann (1992) argued that, from infancy onward, people learn how to communicate in light of the wants and needs they have. From crying when hungry to negotiating the price of a car, we learn communication within the purposes it serves. Kellermann concluded that communication is both *inherently strategic* and *implicitly learned*. Stated differently, people learn strategic communication although they might not know they are being strategic. For example, simply asking to stay home for dinner constitutes a strategy even though it does not appear as one ("What do you want me to cook?" [direct question]). A person could choose alternative communication approaches (e.g., "What do we have to eat around here" [a hint] or "It is your turn to cook" [negotiation]). Because of the implicitly learned and inherently strategic nature of communication, most people remain mindless of the strategies they choose to achieve their desired goals. At this juncture, we discuss what it means to be more mindful and less mindless of your strategic conflict.

Mindfulness as a Prerequisite to Strategic Conflict

People can be mindless, or clueless, regarding their behavior and context. Langer (1989a, 1989b) has long argued that being more *mindful* leads to greater personal success than does being mindless. Burpee and Langer (2005) found that mindfulness increases relational quality more than simply by finding a similar, compatible partner. They observed that "Discussing difficult issues is likely to reveal each partner's perspective and result in a greater mindfulness on both parts" (p. 43). Likewise, Ting-Toomey and Oetzel (2001) hold that being mindful of one's actions during conflict is critical to managing conflict competently. Mindfulness can also help people who are neurotic (predisposed toward negativity) to become more adept at managing conflict (Feltman, Robinson, & Ode, 2009).

Mindlessness refers to the minimal processing of information that relies on past experiences to determine present action (Langer, 1989a, 1989b). For example, how many times have you driven home and not thought once about what you were doing? You arrive home, look at your hands on the steering wheel, and gasp at the thought of being so mindless about driving. Or perhaps you took someone to the airport and say, "Have a great flight," to which your friend replies "you too!" Clearly, these are mindless, rote behaviors. Langer argued that mindless behavior is common. People often do not pay attention to how they are behaving in different situations. That is, mindless people treat information as if context does not matter, and they ignore contingencies they should consider (Langer, 1989b). People who do not adapt their communication behavior to the situation are mindless when interacting with others (e.g., using profanity during a job interview).

On the other hand, *mindfulness* refers to a state of alertness that considers the current situation to determine an effective course of action (Langer, 1989a, 1989b). People tend to become more mindful when (a) an action requires more effort than it has in the past, (b) mindless behavior leads to failure, (c) external factors interfere with completion of a behavior, and/or (d) behavior produces unexpected consequences. Mindful people create options that consider the situation, demonstrating adaptability, flexibility, and creativity (Brown & Langer, 1990).

The cognitive gap between mindlessness and mindfulness occurs at multiple levels. Andersen (1986), for example, described four states of consciousness. The lowest level, *minimal consciousness* refers to simply being awake. Next, *perceptual consciousness* requires a minimum of awareness and is roughly equal to attention and perception. Third, *constructual consciousness* involves planning, direction, and modeling actions. Finally, *articulate consciousness* concerns the rare instances where people can explain their goals and action plans. Managing conflict at levels 1 and 2 reduces your ability to use strategic conflict, whereas managing conflict at levels 3 and 4 promotes strategic conflict. We want to move you from operating at the lower two levels to the third level and perhaps even the fourth level.

Moreover, mindless people engage in their usual communication behaviors and can be offended by someone who objects to their inappropriate behavior. Mindless people may behave defensively and accuse others of starting the conflict. Mindful people, on the other hand, adapt to the rules of appropriateness of the situation and understand his or her role in conflicts. The implication here is that you should take responsibility for your own part of the conflict. With few exceptions, *you are the person who controls your own behavior and should be mindful of that fact.*

The Confusing Nature of Conflict

Conflict is often complex and confusing. Conflict involves (1) multiple and often vague goals that (2) change during the conflict, (3) are structurally incoherent, and (4) occur without warning (Sillars & Weisberg, 1987). In brief, features of conflict resist the thoughtful use of conflict strategies and tactics. Sillars and Weisberg revealed how the emergence of conflict works against developing an effective set of conflict skills that help people manage conflict. Sillars and colleagues have also shown (e.g., Sillars, Roberts, Leonard, & Dun, 2000) that parties to conflict are cognitively challenged and make inaccurate interpretations of what happened in a recent conflict. For example, both parties interpret their partners' intentions and behaviors with only weak connections to what the partners actually did. To obtain a helpful and robust set of strategies, scholars need to account for conflict confusion and complexity.

Examining concrete ways that people manage conflict lends insight into communication tactics and can suggest alternative forms and functions of communication tactics (Putnam, 2006). Confusion about conflict can be better understood by looking at segments of interaction. Such segments are more informative than hypothetical scenarios, recollections of previous conflicts, and interviews because actual interaction shows how conflict strategies and their specific tactics begin, progress, and end. And actual interaction shows how general patterns of behavior emerge (Bakeman & Gottman, 1997, p. 150).

Research shows that dissatisfied couples tend to communicate with more negative messages than do their satisfied counterparts. Negative messages also tend to be reciprocated between partners, making them even more frequent. This might sound obvious to some, so we need to look at specific instances of negative message reciprocation. Ting-Toomey (1983) found, for example, that dissatisfied partners exchange an average of ten attack–defend sequences. Chapter 2 discusses specifics of conflict strategies and tactics to elaborate this discussion for our readers.

At this point, we introduce our model of strategic conflict.

A Model of Strategic Conflict

As mentioned, many researchers have investigated interpersonal conflict. We hold that conflict involves several facets, each of which must be discussed for a presentation of where conflict can be affected by human agency. By "control" then, we do not imply a monolithic force that places other people in irrevocable positions and then dictates their movements. Instead these facets can be seen as "events" that provide opportunities for people to think and act mindfully. Our model emphasizes how people can strategically manage conflict at each event—from the very beginning of conflict until it concludes. Our model illustrates these events in linear form for educational purposes. Finally, the reader might see that we do not have a place labeled "conflict resolution." We believe that even if a conflict is not "resolved," it can be *successfully managed strategically in a way that maximizes outcomes.*

Each event in the model points to different features of conflict that one wants to control. These include episodic control, personal control, attribution control, goal control, strategy control, and interaction control—terms suggested by Brant Burleson (Note 1 in Canary, 2003). Moreover, each event in conflict implies its own strategic objective. Most people do not think of having different strategic objectives for the same conflict. However, people attempt to take control of conflict events as they happen, in addition to attempting to control the final outcome. Here are the various conflict events and their related control objectives:

Conflict Event	*Strategic Objective*
Conflict Instigation	*Episode control* of factors that instigate conflict
Personality Differences	*Personal control* of individual differences
Interpretation of Conflict	*Attribution control* of how to explain conflict issues
Goal Emergence	*Goal control* of how one obtains and maintains goals
Message Production	*Strategy control* over communication strategies and tactics
The Other's Response	*Interaction control* within conflict episodes
Return to Previous Points	*Control issue determined by which previous event is revisited.*

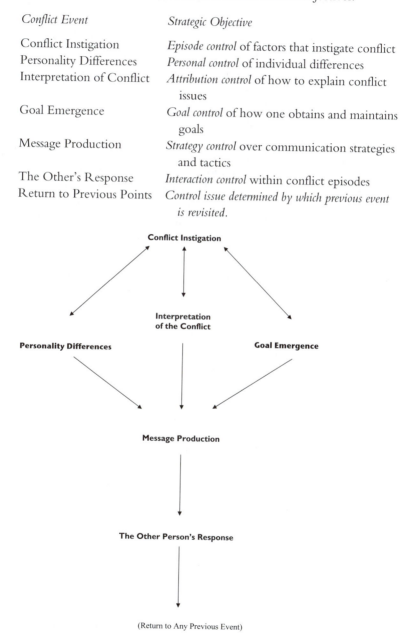

FIGURE 1.1 Model of Strategic Conflict

Conflict Instigation

Conflicts arise from vague to clearly recognized causes. People might perceive a conflict when actually none exists, or what Deutsch (1975) called "false conflict." On the other hand, "veridical" causes for conflict are perceived in the same way by both parties and contain a mutually verifiable cause. And some conflicts should occur but do not, which Deutsch labels "latent" conflict. Conflict can begin for no apparent reason or for clear reasons, as when someone behaves in an objectionable way that has negative consequences for you (Clore, Ortnoy, Dienes, & Fujita, 1993). Of course, causes of conflicts are perceived by each party and do not exist in objective reality.

Consider Siegert and Stamp's (1994) study of "First Big Fights" (FBF) for romantic couples. Various issues led to each couple's first big fight, the most common being uncertainty over the other person's commitment, jealousy, violation of expectations regarding how relationships work, and perceptions of strong differences between the partners. Also, the major differences between survivors and nonsurvivors were seen in whether uncertainty in the relationship increased or decreased, how communication was used to manage the FBF, and differences in the reasons participants gave to explain the FBF. Given all the issues in play, it is no wonder that people agree to disagree.

The chapter on conflict instigators, Chapter 4, reveals instigators that usually evade one's consciousness. We see instigators as flashpoints that ignite when the catalyst of incompatibility occurs. Being mindful of previously unforeseen instigators will help you manage the emergence of conflict. Alcohol, moods, emotions, stress, and even the environment represent common instigators of conflict. The first strategic objective then is to seek *episodic control*.

Three Events that Affect Strategic Communication

Second, people experience three interrelated sets of "events" that filter the link between the initial instigation and use of conflict strategies and tactics. These three events are: individual differences; interpretation of the conflict; and goal assessment/generation (see Figure 1.1). *These three events are interrelated.* However, because we cannot elaborate on their interrelationship, we treat each event separately and present ideas of how the reader can use the research about each event for strategic purposes. We want you to gain knowledge of *personal control*, which reveals how different personality types respond to conflict instigators; *attribution control,* or the ability to perceive conflict episodes more accurately; and *goal control*, which concerns how you see the goals that are in play and how to retain or defend your own goals.

Personality Differences

Individual differences refer to properties of the individual that affect his/her strategy choice; these are discussed in Chapter 7. Although many individual differences exist, we focus on personality variables that research shows have clear relevance to conflict management. As odd as it appears, empirical research has found that sex differences do not affect communication behavior in a robust or consistent manner (for reviews on sex differences, see Dindia & Canary, 2006). Accordingly, we focus on robust and consistent individual effects due to *agreeableness, neuroticism, attachment, narcissism,* and *locus of control.* Because individuals differ on these factors, your composite of personality features (or personality profile) differs from those of other people. At this point, individuals attempt to secure *personal control.*

Interpretation of Conflict

Next, *conflict interpretation* (Chapter 9) concerns how people create explanations for the conflict episode, which in turn affects their strategy selection. Here we mostly rely on attribution theory (Manusov & Harvey, 2001). In this theoretical light, strategic conflict in interpretation of incompatibilities targets *attributional control.* And researchers have variously examined how people's attributions help their constructions and interpretations of conflict situations.

Goal Emergence

Many researchers believe that incompatible goals or perception of incompatibility between people defines interpersonal conflict (Putnam, 2006). To understand conflict, one should acknowledge the central element of goals. Many scholars tie interpersonal goals to communication behavior (Wilson, 2002). Such effort has meant that we had to first identify a set of representative goals that people pursue everyday and then connect those goals to communication behavior.

Conflict points to how social actors' goals are at stake. Also, conflict encounters become complex because each person tends to want more than one goal and so their primary and second goals become enmeshed (Clark & Delia, 1979; Dillard, Segrin, & Harding, 1989). To obtain a complete understanding of how conflict instigation leads to conflict messages, one must know about the intervening nature of goals. Then one can obtain *goal control.*

Message Production

Many researchers in communication and other disciplines have examined conflict communication strategies and tactics (e.g., Cai & Fink, 2002; Conrad, 1991; Kim & Leung, 2000; Newton & Burgoon 1990; Putnam & Wilson, 1982; Rahim, 1983; Sillars, Coletti, Parry, & Rogers, 1982; Weiss, 1984). We examine conflict message behavior in Chapter 2. We discuss the last part of our model (Figure 1.1) early in the book so the reader knows how we view conflict message behaviors that are referenced throughout the book. We briefly review conflict styles and then elaborate more fully on conflict strategies. Such a move is warranted, because people manage conflict when it arises according to the decisions they make (Sillars & Canary, in press). People appear to make two strategic decisions regarding strategic conflict—whether to confront or avoid the other person and whether to be cooperative or competitive (Sillars & Wilmot, 1994). Choices to confront or avoid, and to be cooperative or competitive lead to four strategic approaches and specific conflict tactics that bring those strategies into being (Messman & Canary, 1998; Sillars, Canary, & Tafoya, 2004).

Conflict strategies thus are cooperative and direct, cooperative and indirect, competitive and direct, and competitive and indirect. We discuss these strategies in depth, so you can engage in strategic conflict more effectively by increasing your range of conflict communication strategies and tactics. The mindful selection of conflict communication strategies and tactics refers to *strategy control*.

BOX 1.1 STUDENT STORY

Kung Pao Lunch
by
Lindsey Hedges

I am a hostess in a Chinese restaurant and come face to face with many customers. As a hostess at the restaurant, I am required to not only help seat people at a table, but also do takeout orders.

One Saturday afternoon, a customer ("Ted") called in an order of Kung Pao chicken. As it was lunch-time, I gave him the lunch portion. He was very abrupt, though he did not say anything rude. I was polite and wished him a nice day. Fifteen minutes later he called to complain. After minutes of verbal abuse, I hung up on him.

Two minutes later, his car pulled up in front of the restaurant. He immediately stormed in, threw his takeout bag on the counter, and belligerently asked, "Are you the one I talked to?!! Are you the one I talked to?!!"

Me: "Sir, I was the one who took your order, so I can help you with your problem."
Ted: "I got some [expletive] lettuce and I do not know what this [expletive] food is *but I want my kung pao!*"
Me: "Sir, you received the lunch portion and with that you get a salad, so that is the lettuce item you are probably referring to."
Ted: "Well, I want the dinner portion."
Me: "Well, you were only charged for lunch, and if you would like to come in again I can give you the dinner portion but I will have to charge you for it."

Ted: "No you will [expletive] give me the dinner portion if I want it, and I *refuse to pay for it!*"

Me: "Sir, if you wanted the dinner portion next time you should specify so."

Ted: "No, next time YOU should specify!"

He told me that I was rude. I told him, "Sir, I am sorry but I am going to have talk to my manager about this." I ran into the kitchen crying because I was so scared.

After my manager talked with Ted for a few minutes, he called the police, who escorted him out of the restaurant. Minutes later Ted called again and threatened my manager that he would be after him. We called the police again, and Ted is now not allowed to enter the restaurant ever again.

For the rest of that day, I was scared and shaking because I thought Ted was going to attack me. I do not think that a person ever has the right to put you down. I could have helped Ted with his problem if he talked to me calmly about the situation, without using obscene language. I cannot believe the way people overreact to the most minor things.

Discussion Questions

1. Could Lindsey have anticipated being treated so rudely when Ted first ordered his food and then later cursed at her on the telephone? Could she have used a different tactic to obtain episode control?
2. Imagine you saw this person coming into the restaurant, looking for you. What might be your initial thoughts and feelings?
3. Do you think that Ted might have gotten his way using a different strategic approach? Was this person ethical? Why or why not?
4. Look at the last line: "I cannot believe the way people overreact to the most minor things." Was this a "minor thing" to the customer? What else might this conflict represent to Ted? What general goal might have Ted seen at risk?

The Other's Response

Life would be grand if other people simply did what you asked the first time. Yet conflict involves incompatibility between people, which means that resistance is likely to occur (Wilson, 2002). We examine research on how people engage in conflict sequences and patterns, so that you can increase your *interaction control*. Ongoing patterns of messages strongly affect our work and personal relationships (e.g., withdraw–demand sequences). This material is also covered in Chapter 2.

Return to Any Previous Event

Most conflicts are probably not contained within one episode. Conflicts often continue over time and across situations. The literature on serial argument (Johnson & Roloff, 1998, 2000) is featured to identify factors that perpetuate conflict. In addition, the re-occurrence of conflict implies that parties return to an event already experienced. This means that the strategic objective is identified according to the event where parties to conflict return. Importantly, research reveals that *communication behavior can become a crucible (an instigator) and a catalyst (the source of incompatibility) for ongoing conflict.*

In addition, people can get stuck at any event in the conflict. For example, the argument might initially concern who will cook dinner that night. But one person interprets the conflict as caused by the other person's laziness. In this case, the couple would likely argue about the attribution of laziness and the implications of that attribution for the relationship instead of communicating about the original issue (who will cook dinner that night). Or people might use a hostile question tactic ("Who do you think you are not to cook dinner at least one night a week?"), which would likely prompt the reciprocation of negative behaviors (such as attack–defend, demand–withdraw, disagreement–disagreement, etc.). In such a case, the cooking dinner issue becomes obsolete when the parties focus on the self-presentation of the person who was challenged. Rigid adherence to certain forms of communication (especially avoidance) reflects partner dysfunction that will not change regardless of the issue under discussion (Raush, Barry, Hertel, & Swain, 1974).

We conclude this book with a discussion of forgiveness. Wisdom in strategic conflict includes the willingness to let go of irresolvable conflicts and move on. Resenting the other person and ruminating about what could have happened do nothing to change the events of conflict. Rather, negative thoughts about the harmful event cause wear and tear on you, while the other person is probably oblivious to your ruminations. Strategic conflict here involves a conclusion to the offense, as parties to conflict move through states and stages of forgiveness.

Boundaries to Our Model of Strategic Conflict

Four important scope conditions outline the range and (thus) the applicability of our model. In limiting our boundaries, these scope conditions require a focus on issues that are centrally important for strategic conflict. Here is what we think are our boundaries.

First, we have not exhaustively reviewed or represented research on the topic of conflict management. As the reader can imagine, research on interpersonal conflict is vast and daunting. An academic search for articles on "interpersonal conflict," "marital conflict," "supervisor subordinate conflict," and so on will yield *thousands of studies over the past 50 years*. No book or series of books can possibly exhaust all the studies of conflict. Additionally, the publication dates of the research that we cite represent a span of time wherein researchers have followed their interests. Accordingly, our references include research from the past 50 years. Two personality factors illustrate this observation: locus of control emerged as a hot topic in the 1970s through the 1980s; however, narcissism has emerged as a hot topic since about 2001. We have tried to represent earlier as well as recent research.

Second, we needed to make some painful decisions regarding what literature to include versus to exclude. Our criterion was whether a topic was central to developing the concept of strategic conflict. Several other areas of research hold implications for conflict management and they deserve elaboration. These areas include intrapersonal conflicts dominance behaviors expectation violations (Afifi & Metts, 1998), hurtful messages, relational uncertainty, mediation, negotiation and intergroup conflict peace building, moral conflict, and so on. We certainly hope that our colleagues who research conflict-related areas forgive us for not mentioning their fine work. We also ask scholars whose research on conflict is not referenced to forgive us.

Third, the model we propose relies on interpersonal communication/relational communication research from North America, England and its former colonies (Canada, India, Australia, New Zealand), and Western Europe—countries dominated by Eurocentric attitudes, beliefs, values, and behaviors (Kim & Leung, 2000). In these Western nations, being direct and cooperative typically indicates respect for the other person. Elsewhere, people tend to value *in*direct conflict tactics, which would show respect for the other person much more than direct messages (Ting-Toomey, 2010). Moreover, research regarding family, intercultural, and organizational conflict reveals other contextual factors that affect individual conflict behaviors (e.g., Canary et al., 1995; Oetzel, Arcos, Mabizela, Weinman, & Zhang, 2006; Putnam & Poole, 1987; Ting-Toomey & Oetzel, 2001).

Finally, the reader will likely need other experts for help regarding social and personal conflicts. Psychiatrists, therapists, and mediation experts can look into the specifics of your life and coach you on how to handle demanding and overwhelming problems. For instance, people suffering from severe depression need the help of therapists, ongoing drug protocol, and perhaps hospitalization to recover. When discussing the effects of chronic drinking, we focus on how it affects a person's conflict thoughts and actions. However, ongoing use of alcohol probably means that the person needs help. That person needs to take advantage of one of many hospital-based or clinically-based recovery centers and/or utilize a twelve-step program (e.g., Alcoholics Anonymous), which have proven successful for most problem drinkers and drug abusers. In brief, our book does NOT replace any treatment, therapy, or counseling programs. Our book focuses only on strategic conflict—how individuals can optimally manage their conflicts in a mindful manner.

Concerning material discussed in this first chapter, we offer our conclusions and suggestions for strategic conflict:

Conclusion 1.1: Strategic conflict involves thoughts and behaviors that help one maximize the chance of the best possible outcomes.

Conclusion 1.2: Mindfulness is a necessary requirement for strategic conflict.

Conclusion 1.3: Strategic conflict involves strategic objectives for different events of conflict.

Conclusion 1.4: Strategic conflict works best when the goals and interests of the other person are considered.

Suggestion 1.1: Each person is the one most responsible for his or her own behavior and thus people create their own conflict processes and outcomes.

Suggestion 1.2: People should become more mindful of various conflict events where strategic options change.

Suggestion 1.3: Be mindful that strategic objectives include episodic control, individual control, attribution control, goal control, strategic control, and interaction control.

Suggestion 1.4: Be mindful that this book has boundaries: this is especially important when individuals need professional help; for example, couple counseling and medical intervention provide help to people with specific needs or concerns.

The purpose of this book is to provide you with helpful conclusions and suggestions regarding strategic conflict. In addition to the topics reflected in our Model of Strategic Conflict, we present material that we think is relevant to strategic conflict. Importantly, before we develop elements of our model of strategic conflict we present the "Dual Concern" perspective and factors that work in tandem with strategic conflict to affect relational stability and quality. Also, we offer chapters of different lengths. For example, the accounts chapter (Chapter 6) is double the size of the transgressions chapter (Chapter 5), mostly because responses to transgressions are well represented by how people offer accounts for their failure behaviors.

In conclusion, we want to increase your mindful use of strategies that help you gain control of different conflict events and outcomes. As with all scholarly attempts, this book will be useful for the ideas that you find salient and important. We hope that you will learn and recall the findings, conclusions, and suggestions for strategic conflict that you can apply to your life.

2

SEEKING STRATEGIC CONTROL

Communication Strategies and Tactics

The model of strategic conflict in Figure 1.1 suggests that discussion of communication strategies and tactics should appear toward the back of the book. We want to cover communication strategies and tactics early to show various message behaviors referred to throughout the book. This chapter emphasizes how people manage conflict through communication—communication constituting the primary avenue for managing conflict (or any type of interaction, for that matter).

Paths toward achieving satisfying conflict outcomes are often blocked by the intensity and confusion that underlie many conflicts. Productive communicative strategies can remain oblique or solutions might occur immediately after the interaction, weeks later, or never. Still, people with excellent conflict communication skills are much more likely to obtain their desired goals and simultaneously meet the other person's objectives.

Communication entails symbols to represent objects, events, and behavior. Burgoon (1985) defined symbols as "behaviors that are typically sent with intent, used with regularity among members of a social community, and have consensually recognizable interpretations" (p. 348). As Ruesch and Bateson (1951) and others have noted, the map is not the territory—nor is the thing named the thing itself.

Establish Expectations

Communication provides the means that people use to convey their thoughts about incompatibilities between them through communication. Sure, alternative mechanisms exist, including physical violence, verbal abuse, verbal aggression, or coercion in some other form (e.g., bribery). People who rely on communication, however, rely on strategies and tactics. Strategic conflict requires that individuals "must learn to make social adjustments when faced with opposition from other people. . . . opposition or incompatibility is central to defining conflict. Opposition from other people transforms conflict from an individual, intrapsychic phenomenon to an interpersonal, explicitly social event" (Jensen-Campbell & Graziano, 2001, p. 328).

As mentioned in Chapter 1, conflict interactions involve *two people* who each perceive incompatibility and manage conflict mindlessly or mindfully. Conflicts are managed best when the other person's goals are taken into account, so that adaptation to the other person's ideas can occur (Lakey & Canary, 2002). Parties to conflict who work interdependently can achieve a mutual understanding of the problem(s), to begin solving the mutually defined problem(s) together (Papa & Papa, 2010). Not knowing the other person's goals will handicap your ability to adapt strategically. Stated differently, a lack of perspective-taking prevents social actors from using the other person's goals as information that helps them increase their strategic options.

One also needs to be mindful of rules for conflict behavior. Jones and Gallois (1989) found five rules for conflict interaction: *consideration*, which involves listening to the other person's character or arguments; *rationality* includes remaining calm and not showing one's anger; *self-expression*, or staying on the issue and being honest; *conflict resolution*, which involves problem-solving and creating alternatives; and *positivity*, which concerns relieving tensions, maintaining eye contact, and so forth. Although these rules are rather general, they make imminent sense. Consider how you would react if your conflict partner showed a lack of consideration, demonstrated anger and not reasonableness, changed topics or lied to you, worked against conflict solutions, and/or preferred negativity over positivity. Naturally, people can have different general rules for conflict management. The most important rule for many people is to show concern for the other person's face needs and for both people's face needs, or mutual face (Oetzel, Ting-Toomey, Chew-Sanchez, Harris, Wilcox, & Stumpf, 2003).

Although people might meet the other person's general expectations, they can violate expectations for specific behaviors during conflict interaction (Canary & Spitzberg, 1987). Just one ill-thought comment can ruin an entire conversation. Specific behaviors that violate expectations for conflict interaction include interrupting, swearing, blaming, shouting, not listening or giving eye contact, sarcasm, and so forth. One use of these tactics can damage or sink a prosperous discussion, partly because positive behaviors are normative but negative messages stand out much more and are often remembered longer than positive messages (Canary & Spitzberg, 1990).

A paradox exists here: *How can people succeed at achieving their goals and also meet the expectations of the very person who apparently is blocking their goals?* Your ability to achieve important goals *largely depends* on how well you meets the other person's expectations; when one is aware of and attempts to meet the other person's expectations then the other person becomes more open to acknowledging you, listening to you, and perhaps will be persuaded by you (Canary & Spitzberg, 1987). Referring to the model driving this book, by being mindful of what prompts conflicts, of the other person's personality, of interpretations of the conflict, and of goals at stake, the reader can assess the situation and adapt to it. Not meeting the other person's needs and expectations would dissuade that person from being interested in what you want. Remember the Golden Rule: treat others as you would have them treat you. This rule is ingenious because it advises you to communicate in positive and caring ways (as you would be treated), and it creates a joint expectation of engaging in positive, caring behavior. We offer the following, which reflects the wisdom of the Golden Rule.

Conclusion 2.1: Assessments of communicative competence depend on the extent to which you meet other people's expectations for communicating during conflict.

Suggestion 2.1: Establish expectations by using this simple strategy: communicate with other people the way you want other people to communicate with you.

Selective Perception (Short Take) and Communication

When looking at their own communication during conflict, people have a surreal view of what exists. However, people most often believe that their view is real; people tend to believe that their reality is other people's reality. The more a person thinks that he or she sees reality as it really is, then the more subjective and surreal that person becomes—adding another layer to the myth that people can view the world objectively.

We will elaborate how people make sense of their conflicts later (Chapter 9). For now, however, we simply offer a couple of reasons why objectivity in recalling conflict cannot possibly exist. First, and according to a review of the literature (Berscheid & Regan, 2005) people can sense approximately 7 *million bytes of information each second* but can only attend to ten bytes of information per second. Naturally, then, people must engage in selective perception. In recollections of brief conflict interactions, people can recall only about one third of message sequences an hour after their interactions and only 2% a month later (Sillars, Weisberg, Burggraf, & Zietlow, 1990). And when people view their conflicts on videotape immediately following their interactions, their recollections and interpretations of messages overlap minimally with the other person's recollections and interpretations (between 1 and 3%; Sillars et al., 2000).

People's shortcomings for perceiving and managing conflict might lead you to give up on communicative strategies that can help bring about positive outcomes. However, giving up control over one's life due to its complexity is not an option for successful living. Research shows that message behaviors can lead to productive or destructive conflict outcomes. The question becomes which conflict strategies and tactics are most effective and simultaneously appropriate given people's incompatibilities.

The following section provides many strategies and tactics that you can use to manage conflict. In addition, this chapter discusses several strategies and tactics that many of us would not appreciate or respect. By learning about these strategies and tactics, your options for strategic communication can increase dramatically.

The Styles Approach for Assessing Conflict Communication

A *styles approach* to managing conflict was a hot topic in the 1970s and 1980s, and it remains popular today. A person's conflict style represents that individual's propensity to engage in the same conflict behavior across situations. A style is typically determined by the extent to which a person is concerned with self and concerned with other. The combination of these two concerns is said to lead to one's conflict management styles. An important measurement tool of conflict styles approach has been the Management of Differences Exercise (MODE) instrument developed by Kilmann and Thomas (1977; Rahim, 1983), which labels the five styles as competing, collaborating, compromising, avoiding, and accommodating. Figure 2.1 represents the styles approach, indicating where each style is placed given its concern for self and concern for other.

It would be informative to examine the items that are used to measure these styles. For this exercise, we used items from Rahim's (1983) measure. For each item, you would be asked to write the name or the role relationship of the other person (e.g., "my supervisor"). Collaboration refers to having a high concern for

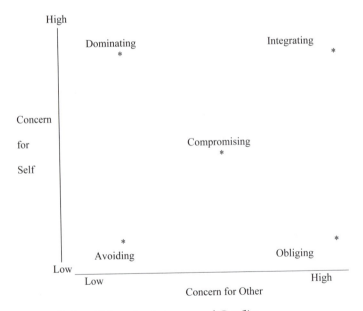

FIGURE 2.1 Styles of Managing Interpersonal Conflict

Adapted from Rahim (1983)

self and a high concern for others. It is measured by items such as "I try to work with my _____ to find solutions to a problem which satisfy our expectations," and "I exchange accurate information with my _____ to solve a problem together." Avoidance means having a low concern for both others and self. Example items include, "I usually avoid open discussion of my differences with my _____," and "I try to stay away from disagreement with my _____." Dominating reflects having high concern for self but a low concern for others, as seen in such items as "I use my influence to get my ideas accepted," and "I use my authority to make a decision in my favor." Next, Obliging refers to having low concern for self but a high concern for others. Obliging items include "I generally try to satisfy the needs of my _____" and "I usually accommodate the wishes of my _____." Finally, a moderate amount of concern for self and other indicates a compromise style. Example items for Compromise are "I try to find a middle course to resolve an impasse," and "I usually propose a middle ground for breaking deadlocks."

The styles approach is memorable, easily testable, and interesting for people's self-assessment of how they normally behave. Pros and cons of each style offer topics for discussion. However, in our view, the styles approach is not very useful in representing people's actual strategic decisions and behaviors. With the same individual, you might avoid conflict in one situation but confront that person in a different time and space. In addition, the styles approach assumes that conflict messages are linked to caring for self and caring for the other person. Avoidance in this research reflects low care for self and low care for others. But such is not the case. Avoidance can instead reflect a high care for others *and* high care for self. For example, not saying something in anger implies caring for the other person and yourself. Moreover, people often prefer to be left alone than forced to discuss problems that are better left for a different place and time. In such cases, avoidance would be a smart and a considerate strategy.

A Strategic Approach

Before we discuss the strategic approach, we need to underscore how people simply do not perceive an incompatibility and then respond with messages. As mentioned in Chapter 1, conflict instigation occurs first and the individual reacts to it cognitively, emotionally, and behaviorally. Following conflict instigation, three factors intervene between conflict instigation and choices on how to manage the conflict: personality factors, interpretation of the conflict, and assessment of the goals at stake. These three factors inform people (sometimes within a tenth of a second) regarding which strategic choice is best. More of each of these elements of conflict is discussed in later chapters. However, we wanted to discuss conflict communication strategies early so you can have a concrete sense of what we mean by "conflict strategies" or "communication strategies."

A strategic approach ties communication behaviors to decisions that people make for handling a conflict situation. From a strategic point of view, then, conflict strategies and their related tactics are born from *people's decisions*—decisions that you, we, and everyone makes regarding how to communicate in the face of incompatibility. Specifically, theory and research has shown that people's decisions involve (1) whether to be direct or indirect (whether to approach or avoid), and (2) whether to cooperate or compete (whether to be positive or negative) (Putnam & Wilson, 1982; Sillars & Canary, in press; Sillars & Wilmot, 1994). These two decisions then most directly lead to the intention of using particular conflict strategies and their specific tactics.

People can make these two decisions in a flash or over a sustained period of time. For example, how much time is needed to decide how to respond to another driver who aggressively cuts you off on the highway? Or how much time do you need to respond strategically to your partner's demands, deal with an overbearing supervisor, talk to a former partner who makes it very difficult for you to visit your children, or decide what to say to his or her parents after 20 years of neglect? The time you need to decide which communication strategy to use can vary immensely.

Intensive observational research of actual interactions has uncovered various conflict strategies and tactics that can be readily grouped into the dimensions of directness and cooperation (Sillars, Canary, & Tafoya, 2004). Crossing directness and cooperation at 90 degrees shows how people's strategic choices bring about various communication strategies and tactics. These dimensions closely resemble those that van de Vliert and Euwema (1994) discovered—activeness and agreeableness.

Van de Vliert and Euwema reviewed the conflict literature to discover how conflict behaviors and outcomes can be grouped. They found four approaches that integrate research on conflict processes and outcomes: *negotiation, nonconfrontation, direct fighting,* and *indirect fighting.* Negotiation includes tactics that are direct and cooperative; nonconfrontation comprises tactics that are positive or neutral, and they seek to minimize the conflict's importance; direct fighting involves tactics that compete with the other person, such as ridicule, threats, intimidation, and the like. Finally, indirect fighting includes tactics that attempt to remove oneself from the conflict in a negative manner—stonewalling is a form of indirect fighting. We adopt van de Vliert and Euwema's labels to discuss conflict communication strategies and tactics.

One interesting (and confusing) feature of conflict categories is that they are not always discrete, separate message behaviors. Specific conflict behaviors can represent more than one set of meanings. The statement, "I really like the way you drive," can represent praise or criticism (if said with a sarcastic, negative tone). Also, the statement "let's get together sometime" can indicate that you want to see more or less of another person (depending on whether the time and place are clear). In a word, conflict messages are *polysemous*—that is, message codes can take on different meanings depending on the relational history of the conversational partners and the context in which the statement is expressed (Sillars & Canary, in press).

What should you do when the meaning of someone's statement is unclear to you? One smart decision is to behave in a normative manner. *That is, behave as most people do and interpret the other person's comment literally.* For example, if someone says "Hello [your name]" in a condescending voice, you could reply with a "Hello [their name]" as most people would do and *as if* that person was literally genuine.

> *Conclusion 2.2: Decisions you make about how to approach the other person in conflict will most likely lead to your use of related communication strategies and tactics.*

> *Suggestion 2.2: Use strategies that reflect a mindful, intelligent individual; the best "bet" for mindful strategy use is negotiation, then nonconfrontation, and then the two fighting strategies.*

The DINN of Conflict

Using van de Vliert and Euwema's categories of *negotiation, nonconfrontation, direct fighting,* and *indirect fighting,* Gustafson (Pennsylvania State University) and Canary created a coding system for use in training, education, and research. We labeled this the DINN system (Direct–Indirect, Nice–Nasty). Later (2007), in collaboration with Beth Babin (Cleveland State), Perry Pauley (California State, Fullerton), and Shannon L. Johnson (James Madison University) we revised the DINN category scheme to include other tactics that we discovered in the research (for parallels to these behaviors, see Sillars et al., 2004). We do not claim these behaviors exhaust the numerous communication strategies and tactics reported in the literature. Instead, we claim the communication strategies and tactics as reported in the DINN clearly *represent* communication strategies and tactics that people choose to use. Moreover, the reader can readily use the DINN coding scheme to identify different ways they can learn many tactics to achieve their goals to be effective as well as appropriate.

According to the DINN of conflict, message behavior can be grouped according to four general strategies of: negotiation, nonconfrontation, direct fighting, and indirect fighting (Van de Vliert & Euwema, 1994).

Examples of these strategies below show that various conflict strategies and tactics do not occur once or in isolation from other behaviors. That is, one person uses a particular tactic followed by the other person's response, which in turn leads the first person to communicate again and so forth. Accordingly, we need to examine how one person responds to another to find conflict patterns (Messman & Canary, 1998). In the progression of conflict, people are largely unaware of these levels of communication, let alone the specific tactics that reflect the higher-ordered strategies.

In addition, tactics unfold in various ways. That is, one person might adopt the negotiation sub-strategy of "seeks disclosure by using a solicitation of disclosure." This tactic might not work, for instance, if the other person relies on nonconfrontation and uses a vague or distraction disengagement tactic. Hypothetically, the first person might enact the same tactic (solicitation of disclosure) or rely on a different tactic (such as personal criticism). Let us now examine the four strategic approaches and examples of how they unfold in real interaction.

Negotiation Tactics

Negotiation refers to various tactics that people use to make their points directly but in a cooperative manner. Table 2.1 lists the subcategories and tactics that compose negotiation. Of course, people can still disagree with each other, but they do so in ways not to offend or to cause the other to respond in a hostile manner. More positive outcomes emerge by using negotiation rather than other strategies, at least in the US and similar countries. The following strategies and tactics represent negotiation behaviors.

TABLE 2.1 Negotiation Tactics

Shows Willingness to Manage the Problem

- Acceptance of responsibility—showing "ownership" (part or whole) of cause of conflict. ("I shouldn't show so much anger." "Maybe we're both at fault.")
- Discussing courses of action—exploring consequences for courses of action in a nonhostile way. (Discussing pros and cons.)
- External problem description—one or both parties attributes the conflict to an external source for the problem. ("I can't play with a sprained ankle." "Yeah, I know.")
- Concession—expression of willingness to change behavior (includes apologies) ("Okay, I'll cook on the weekends too.")
- Compromise—proposal of mutual exchange of behaviors. ("If you do the cooking, I'll clean up.")
- Pleading and coaxing—appeals to fairness, appeals to love, appeals to the other's motives.
- Nonhostile proposal: nonhostile proposal for termination/decrease OR initiation/increase of some behavior.

Supports the Partner

- Agreement—direct and clear agreement.
- Approval—responding favorably to attributes, actions, or statements of the speaker, including assents. ("Yeah," clearly in support ofspeaker.)
- Excusing of other—excusing behavior of other. ("You wouldn't fight, if your mother didn't bring it on.")
- Paraphrase reflection—nonhostile statement mirroring the preceding

---

statement. ("I hear you saying . . .," "I think you're saying . . .," "What you're saying . . .")

- Positive mind reading—statement of "fact" assuming positive mind-set or motive of partner. ("You really enjoy playing golf." "You like being a generous person.")
- Supportive remarks—statements reflecting support, acceptance, and positive regard for partner. Offering assistance. ("You are so sweet.")
- Laughter (at something that was intended to be funny, nonhostile).
- Positive physical interaction—affectionate touch, hug, or kiss.
- Positive interruption—statement that provides support for partner's thoughts.
- Constructive metacommunication—nonhostile statement about the conversation, said in a neutral or positive tone. ("I think we have drifted away from the problem at hand." "I like how you said that.")

Seeks Disclosure

- Solicitation of disclosure—nonhostile request for the partner to reveal feelings or attitudes/seeking reassurance.
- Solicitation of criticism—nonhostile request for criticism. ("Do you think I am spending too much time away from you and the family?")

Offers Disclosure

- Disclosive statements—nonhostile reporting of feelings, attitudes, motives, actions, etc. ("I'm not too crazy about the way your brother talks to me.")
- Descriptive statements—nonhostile observation. ("Sometimes the garbage can sit there for days.")
- Internal problem description—description of a problem residing inside the speaker. ("I know I have a tough time discussing money.")
- Disapproval—nonhostile statement of dislike or disapproval of a behavior. ("It hurts my eyes when you smoke.")
- Disagreement—nonhostile statement expressing disagreement. ("I don't think that is entirely the situation.")

Because people largely experience conflict in a negative manner, the use of negotiation can be difficult. However, negotiation allows one to maintain his or her emotional regulation, the ability to edit one's messages, and avoid negative health consequences from using negative emotions. Moreover, the use of negotiation permits the social actor to retain his/her dignity. The following exchange shows how negotiation occurs between these partners (from CA couple 32).

More specifically, note how the husband excuses his wife's lack of financial responsibility in turns 15.3–15.8; and she acknowledges her role in the conflict in turn 16. The husband then states she has become more responsible and that his money is actually hers as well.

Turn	Speaker	Message
15.1	M	Next question.
15.2		To what extent do you have problems with or disagreements about money? For example, how much to spend, how much to save, one person spends too much money?
15.3		Well, Laura, she doesn't have a lot of fiscal responsibility,
15.4		because she never had to have it
15.5		because her parents gave her money all the time and she really didn't have to <u>earn</u> it or she didn't really have to a, manage her money really well.
15.6		It's not her fault
15.7		but she never was taught or never had the opportunity to do that.
16.1	F	Well, but though since we've been married . . . I have, I've been a full time student
16.2		so I haven't made money
16.3		and I have taken into consideration that you're the one who makes the money
16.4		and I don't buy anything that's a lot of money without asking you first.
17.1	M	That's good.
17.2		I'm not saying you're not doing a good job.
17.3		You're doing a good job, now.
17.4		I'm just saying, it took a while . . . [lengthy pause]
17.5		for you to get used to it.
17.6		And now you're doing pretty good.
17.7		And now you're responsible.
18.1	F	Now I'm getting ready to make my own money,
17.2		I'm gonna have to start all over again.
18.1	M	No.
18.2		There's no my money or your money.
18.3		It's our money.

Nonconfrontation Tactics

Nonconfrontation tactics involve efforts to minimize the severity and/or consequences of conflict in a nonhostile manner (see Table 2.2). However, people are more aware of the use of nonconfrontation than the communicator realizes. For example, Canary and Spitzberg (1990) found that people in conflict more readily see their partners' use of nonconfrontation than they do the use of negotiation and direct fighting tactics.

In addition, people often prefer to hear nonconfrontation tactics because they do not reduce people's wishes to be seen as competent and likeable. Also, nonconfrontation is the least likely strategy to confine people and burden them

---

TABLE 2.2 Nonconfrontation Tactics

Minimizes Problem/Responsibility in a Nonhostile Fashion

- Implicit denial—implying that conflict is not a problem or rationalizing that it doesn't exist. ("Yeah she's cute, but she's not my type.")
- Qualifying statements—explicitly qualifying the extent or nature of conflict. ("Well that was just that once," "This is a problem, but it's no big deal.")
- Excuse—offering a reason for problematic behavior. Excuse weak or reasoning faulty. ("I was late because every light was red.")

Vague or Distracting Comments

- Noncommittal questions—asking unfocused or general questions. ("What do you think?")
- Abstract remarks—making general remarks about the nature of things. ("Everybody gets irritable sometimes." "It is important for people to compromise.")
- Distraction—says something to distract the other person. ("You have a crumb on your shoulder.")
- Disengagement—nonhostile statement expressing desire not to talk about conflict. ("I'd rather not talk about that now. How about tomorrow?")

Uses Humor or Teasing

- Friendly jokes—joking *not* at the expense of the partner. ("That reminds me of a joke: You know how to catch a unique rabbit? Unique up on it." [Laughter])
- Humor—lighthearted humor, not sarcastic. ("We don't argue about money, because we don't have any." [Laughter])

with the need to respond. That is, the positive but indirect nature of non-confrontation offers a polite way to communicate during conflict.

Here are two examples of nonconfrontation. The first, short example illustrates how partners can lighten the intensity of a conversation through distraction (with cajoling and teasing; from AZ Couple # 77):

Turn	Speaker	Message
49	W	I'm fine, I'll be fine. I keep telling you I'm fine, and I will be. Did you get me ice tea or a Diet Coke?
50	M	Ice tea.
51	W	I asked for Diet.
52	M	You always drink ice tea.
53	W	(Laughs) I wanted Diet. Didn't you hear me say that?
54	M	Take mine.
55	W	I certainly will. Thank you.

The next example shows that nonconfrontation can reduce the severity of the issue. The partners collude to broaden the issue so much that no concrete ideas or behaviors emerge. Specifically, the wife begins with a general description of the problem and then she *qualifies* it, to say that the problems at home are probably created at work. But the problems at home require her to verbalize, because that allows her to think (turns 5.5–5.6) whereas he tends to be quiet when he thinks (turns 5.7–5.8). Next, she excuses his quietness in *abstract* terms to explain his usual way to solve problems such that she does not need to participate in his work problems. The man uses the tactics of implicit denial as well as abstraction (turns 6.1–6.2).

Although she articulates her desire to hear whether the "problems" at work actually spill over into the home, she engages in *abstraction* and *excuse* for diagnosing his quietness. From that point, the woman accepts blame for the problem, again using *qualifying* and *abstract* remarks. The man simply agrees, which validates her nonconfrontation tactics and concludes with an abstract solution that lacks any concrete commitment on his part (turn 8.2).

Turn	Speaker	Message
5.2	F	I think sometimes these um, problems that you are referring to, many times they are work related, where they wouldn't really involve me.
5.3		But it would I think help me to know that that's what you are doing, that you are mulling over this problem at work,

5.4		so that I'm not wondering why is he so quiet or is there something bothering him that he is not comfortable talking about.
5.5		But I think when it's an issue that involves us, or a joint decision, I tend to want to talk about it more and verbalize about it more,
5.6		whereas I know you know, I kind of think out loud as I am verbalizing.
5.7		Whereas you do your thinking internally,
5.8		and then when you've come to some conclusions or some ideas, *then* you verbalize them.
5.9		And then you *talk* about them.
5.10		It's not like you're making the decisions all by yourself,
5.11		You're just coming to terms, I think, with what you think we should do when it's kind of a joint decision.
6.1	M	Right.
6.2		Well, I don't think I make, maybe I do sometimes, I don't know, but generally I don't think it's, after analyzing internally and not being collaborative, I don't think I make a decision and then um force the decision on you.
7.1	F	Oh no, not at all.
7.2		But I think you come to terms with maybe how you think we should lean.
7.3		Whereas before I come to terms with how I think we should go, I verbalize about it.
7.5		And I bounce more ideas off you and sometimes just kind of rattle on because it helps me to think to just be talking about it.
8.1	M	I agree.
9.1	F	But I think, and we've kind of talked about this issue, you know a couple of other times, I think it has to do with just sort of respecting each other's different ways of problem solving.
9.2		I mean when I know you have something on your mind that you're quiet about I don't feel . . . threatened or less loved.
8.3		I've just learned that this is your way of dealing with it.
8.1	M	Yeah, I appreciate that.
8.2		You know it's something that I can try and be more cognizant of and be more open.

This latter segment reveals how avoidance, even polite avoidance, hides problems and disables solutions. Using chronic avoidance can create a dysfunctional system. nonconfrontation can resemble cotton candy—it tastes good but is not something you want to take home for dinner.

Direct Fighting Tactics

As the label implies, direct fighting refers to direct and competitive ways to communicate during conflict. Another popular term for direct fighting is "distributive behavior" (e.g., Canary & Cupach, 1988; Sillars et al., 1982). Distributive behavior attempts to divide the resources and outcomes of both people so the communicator achieves more than the other person. In other words, direct fighting involves ways to win the conflict regardless of the other person's conversational goals. Table 2.3 presents various subcategories and tactics of direct fighting.

TABLE 2.3 Direct Fighting Tactics

Makes Accusations about Other's Behavior(s), Attitude(s), Thought(s), or Feeling(s). Sometimes Characterized by "You" Statements

- Presumptive remarks/negative mind reading—statements (including predictions) that attribute negative qualities to the other. ("You don't care about me." "You purposefully do this to yourself.")
- Personal criticisms—direct criticism of another's behavior, thoughts, attitudes, feelings, etc. ("That's silly.")
- Blaming the other person for causing the conflict. ("This is your fault/problem.")

Shows Hostility

- Hostile imperatives—statements that blame the partner or demand change. ("If you wouldn't spend the money, we wouldn't be in this mess.")
- Threat—physical and/or emotional harm that is contingent on compliance of the other. ("If you don't change, I'm leaving." "Shut up, if you know what's good for you.")
- Intimidation—attempt to induce fear and/or respect without clear reference to compliance. ("Watch it." said in a threatening way)
- Command—direct command of specific behavior that could be fulfilled in the next ten seconds. ("Stop whining." "Put out that cigarette.")
- Hostile questioning—questioning in a hostile tone that tends to lead an answer. ("Who does all the work around here anyway?" "Who do you think you are?")

Puts Down/Rejects

- Put-down—demeaning or mocking the other. ("Thanks for making me look like a total ass in front of my boss." Laughter while other is making point.)

- Sarcasm—using negative or ironic tone to demean the other person. ("Boy if you weren't the life of the party last night.")
- Rejection—hostile statement reacting to a personal criticism or description of a conflict. ("You can't be serious!" "Nonsense.")
- Disagreement—explicit disagreement or objections (can be "yes-but" statements).
- Turnoff—nonverbal gesture suggesting disgust or disapproval. (Nonverbal behavior like shaking of one's head in disgust or audible groan.)

Competes Conversationally

- Negative metacommunication—talk about talk, said with negative intonation. ("You said, 'I don't care'?" [in a negative tone])
- Hostile interruption—breaking in and not allowing other to finish point.
- Withhold information—unwillingness to disclose information that one has access to ("I can't say." "But that's a personal question.")
- Refusal to Comply—refusing to engage in behavior that partner requests/demands. ("I will not stop this.")

The Demand–Withdraw Pattern

One pattern of direct fighting has received much attention recently—the demand–withdraw pattern. Perhaps the primary reason for this attention concerns how the demand–withdraw pattern summarizes in one exchange how people can be direct and hostile with each other. Different forms of demand–withdraw occur. Papp, Kouros, and Cummings (2009) define **demanding behavior** with the subcategories of *pursuit and personal insult*. *Pursuit* refers to not letting the issue or the other person go away, whereas *personal insult* refers to direct fighting tactics, including making accusations, insulting the partner, blaming, rejecting, and use of sarcasm. Papp et al. (2009) define **withdrawal behavior** in terms of three subcategories. First, *defensiveness* involves escaping blame, refusing responsibility, and offering excuses for one's behavior, reacting to criticism with criticism, and so forth. Second, *change topic* simply is defined as "changing the topic to avoid the interaction" (p. 291). Finally, *withdraw* involves attempts to create both emotional and physical distance from the interaction partner; these include stonewalling, leaving the scene, avoiding eye contact, and so forth.

These message behaviors clearly coincide with most of the DINN behaviors. Yet the DINN appears to cover more ground and is consistent with this text. Accordingly, we will describe the various tactics and sequences by using the DINN coding scheme (see Table 2.3).

In showing how direct tactics are countered, the demand–withdraw summarizes important information about the ebbs and flows of distributive conflict. An example of this can be found in the literature examining demand–withdrawal patterns in married couples, which has found that partners begin to reflect each other's demands in their own behaviors (e.g., Caughlin & Vangelisti, 2000). In other words, even though one person is unhappy with an issue and complains about it, the other person is more likely to complain as well, even when the second person wants to maintain the way things are. Accordingly, each person can believe that he or she is the "victim" and the other person is the "perpetrator."

The following sequence illustrates how specific tactics are used to construct a demand–withdraw pattern. The woman initiates the pattern in turn 1 by proposing that her husband listen to her deal, which represents the negotiation tactic of *compromise* (see Table 2.1). Instead of listening to her "deal," the husband responds in a hostile manner that she should cook if she had "you know, kids to feed and stuff." This message is clearly direct and competitive, and is a *hostile imperative*. In turn 9, the wife responds with a *hostile question* that is followed by a *rejection* of the husband's argument (we have one child, and he is an adult). The husband counters that the boy is only 16 and cooks for himself "all the time" (a *rejection*). Finally, in turn 11.1 the wife *rejects* the legitimacy of the husband's argument but is interrupted before she can offer another thought (turn 11.2).

[M: You start first. What is your issue?]

F1.1:   Cooking meals, let's just start with cooking meals.
1.2   Okay I'll make you a deal. I'll make you a deal on cooking meals.

M2:   [loudly] NO! I AM <u>NOT</u> <u>GOING</u> <u>TO STOP</u> <u>WATCHING</u> (brief pause, softer) baseball games just because . . .

F3.1:   [interrupting] No, I wasn't go to say that.
3.2   I wasn't going to say that.

M4:   It's not like . . . . Okay . . .

F5.1:   I mean, do you want to <u>solve</u> the cooking meal problem
5.2   or do we just want to fight about it?

M6:   No because . . .

F7.1:   [interrupting] Would you like me to make the meals?
7.2   Then I want something back,
7.3   that's all.
7.4   I'll make you a deal.

M8.1:   <u>No</u>!
8.2   I think you just <u>do</u> it,
8.3   because it's your responsibility if you had, you know, kids to feed and stuff.

F9.1   Why do you say that kids to feed thing?

9.2   We have one kid;

9.3   he's a grown-up.

9.4   He can cook for himself.

M10.1   He is sixteen.

10.2:   He's cooking for himself all the time.

F11.1:   He <u>doesn't</u> all the time.

11.2   Anyway, I mean, we are supposed to discuss our problem so I . . .

As the reader can imagine, this conflict continues. But in the next turn the husband reverses his role to demand something from the wife (turn 12.1), which is an interesting ploy. Caughlin and Vangelisti's research (1999, 2000) suggests this switching of roles—in the same interaction—can be demanded by both partners.

M12:   [interrupting wife at turn 11.2] At least you could, um, go grocery shopping.

F13:   I buy *lots* of ready to eat things . . .

M14:   Yeah [sarcastically]

F15:   that people don't eat.

M16.1:   Like WHAT? [loudly]

16.2   Like, like corn in a <u>baaaag</u> (in disgust).

F17.1:   That's not true!

17.2   There is T.V. dinners in there.

17.3   There's pot pies.

17.4   There's . . .

M18:   [interrupting] Burritos.

F19.1:   Burritos.

19.2   There's plenty of sandwich meat and, and stuff.

19.3   There's a lot of things if people would take ten minutes they can make their own meal.

19.4   Nobody is starving here.

The wife then pivots on his demands and re-takes the offensive, which leads to another demand–withdraw segment. She makes a *presumptive remark* in 19.5 about the husband's motive, to which he replies defensively, citing how he was raised. Then the wife uses *sarcasm* and *put-downs* regarding the husband's weight: he does not need big meals—rather he needs "*little bitty* meals" and salads. So, she offers to make him a salad (a combination of *put-down* and *sarcasm*).

F19.5   I think you just need to see me cook for some reason.

M20:   I just, it's just that I grew up eating nice, full, healthy, well-balanced meals.

F21:   You don't need full meals anymore, Bob—you need *little bitty meals*.

M22:   Don't say my name. This is going to be broadcast on the internet.

F23.1:   (laughing) You don't need big meals—you need *little* meals.

F23.2:   You need to have *salads* for dinner.

F23.3:   That's it. I'll make a salad.

In brief, the demand–withdraw pattern is a major type of negative conflict pattern. This sequence, as do many sequences, represents the use of negative complementarity.

Indirect Fighting Tactics

Indirect fighting refers to competitive ways that people attempt to dislodge themselves from the issue at hand without concern for the other person's goals. It is an indirect and competitive strategy. By "indirect" here, we refer to both explicit as well as implicit attempts to deny a conflict exists and, if it did, the person certainly does not want to own part of it. Table 2.4 lists message subcategories and tactical behaviors associated with indirect fighting.

TABLE 2.4 Indirect Fighting Tactics

Minimizes Seriousness or Personal Responsibility

- Evasive remarks—failing to acknowledge or speaking with a degree of tentativeness. ("I guess that could be a problem." "How could *I* know?")
- Defensiveness—giving reasons for a course of action in a hostile way. ("It's not like I have all the time in the world.")
- Noncommittal remark—remark that does not deny or affirm existence of conflict. ("Whatever.")
- Implicit denial—statements that imply denial by providing a rationale for a denial statement, although the denial is not explicit. ("We really don't have a problem with being in a rut. Of course, we are not passionate as we used to be, and we spend our weekends doing the same thing every weekend. But everything is fine.")

Attempts to Change Path of Discussion

- Procedural remark—remark that brings attention to procedural matters in a fashion that overshadows the discussion at hand. ("I can't talk to you when you are like that.")

- Topic avoidance—hostile demand to stop discussing the conflict. ("I don't want to talk about this!")
- Topic shifts—statements that derail focus of conversation before one can fully express him- or herself. ("I can't tell you about that unless you listen to my other point.")

Implies Negativity

- Dysphoric affect—expressing of depression in a whiny voice. (e.g., [Bitter voice] "I always have to pick up the kids.")
- Stonewalling—clear withdrawal from the conversation or topic discussion. (Silence followed by partner's attempt to engage in conversation. For example, [silence]. . . . "Well, are you going to say something?")
- Negative attitude—hints or implied subtle threats (indirect) that reveal a negative attitude
- Contempt/Condescension—sings of superiority or arrogance.
- Guilt induction—indirect statements intended to induce guilt in the other party ("I guess nobody appreciates what I do around here.")

From Gustafson, Canary, Farinelli, Johnson, and Eden (2007), *DINN II*. Unpublished coding manual, Arizona State University.

The following example shows how frustrating indirect fighting can be. The woman complains about her partner's drinking and driving. However, he will have none of the conversation and resorts mostly to using the strategic subcategory of Minimizes Seriousness or Personal Responsibility. Also, we see his tactical use of evasion and defensiveness. This portion takes only one minute.

Turn	Speaker	Message
175	F	[I do not like] your drinking habits.
176	M	I don't have any drinking habits.
177	F	Getting into the car irresponsibly with people that drink not only is that selfish . . . stop it. . . Not only is it selfish to be like that because you're hurtin' me and everybody else that's close to you if something happens to you. It's *stupid!* And it's illegal for you . . .
178	M	No, because listen . . .
179	F	'Cause listen . . .
180	M	You say, if I'm over a friend's house . . . Well, yeah, *we* stay and we'll have a beer. But it's different?

181	F	*I'm* not drivin'. *I'm* not puttin' anybody's life in danger!
182	M	But you say, "Let's have a beer" and I have *one* beer. One beer does nothing to me.
183	F	Yeah, but then you go . . .
184	M	So, that's not putting your life in danger.
185	F	Then you wanna go someplace else and have another beer with somebody else.
186	M	Yeah, and what's wrong with that?
187	F	And therefore, it's *two!*
188	M	It doesn't make any sense.
189	F	Yeah, because you're addin' on.
190	M	No, I'm not, because I've sat down at home or anywhere else and had one beer. That's it.
191	F	Yeah, but what I'm saying is that . . .

These two lovebirds continue this pattern for another 20 minutes! Moreover, these people are so keen on maintaining this attack–defend pattern that they often do not make sense. For example, the man argues that if he has a drink at one house and then goes somewhere else to drink, the effects of alcohol do not occur. Another feature of this conversation concerns how they do not listen to each other. The interruption in turns 178–9 is revealing ("No, because listen . . ." "'Cause, listen . . . .") because it shows they are *not* listening to each other. Such examples of interaction help us make sense of the scrambled mess of conflict.

> *Conclusion 2.3: Strategies are executed in tactics such that one person's tactics are followed by the other person.*
>
> *Suggestion 2.3: Avoid the demand–withdraw pattern, either as the person demanding change or the person defending against change.*

The Danger of Reciprocating or Complementing Negative Tactics

Tactical reciprocation during conflict occurs when the partner mirrors the actor's conflict behavior (Burggraf & Sillars, 1987). Parties to conflict can also continue the pattern of their exchange by complementing each other's behavior. *Tactical complementarity* during conflict thus occurs when the partner engages in a way that promotes the first person's tactics, both positive and negative. Earlier, we discussed the demand–withdraw pattern, perhaps the most researched of all complementary patterns.

TABLE 2.5 Examples of Negative Reciprocation Patterns

---

1. Demand–withdraw: one person attempts to discuss an issue, often negatively; the other person refuses or otherwise denies the problem or deflects the issue.
2. Complaint–counter-complaint: a complaint by one person is followed by a counter-complaint by the other (Gottman, 1982).
3. Proposal–counter-proposal: a proposal by one partner is met immediately by a proposal by the other partner (Gottman, 1982).
4. Disagreement–disagreement: disagreement is reciprocated and/or develops refutations against another person's points (Canary, Weger, & Stafford, 1991).
5. Defensiveness–defensiveness (indifference): behaviors that are threatening or punishing to others and reciprocally invite and produce defensive behaviors in return (Alexander, 1973).
6. Attack–counter-attack: one person's criticism, showing contempt and so forth are countered by the second person doing the same.
7. Metacommunication–metacommunication (with negative feelings): statements about the process of communication are continuous (Gottman, 1982).
8. Mind-reading (negative affect): making attributions of emotions, opinions, states of mind, etc., to a spouse, delivered with negative affect, it is responded to as if it were a criticism; it is disagreed with and elaborated upon, usually with negative affect (Gottman, 1982).
9. Summarizing self: a statement by one spouse, followed by a statement from the other spouse that evaluates the speaker's previous statements (Gottman, 1979).
10. Complain–Justification: individual-oriented blaming that discloses discontentment and resentment indirectly, followed by the other's individual-oriented act which persists in clarifying one's own position regardless of other's feelings/idea (Ting-Toomey, 1983).

Note: Reprinted by permission of Wavelanad Press, Inc. from Cupach, Canary, and Spitzberg with the assistance of Melissa Marks, *Competence in Interpersonal Conflict*, 2nd edn (Long Grove, IL: Waveland Press, Inc. 2010). All rights reserved.

Reciprocating or complementing negative, competitive behavior can destroy people's social and personal relationships. The reciprocity of negative message behavior confounds the clear separation of one person's conflict messages from the partner's conflict messages. People who reciprocate each other's behavior only need to look at the other person to gain insight into their own conflict communication. When negative reciprocation occurs, then the sheer amount of that behavior rises. For dissatisfied partners, the reciprocation of negative behavior

TABLE 2.6 Examples of Positive Reciprocation Patterns

1. Validation (argument exchange): comment followed by the other with "assent codes" (Gottman, 1982).
2. Contracting: direct modification of one's own point of view (Gottman, 1982).
3. Convergence: understanding and/or agreement with one another's arguables, the convergence is either explained and/or leads to new ideas (Canary, Weger, & Stafford, 1991).
4. Supportiveness–supportiveness: genuine information seeking and information giving are reciprocated (Alexander, 1973).
5. Cajoling (coaxing–coaxing): mutual-oriented act that attempts to make the partner feel good about himself/herself before making explicit any other motivation behind the act (e.g., flattering other, gentle appealing., jokes) (Ting-Toomey, 1983).
6. Metacommunication–metacommunication (with positive feelings): brief statements about the constructive process of communication (Gottman, 1979).
7. Socioemotional (description–question): descriptive statements concerning one's feelings, followed by statements that inquire about the affective state of the partner (Ting-Toomey, 1983).
8. Task-oriented (question–question): statements that ask for factual information or request further elaboration of task-oriented points, followed by asking for information or further elaboration from the other spouse criterion (Ting-Toomey, 1983).
9. Task-oriented (question–description): statements that ask for factual information or request further elaboration of task-oriented points, followed by issue-oriented factual statements concerning the past, present, or future (Ting-Toomey, 1983).
10. Mind-reading (neutral, positive affect): making attributions of emotions, opinions, states of mind, etc., to a spouse with neutral or positive affect, it is then responded to as if it were a question about feelings; it is agreed with and elaborated (Gottman, 1982).
11. Summarizing (spouse or both): any statement by the other speaker that summarizes the previous statements of the other person and/or a statement that prevents a review of the conversation (Gottman, 1979).
12. Confirm–agree: reveals one's understanding of the situation and openly conveys acknowledgement, empathy and/or acceptance of partner's feelings/ideas, followed by the spouse's assent, explicit agreement, and/or compliance which indicates one's concurrence and support for the other's ideas (Ting-Toomey, 1983).

increases within the episode of conflict (Billings, 1979; Gottman, 1994). The urge to respond in kind can be all-consuming. People in conflict can reciprocate or complement each other's behavior for an extraordinary amount of time.

Why do people reciprocate/complement each other's negative tactics? The truth is that several factors promote reciprocation and complementarity. First, people value fairness, want to be treated fairly, and resent partners who appear to want more than they deserve. Unfair treatment rattles even the self-composed. For example, people who are treated unfairly rely more on *distributive-aggression* tactics than fairly treated people.

Second, people will engage in reciprocation of negative messages when they believe their identity is being questioned. Indeed, Spitzberg (2010) argues that refusing someone's account, or explanation, for a negative behavior escalates conflict because not believing what someone says suggests that the person is a liar or a coward, or worse. The notion that someone else disrespects you is implied in this hostile question: "Who the ____do you think you are?!"

Third, people implicitly use the other person's behavior as a barometer for how much pressure the conversation can hold. Responding politely to your partner's claim that she or he is right is difficult. Responding politely to your partner's ugly stare and twisted face in anger can be almost impossible.

Given the above material we offer:

Conclusion 2.4: People tend to reciprocate or complement conflict strategies and tactics.

Suggestion 2.4: Do not reciprocate or complement negative messages! Do reciprocate or complement positive messages.

3

MAINTENANCE AND CONFLICT

A Dual Process View

More than 40 years ago, Orden and Bradburn (1968) observed that relational happiness derives from two factors—"satisfactions" and "tensions" (or *rewards* and *incompatibilities*). Rewards positively affect relational happiness and incompatibilities negatively affect happiness. However, rewards and incompatibilities do not necessarily associate with each other. According to Orden and Bradburn, maintaining quality relationships requires the provision of rewards and the reduction of incompatibilities, because the removal of one does not necessarily lead to an increase in the other (p. 715). Couples cannot simply decrease incompatibilities to increase rewards; rewards require behaviors other than eliminating incompatibilities. According to Orden and Bradburn, more current assessments have determined that two processes represent (1) the reduction of antagonism and (2) the increase of nurturance.

Recently, researchers have explored how conflict behaviors specifically combine with other contexts and domains of communication to affect relational quality (e.g., Caughlin & Huston, 2006; Ellis & Malamuth, 2000). This research holds that conflict communication does not operate as a monolithic determinant of relational quality. Rather, other forms of communication in the home affect relational quality. This perspective of how conflict affects relational quality and outcomes is known as the "Dual Concerns" approach.

The Dual Concerns view examines conflict and various other domains of behavior, including playfulness and enthusiasm (Driver & Gottman, 2004), social support, love and responsiveness (Ellis & Malamuth, 2000; Huston, Caughlin, Houts, Smith, & George, 2001), and other proactive behaviors. In addition, positive and negative behaviors function differently as marriages continue (Gottman & Levenson, 2002; Huston et al., 2001; Rogge and Bradbury, 1999). Processes that predict divorce in the early years differ from the processes that predict relational quality and divorce later. Stable and satisfied partners engage in a variety of positive behaviors that affect and reflect how conflict behaviors function in close relationships as well as work relationships (Waldron, 2003).

We focus on how selected relational maintenance behaviors complement conflict strategies to affect relational quality. Positive and proactive maintenance behaviors are strongly associated with quality indicators such as trust, commitment, and satisfaction (Canary, Stafford & Semic, 2002). In this chapter we show how shared activities, social support, and positivity complement conflict management in predicting relational quality. (Elsewhere we review how sharing tasks reduces conflict; Canary & Stafford, 2001.) Figure 3.1 presents the dual process model involving maintenance and conflict strategies.

The key assumptions of this model are that (1) managing conflict cooperatively can reduce aversion, whereas (2) promoting the relationship through maintenance behaviors increases relational quality. Relational quality reflects in important factors such as stability, satisfaction, commitment, and so forth. Relational maintenance behaviors promote cooperative conflict communication and change the course of destructive messages. In turn, direct fighting and indirect fighting negatively affect one's motivation to share activities, show support, and use positivity. Finally, both conflict communication and maintenance behaviors directly affect personal and relational outcomes. See Figure 3.1.

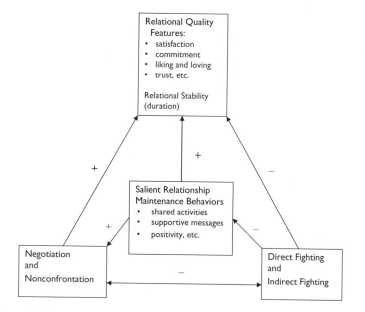

FIGURE 3.1 Links among Cooperative and Competitive Conflict, Relationship Maintenance Behaviors, Stability and Relational Quality Features

Note: A positive sign indicates a positive association between factors; a negative sign indicates an inverse association between factors.

We first discuss how spending activities together during leisure time provides opportunities to develop a nurturing relational environment. Next we examine how participation in shared activities mitigates against aversion, negative conflict behaviors, and potential harms that sometime arise from conflict. Finally, we touch on the roles of positivity and supportiveness as maintenance behaviors.

Balancing Conflict and Shared Activities

Researchers have identified *shared activities* as quite important in maintaining various kinds of work and personal relationships (Canary et al., 2002; Canary, Stafford, Hause, & Wallace, 1993; Dindia & Baxter, 1987; Waldron, 2003). Spending time with one's partner in an inclusive manner helps to nurture a positive relational environment (Waller & McLanahan, 2005). In turn, one's relational environment establishes a context for dealing with incompatibilities when they emerge.

Overall, partners tend to be *unhappy* about the amount of time they spend together and the types of activities they pursue (Huston, Robins, Atkinson, & McHale, 1987). Differences in types of shared activities can make a difference. Friends tend to spend more time involved in *interactive activities*, where partners interact with each other; and married partners tend to spend less time pursuing *parallel activities*, where partners are together but do not interact, and *individual activities*, or activities done alone (Orthner, 1975).

Although partners tend to be unhappy with the time spent together, Yet Voorpostel, Gershuny and van der Lippe (2007) found that partners actually participate in more shared activities than they did 50 years ago. Such activities include going to the cinema, theatre, concerts, museums, sporting events, restaurants, parties, and so forth. And partners play games (e.g., cards; board games) and simply spend time together at home. A much smaller increase in satisfaction was due to sharing arts, crafts, and hobbies. *Decreases* in satisfaction occurred with increases in shared use of television, radio, and music (Voorpostel et al., 2007).

That partners find some of their shared activities dissatisfying merits comment. First, individuals simply want to do some activities alone (Orthner, 1975). Still, spending time alone could imply that one person is purposefully excluding their partner from events (Beck & Beck-Gernsheim, 2001). Second, women opting to spend time in the workforce, as men do and have done, means less time for couple activities (Emmers-Sommer, 2004). Next, couples' time together can be negatively impacted by the number of hours at paid labor (e.g., Kingston & Nock, 1987). Last, the presence of children in the home decreases the amount of time partners can spend with each other (Hill, 1988; White, 1983).

Shared Activities and Conflict

Shared activities also act as "shock absorbers" during conflict (Orthner, 1975, p. 93). Sampling participants from 11 countries, Varga (1972) reported a strong and negative correlation between the amount of joint activities and divorce. Partners who perceive more joint activities are more likely to experience higher levels of marital satisfaction and quality but lower levels of marital distress and separation (Hill, 1988; Locke, 1951; Orthner, 1975; Orthner & Mancini, 1990, 1991; Smith, Snyder, & Monsma, 1988).

Several researchers have examined the link between shared activities and conflict in marriage. Findings support the idea that jointly shared activities act as a *buffer* against relational tensions and conflict. For example, Hill (1988) observed that couples can decrease the amount of conflict if they increase shared activities. Likewise, Waller and Mclanahan (2005) found that low levels of conflict and high levels of shared activities increase partner commitment. Similarly, Crawford, Houts, Huston, and George (2002) found that engaging in shared activities suppressed individuals' desire to pursue independent activities. However, if couples pursue activities that only one partner enjoys, more conflict can emerge (Crawford et al., 2002). Additionally, Orden and Bradburn (1968) found that the happiest couples experienced few tensions but engaged in several interactive activities; couples with high tension cannot offset lower levels of happiness unless they have high levels of interactive-based shared activities.

As suggested above, certain forms of shared activity appear more beneficial than others. Excitement appears to make the heart grow fonder—not the mere presence of the partner. Aron and colleagues differentiated between "exciting" or "challenging" shared activities versus "mundane" shared activities. They found that engaging in exciting activities (vs. mundane ones) brought about significantly higher levels of relational quality and satisfaction (Aron, Norman, & Aron, 2000; Aron, Norman, McKenna, & Heyman, 2001). Challenging and novel activities in particular increase satisfaction (Aron, Norman, Aron, & Lewandowski, 2002). Strong and Aron (2006) pointed out that, "when the couple is no longer engaging in a novel and challenging activity, positive affect is reduced and conflict returns" (p. 354). This research implies that couples should engage in exciting, challenging, novel activities.

Sex as a "Shared Activity"

One shared activity involves sex. Having sex satisfies a number of needs as well as relational quality. Although sex most often occurs within positive episodes, sex can reduce tensions arising from conflict. Partners can use sex "to reconnect after a period of alienation or soothe disappointment," and to offer a "port in the storm" following a stressful encounter (McCarthy & McCarthy, 2009, p. 52). Sometimes, partners intentionally start conflict so they can enjoy "make-up sex" (Goldner, 2004). Goldner also indicated that sex after conflict offers erotic mystery and novelty. One ironic reason why sexual intimacy has not been popularly tied to conflict communication is that researchers have subordinated the importance of sex to the study of conflict behaviors (Sullivan et al., 2010).

Sex Differences in Shared Activities

A few important sex differences affect shared activities. For example, Claxton and Perry-Jenkins (2008) found that wives who reported more interactive-based shared activities also reported more marital love and less conflict one year later as opposed to their husbands. Other research shows that wives who engage in independent leisure report lower levels of marital satisfaction (Crawford et al., 2002; Orthner, 1975). Marks, Huston, Johnson, and MacDermid (2001) found that husbands who engage in more independent activities experience more role strain (i.e., anxiety as different roles compete for one's time and energy). Marks et al. (2001) noted that interdependent shared activities benefit both husbands and wives.

Gager and Sanchez (2003) found that shared time for wives increases marital solidarity and buffers against divorce and conflict. For husbands, however, shared activities *positively* associated with the likelihood of divorce. In brief, shared activities consistently associate with relational quality for women—but not for men.

Several explanations exist regarding how shared activities as a buffer to conflict might have negative repercussions for partners. First, as Aron et al. (2000) point out, challenging and exciting activities—not ordinary or mundane activities—help promote relational quality. Second, engaging in shared activities might reveal to partners (esp. men) that their relationship has become boring. Such would certainly be the case if couples share an activity that only one person enjoys (e.g., who likes board games?). Third, trying to cooperate in shared activities could create conflict, especially if one person sees the same event as an individual versus interdependent activity (e.g., one person sees golf as a competitive sport, and the other views golf as an opportunity to interact). Sharing activities could increase conflict, which might deter them from wanting to engage in further shared activities (Orthner & Mancini, 1990). Finally, women's involvement in shared activities tends to utilize their communication skills; men's engagement in shared activities tends to reflect an obligation to meet an expectation (Canary & Wahba, 2006). Thus, men might find interactive shared activities more taxing than women.

Most research supports the idea that sharing activities help minimize destructive conflicts. As Orthner (1975) noted, the primary relational function of shared activities for marriage is that it facilitates cooperative communication during times of conflict. At the same time, sex difference findings suggest that interactive-based shared activities present a positive buffer against conflict, particularly for women. The view of shared activities as a buffer to conflict is not as robust for men. Given the above review, we offer the following:

> *Conclusion 3.1: Conflict strategies operate in conjunction with proactive and positive maintenance behaviors to affect relational stability and quality.*
>
> *Conclusion 3.2: Sharing activities can buffer the use and effects of competitive conflict.*

Conclusion 3.3: Men tend to prefer independent activities more than women do, whereas women tend to prefer interdependent activities more than men do.

Suggestion 3.1: Be mindful that conflict episodes occur within a larger relational context, which includes shared activities and other communicative behaviors such as social support, positivity, sharing tasks, and so forth.

Suggestion 3.2: Engage in novel and exciting shared activities in addition to routine shared activities.

Suggestion 3.3: Attempt to accommodate to the other person's preference for independent and interdependent leisure activities.

Supportive Messages

Relational partners provide a critical source of assurances, including social support (Beach, Martin, Blum, & Roman, 1993; Julien & Markman, 1991; Sullivan, Pasch, Johnson, & Bradbury, 2010). People who receive high partner support enjoy greater relational satisfaction than do partners who report lower levels of support (Acitelli & Antonucci, 1994; Cutrona & Suhr, 1993; Julien & Markman, 1991). In addition, couples often cite lack of support as a reason for relational dissatisfaction and dissolution (Baxter, 1986). Furthermore, supportive messages correlate inversely with nonverbal messages during conflict (Sullivan et al., 2010). Moreover, supportive messages can help the partner overcome a variety of debilitating experiences to the extent they are used skillfully (e.g., are person-centered, include helpful appraisals; see Burleson, 2003; Burleson & Goldsmith, 1998; Burleson & Samter, 1985; MacGeorge & Burleson, 2003).

Supportive behaviors include expressions of love and concern, providing practical advice, and showing one self as being loyal; overprotection, insensitive comments, and lack of care are nonsupportive behaviors (Burleson & Goldsmith, 1995; Goldsmith, 2004; MacGeorge & Burleson, 2003). In addition, empathic statements that display concern and understanding, responses that promote trust and appreciation, and showing feelings of goodwill, thoughtfulness and helpfulness reflect positive relational behaviors (Cutrona, 1996). Supportive behaviors function to build a nurturing relational context and to repair damage done (Burleson & Goldsmith, 1995). The positive effects of support can reduce the impacts of negative conflict and stress (Sullivan et al., 2010; Vangelisti, 2009). Using more supportive than unsupportive behaviors also helps people to cope with conflict and stress (Cutrona, 1996; Gottman & Levenson, 1992; Sullivan et al., 2010).

Even in the first year of marriage, however, a lack of supportive behavior can exacerbate negative emotions expressed during conflict to affect relational satisfaction negatively (Pasch & Bradbury, 1998). Empirical evidence consistently shows that both higher levels of marital conflict and lower levels of supportive communication associate with poorer mental and physical health (Kiecolt-Glaser & Newton, 2001). As with shared activities and positivity, supportive messages and conflict operate independently; for instance, supportive messages contribute to satisfaction after the effects due to negative conflict are removed (Pasch & Bradbury, 1998; Sullivan et al., 2010). Supportive communication can function as a buffer against the negative effects of conflict. Pasch and Bradbury's (1998; see also Sullivan et al., 2010) findings indicate that stable and satisfied couples report higher levels of support and lower of levels of conflict than do their counterparts. Similarly, Pierce, Sarason, and Sarason (1992) found that relationships characterized by conflict contain fewer supportive behavior. Moreover, lower levels of support associate with greater relational problems (Cutrona, 1996).

Pasch, Bradbury, Davila, and Sullivan (1999) examined some implications that supportive communication has on relational characteristics. These researchers found that supportive communication predicted satisfaction in couples four years later. Likewise, Julien, Chartrand, Simard, Bouthillier, and Begin (2003) found that supportive communication positively correlates with relational quality. Additionally, supportive communication conveys new information not expressed during conflict. Thus, supportive messages post-conflict benefited partners who could provide information that was left unsaid during conflict episodes. As is evident, engaging in supportive communication before, during, and after conflict is pertinent to maintaining the relationship and buffering the effects of conflict.

Caughlin and Huston (2002) examined supportive messages pertaining to the demand–withdraw pattern. They found that positive affection buffers the negative relationship between relational satisfaction and demand–withdraw patterns. The negative effects the demand–withdraw pattern has on couples, particularly when engaging in serial arguing, is reduced by supportive messages—particularly those that contain affection.

As Cutrona (1996) found, supportive communication provides a positive emotional tone to the relationship that might "actually prevent the occurrence of frequent and intense conflicts by virtue of the positive emotional tone that they establish in the relationship" (Cutrona, 1996, p. 180). In particular, expressions of understanding and recognition of a partner's emotions constitute supportive messages that happily married couples used to moderate the effects of conflict. Sullivan et al. (2010) also found that supportive messages reduced the effects of conflict over time. Thus, supportive communication aides couples to express themselves honestly when conflict arises, leading to likelihood of effectively managing the conflict. In addition, supportive communication increases feelings of closeness. Moreover, the positive emotional climate that is created by supportive messages promotes the couple working together as a team, instead of approaching conflicts individually. This emphasis on the dyad can be highly effective for conflict resolution as well as countering the negative outcomes of conflict. Finally, sharing positive experiences often results in greater levels of companionship and time together in shared activities (Vangelisti, 2009).

Conclusion 3.4: Supportive messages are positively correlated with relational stability and quality and provide an atmosphere of nurturance.

Suggestion 3.4: Use supportive messages to mitigate direct fighting and indirect fighting.

Positivity and Conflict

As a maintenance strategy, positivity can affect conflict in various ways. As indicated above, positivity provides a source for building a nurturing relational climate that encases conflict when they arise. Positivity as a maintenance behavior includes: being upbeat and cheerful though one does not want to, asking how the partner's day has been, being spontaneous, doing favors for the other, complimenting the other, and so forth (Stafford & Canary, 1991). Moreover, positivity has been found to be a strong predictor of liking, commitment, and relational satisfaction (e.g., Canary et al., 2002). Also, one can use positivity within conflict interaction, for example, by acknowledging the partner, seeking areas of agreement, offering statements of affection, and the like. We focus on two ways that positivity complements conflict behaviors to predict relational quality: positivity that occurs outside of conflict and during conflict.

Researchers have recently noted that the combination of positive behaviors and conflict communication predicts divorce. For example, Caughlin and Huston (2006) summarized their program of research on the topic and argued that two factors predict divorce: affection and antagonism. They argued that high levels of affection are needed at the outset of marriage as well as over the course of marriage. Not surprisingly, high levels of antagonism disrupt marriages. These authors examined couples who had been married 14 years and they found that the combination of positive affect and antagonism combined to predict stability and relational quality.

Stable and satisfied couples experience a high amount of positive affect and a low amount of antagonism. These people remained together at the end of the study (14 years). Conversely, *unstable and dissatisfied* couples have a high amount of antagonism but low affection. As one might expect, such marriages did not survive beyond two years. Next, *stable but dissatisfied* partners remain together after 13 years. These partners experience above average antagonism but, relative to stable and satisfied couples, a low degree of affection. The *lifeless marriage* represents a fourth type wherein partners divorce between 2–7 years; lifeless marriage contains an average amount of antagonism but, of all couple types, the lowest levels of affection. Similar to the lifeless couple, a *disenchanted marriage* contains an average amount of antagonism. However, at the beginning of the marriage they enjoy a high degree of affection; but such affection gradually and clearly declines over the years. *Disenchanted* partners tend to divorce between 7–14 years of marriage. Note how antagonism and affection can operate in tandem; for instance, too much antagonism coupled with too little affection predict early divorce, whereas declines in affection (but not antagonism) predict later divorce.

Examining how couples manage conflict, Gottman and Levenson (2000, 2002) found that different behaviors predicted the timing of divorce. More precisely, they found that expressiveness and negative behavior during conflict management predicted divorce the first seven years of marriage. Similar to Caughlin and Huston's research, a high amount of negativity, in particular, predicts early divorce. After seven years, however, decreases in positive emotional expression prompts people to leave. Gottman and Levenson (2002) noted that, after seven years the primary behavioral predictors of divorce revealed an "affectless" relationship—where a lifeless bond exists between partners. Gottman and Levenson (2002) concluded, "Intense marital conflict likely makes it difficult to stay in the marriage for long, but its absence makes marriage somewhat more acceptable. Nonetheless, the absence of positive affect eventually takes its toll" (p. 743). Accordingly, being positive during even routine discussions is vital to a lasting marriage, but a lack of such positivity erodes marriage even after the effects of negative conflict have done their damage.

Turn	Speaker	Message
225	Wife	And you might ask nicely just as many times as you do unnicely [sic] and end-up with the same results. Whether you ask them five times . . .
226	Husband	I don't agree with that, because I ask them once nicely and they don't comply, and then I bark and then they comply.
227	Wife	And you know what? You *taught* them "I don't have to comply unless dad barks at me. Until dad's voice changes and he's pissed, then I *have* to comply!" And you've trained them to do that.
228	Husband	No.
229	Wife	What you have to do is retrain them . . . we have to retrain them to show we're serious.
230	Husband	How do we do that?
231	Wife	One day at a time.
232	Husband	That is not an answer.

Note that this couple reaches no satisfactory outcome and lacks positive emotional tone.

In contrast, see how this couple flirts with each other during a conflict about how much affection exists between partners.

Turn	Speaker	Message
12	Husband	Intimate affection, uh, I've been described as a sex maniac from time to time. . . . Uh, I like sex and sometimes, you know I'm not complaining—I think we have a good sex life—but I'd like to see a little bit more of it every now and then.
13	Wife	Well, um, I guess that would probably fall back to being so discouraged with my job and being depressed over my job and bringing that home. And I should not bring that home. But I have a lot of responsibility and a lot of stress, and they wear me down. I have asked to step down and they will not allow me to do it. And so it does depress me, which makes me tired, and I don't have the proper energy and motivation sometimes. But I don't think that we have an inactive sex life, either.
14	Husband	No, not by any means, but . . .
15	Wife	I just think you have a high level of testosterone and I'm just *so* cute that you're very turned on by me. And I can't help that.
16	Husband	(laughs) Well that's, that's all true, that's very true. But uh, I guess that goes back to the first issue of the job change. It affects, it affects a lot of things, and that's one of them.
17	Wife	And I'll agree with that. I'll try to work on that.
18	Husband	That'd be good.

In turn 12, the husband states his desire for more sex but minimizes its relational impact by stating "you know I'm not complaining—I think we have a good sex life." The wife then blames their decreased sex on her own work pressures but also discloses in a nonhostile manner "I don't have the proper energy and motivation sometimes. But I don't think that we have an inactive sex life, either." And the husband immediately agrees with this assessment (turn 14). Then notice the previous conversation above differs from this latter example: it contains some creativity; that is, the woman throws her husband in a loop with a teasing and provocative statement in turn 15, which reduces the tension. Importantly, compare the final comment by the husband in this example ("That'd be good") to the final statement by the husband in the previous example ("That is not an answer"). Whereas the former issue ended in a deadlock, the more recent issue ends on a positive note. Ending a conflict discussion in an affectively positive manner provides each partner reason for hope, a sense of well-being, and relief.

From the research on positivity as a productive conflict management strategy, we present the following:

> *Conclusion 3.4: Positivity as an ongoing maintenance strategy coincides strongly with relational stability and quality.*
>
> *Conclusion 3.5: Positivity during conflict proportionally diffuses the effects of negative conflict tactics; that is, the association between the ratio of positive/negative communication is strongly correlated with relational stability and quality.*
>
> *Suggestion 3.4: Use relational maintenance strategies, including positivity, on a routine basis.*
>
> *Suggestion 3.5: Use negotiation tactics, especially those in the support other category (e.g., agreement, approval, positive mind-reading, etc.).*

Although one might believe that high levels of conflict episodes prevent partners from engaging in positive episodes at other times, Fincham and Linfield (1997) found this to not be true. Rather, engagement in joint activities, supportive messages, and positivity counteracts the effects of competitive conflict. More importantly, the effects of countering conflict through interactive and interesting shared activities lead to higher levels of relational stability and relational quality. Shared activities help increase positive emotions and prompts partners to polish their constructive communication skills. Showing supportiveness to one's partner underscores one's personal commitment to the partner's well-being. Finally, positivity both within and outside conflict episodes promotes a nurturing relational environment. In brief, the management of conflict does not occur in a relational vacuum but rather can be complemented by proactive and positive behaviors that help to create a healthy and responsive relational environment for strategic conflict.

4

SEEKING EPISODE CONTROL

Conflict Instigation Due to Alcohol, Moods, Emotions, Stress, and the Environment

Our model of strategic conflict begins by considering how conflict begins. Many texts would begin this chapter by talking about issues that lead to conflict. We do not cover different issues in conflict because, with few exceptions (e.g., disagreement about household labor; e.g., Kluwer, Heesink, & van de Vliert, 1997), issues of conflict do not matter as much as how conflict is managed. Instead, we discuss the crucibles of conflict—locations where the catalyst of incompatibilities can ignite interpersonal arguments.

Research suggests that people can gain more episodic control by knowing the crucibles for conflict and strategically accounting for them. People often think that another person causes their problems and that they have little agency in how conflict emerges. This is simply not true. Parties to conflict indeed have agency in how conflict emerges and how they manage conflict right off the bat. By being more mindful of conflict instigators, you can anticipate them and strategically change them (if you wish).

At the same time, we do not underestimate the initial shock that people experience when confronted by someone else. Conflict is often negative. Anger, frustration, defensiveness, disappointment, resentment are a few of the normal responses we have to another person's negative behaviors. These are some of the crucibles for conflict.

Our objective in this chapter is to identify several factors that constitute crucibles for escalating and possibly destructive conflict. First, we focus on the effects of alcohol. Next we analyze moods and emotions, specifically anger and depression. Third we discuss how stress promotes conflict. Finally, we discuss environmental factors that lead to conflict. The reader will discover that these instigators can work alone or in combination and how strategic conflict can change the mindless influence of these instigators.

Alcohol

Effects of Alcohol

Approximately 45% of college students binge drink two times a month on average (Crews & Boettinnzer, 2009). Of course, many people enjoy alcohol for its taste and/or because it can elevate one's mood, increase sensations of warmth-glow, and remove social inhibitions (Bushman & Cooper, 1990). Also, the mere *expectation* of drinking can lead to decreased inhibitions (Hull & Bond, 1986). Still, some people drink to get drunk. Reasons why people drink to get drunk are varied (e.g., genetic versus social learning). The effects of drinking, however, remain the same.

Alcohol negatively affects the brain in dramatic ways (for reviews, see Bushman & Cooper, 1990; Crews & Boettinnzer, 2009; Hull & Bond, 1986; Scaife & Duka, 2009). We consider effects on the brain and not other organs, such as the stomach, liver, etc. More specifically, alcohol negatively affects the frontal lobes that include the *bisolateral prefrontal cortex* (bPFC), the *anterior cingulate cortex* (ACC), and the *orbital frontal cortex* (OFC). These three areas serve as "executive functions." Executive functions in the frontal cortex allow you to do the following: attend to perceptions selectively, reason and make judgments, consider the consequences of your behavior, use delayed discounting (i.e., value long-term superior rewards more than short-term inferior rewards), inhibit impulsive behavior (e.g., scratching an itch), remember an idea, keep memories over time, and other important functions.

Experts define *binge drinking* as five drinks for men and four drinks for women within a two-hour frame, give or take other factors such as body mass. Over time, binge drinking brings about severe damage to our brain and other organs. Binge drinking increases neurodegeneration of the brain, damages the frontal cortex so the executive functions are compromised, disorganizes brain processes, shrinks the size of the brain, severely damages short-term memory, impedes motor skills (e.g., shaking, swaying when walking), and so forth. Alcohol's damage to the brain also includes less connection between the frontal cortex and the *amygdala* (the part of the brain that drives impulsive behaviors), so impulsive behaviors (e.g., scratching an itch) increase and dominate executive functions. So one is less likely to make good judgments and dismiss the negative consequences from drinking (sure I'll have a hangover for my test, but who cares right now?). Greater control by the *amygdala* is why you might begin with an intention only to have a couple of drinks and then end up having several more.

These mental and other negative effects (including personal appearance, damage to liver) can continue years *after* a person stops drinking (Crews & Boettinnzer, 2009; Scaife & Duka, 2009). Moreover, continued use of alcohol indicates that you likely drink to get drunk, think a lot about drinking, crave alcohol, and behave impulsively to drink. Such behaviors, in concert with one's family history, each lead to a diagnosis of alcoholism. Yet, people behaving these ways tend to deny anything is wrong with these behaviors. Chronic use of alcohol most likely indicates the person is suffering from alcoholism and needs help (e.g., from a hospital or health clinic that cares for alcohol and drug abuse, or AA). However, only the individual can admit that he or she suffers from this terrible disease.

Alcohol as a Conflict Instigator

Alcohol challenges the best people to maintain control of their conflict episodes. Alcohol directly and indirectly increases the possibility that someone will instigate a conflict. Directly, alcohol plays a role in escalating conflict from bad to worse (MacDonald, Zanna, & Holmes, 2000). Men's and women's alcohol use leads to increased likelihood of physical, psychological, and/or sexual abuse (e.g., Cunradi, Caetano, & Schafer, 2002; Thompson, Saltzman, & Johnson, 2003). Alcohol also produces mood swings and outbursts (Lubit & Russett, 1984). Alcohol diminishes your ability to read other people's nonverbal signals and interpret messages accurately, which leads drinkers to behave irrationally (Zillman, 1990). Indirectly, people often use alcohol to reduce anxiety or to increase a sense of power, either of which may prompt more assertive communication and aggressive behavior (Bushman & Cooper, 1990). Alcohol can indirectly instigate conflict when triggered by friends, a social group, or situation—such as a particular bar. Such links to alcohol and anticipation of drinking can diminish inhibitions and responsibility. Either directly or indirectly, alcohol use and aggression appear to be good friends.

One's ability to gain and maintain episodic control dramatically depends on the amount of alcohol one takes. Simply put, excessive alcohol dismantles the frontal cortex and its executive functions that control judgment, consider consequences, and limit impulsive thinking.

This research leads to:

> *Conclusion 4.1: Increases in alcohol use damages the brain's ability to govern one's behavior and maintain episodic control.*
>
> *Suggestion 4.1: If intoxicated, avoid conflict entirely, because you have limited your ability to interpret events and communicate rationally.*
>
> *Suggestion 4.2: Do not argue with a person who is drunk.*

The Nature of Moods and Emotions

Although most people tend to view moods and emotions as similar states, differences exist between the two (Forgas, 1983). A *mood* is a state of mind that involves diffuse and general information (Forgas, 1983). You may recognize that you are in a "good mood" or a "bad mood" but not know exactly how to label your feelings or their causes. To identify their moods, people ask themselves basic questions about the situation; in turn, the questions they ask can affect the mood they identify. For example, you might be in a sour mood if wondering whether the large amount of work you do is fair because other people work less for the same pay. After reappraising the question, you can create a better mood, for example, if you focus on your enjoyment of the task, or how your work offers something important to people, or that you are fortunate to have that job (Martin, Achee, Ward, & Harlow, 1993).

Emotion, on the other hand, is more specific and includes fewer behaviors. *Emotions* entail distinct reactions to specific situations; people process certain information about an event and then react to those perceptions. Their emotion then influences behavior choices. For example, if you experience sadness, you will select different strategies than if you feel anger (Ellis & Malamuth, 2000). Because moods are more diffuse, they are easier to change than emotions (Forgas, 1983). Being sad because you move away from your friends and family is hard to change because, no matter what you do, the situation remains the same.

The Role of Moods and Emotions in Communication

Emotions influence communication in multiple ways during strategic communicating and message interpretation. Mood and emotion are involved in communication in three interrelated ways. First, in *emotion-motivated* communication, emotion precedes the communication and forms the basis for it (Dillard & Wilson, 1993). If you are relieved that your mother has successfully undergone a major operation for her cancer, then you might want to convey your relief. Next, *emotion-manifested* communication involves people's revealing their internal states implicitly or explicitly. For instance, you could explicitly disclose the good news or you might simply smile in gratitude (which can be seen by others). Finally, during *emotion-inducing* communication one person elicits an emotional response from another person. So your friends might react emotionally in a positive way to your joy. Dillard and Wilson (1993) state that friends' emotions reflect a direct response to the first person's message.

Reactions to Moods and Emotions

Moods and emotions initially influence behavior through priming, or by increasing normal base-state level of arousal to levels that can be readily triggered into an emotional reaction. Priming can occur before or during conflict, but it affects people similarly in two ways: first, *arousal* occurs when people experience perceptual discrepancies or when a force interrupts or blocks some activity they are doing (Mandler, 1993); second, *physiological arousal* occurs when people experience an interruption of goal-relevant actions. Because people cannot easily identify strategic paths to complete their plans, they experience emotional priming. The positive or negative feature of the emotion depends on several factors, such as the importance and urgency of the goal.

One communication-based emotional priming involves positive versus negative interruptions. Conflict challenges people to make coherent sense of their thoughts when they might feel emotionally strained (Sillars & Weisberg, 1983). Not allowing someone to complete his or her thoughts adds to the challenge. Moreover, interruptions during conflict typically emerge in direct fighting tactics that bewilders and frustrates the conversational partner (Sillars et al., 2003). More helpful interruptions assist the partner to complete his or her thoughts with clarification, organization, evidence, and other forms of support (Robey, Canary, & Burggraf, 1998). Conversations proceed more smoothly when interdependent people work together in problem solving communication (a negotiation tactic), and they perceive fewer interruptions than people who function more independently. Consider how this couple engage in interruptions that prevent the partner from completing his/her point of view.

Turn	Speaker	Message
94	Husband	Well, look at what you did. Look at the scene you made!
95	Wife	Yeah, well you deserved it.
96	Husband	No, I didn't . . .
97	Wife	Everybody fights.
98	Husband	deserve that.
99	Wife	So . . .
100	Husband	No, everybody . . .
101	Wife	Yeah, everybody fights dear. 'cause if they don't . . .
102	Husband	Yeah, but not in the presence of company. Not when, honey, we had 15 people.
103	Wife	See, I'm a very prompt [sic] person. I don't care . . .
104	Husband	But I do.

With regard to mood and functions of interruptions, we offer the following:

> *Conclusion 4.2: Become mindful that moods are diffuse but can change by altering your interpretation of events, and emotions are more difficult to change.*
>
> *Suggestion 4.3: Interrupt other people primarily to help them develop their ideas.*

The Role of Moods in Thought and Action

Mood affects people in various ways. Happy people tend to be more confident, set higher goals for themselves, and overestimate the likelihood that they will succeed (Forgas, 1999). People in positive moods more likely comply with a request—if it does not interfere with their own positive mood (Forgas, 1998a). Happy people tend to use negotiation tactics more and direct fighting less (Forgas, 1998b). In contrast, people in negative moods make negative assessments of themselves and of others, have reduced levels of self-confidence and self-efficacy, increased self-deprecating messages, and reliance on pessimistic judgments of other people's behavior (Forgas, 1999). These people also are less likely to comply with requests and to be more critical of requests (Forgas, 1998a). In addition, people in negative moods tend to be more competitive and less cooperative.

Naturally, moods affect how people process information. Happy people, who have no need to change to their mood state, tend to use *heuristic processing* (e.g., "She's wearing glasses, so she must know what she is saying"). *Heuristic* thinking is a type of mindless thinking largely formed by schemata or ready-made explanations for how behavior unfolds. Sad people tend toward more complex *systematic processing* (Forgas, 1995), and they tend to take an analytical approach to explaining events (e.g., "His data do not support his claim") (Keltner, Ellsworth, & Edwards, 1993). As a result of their unconscious awareness, happy people generally recall less information from interactions than do people in a negative mood.

However, here is a situation where systematic processing works against strategic conflict. The reason is that people mindlessly, unconsciously distort evaluations of interactions to coincide with their moods (Forgas, Levinger, & Moylan, 1994). Even temporary moods affect our judgments, such as attributions we make about who is responsible for the conflict, a phenomenon we discuss with more development in Chapter 10. Happy people tend to use explanations that do not blame the partner—the causes are external, unstable, and unique to the specific conflict. Such judgments are optimistic and lenient. Conversely, sad people tend to explain the cause of their sadness as something that resides in the other person, is stable over time, and can be linked to the other person's personality (e.g., "he is stupid") (Forgas, 1994). Sad people tend to think about their perceptions over and over, or what scholars call *rumination* (e.g., Burnette, Davis, Green, Worhington, & Bradfield, 2009).

Such biases no doubt affect responses to conflict (Forgas, 1998c). Judgments about our relationships tend to be favorable when we are in good moods and unfavorable when we are in negative moods. Clearly, mood-congruent judgments (when negative) can set up conflict situations that can quickly escalate (Forgas et al., 1994). For example, an individual can have radically different reactions to teasing. When in a good mood, teasing can be seen as good fun; when in a bad mood, teasing can be taken as provocation.

Regulating Negative Moods

People can learn to recognize their positive and negative moods and to understand the distortion these moods can cause. This recognition allows people to compensate for their current mood (Forgas, 1999). Indeed, the simple recognition of your ability to change negative mood states can improve your negative moods.

Catanzaro and Mearns (1990) argued that mood regulation largely depends on people's belief that they can change their negative moods. They proposed three factors of negative mood regulation. *General negative mood regulation (NMR)* refers to one's thoughts about cheering oneself. *Cognitive NMR* concerns thinking of happier times and faith in happier times again and soon. *Behavioral NMR* refers to being with friends and sharing pleasurable activities with friends. Catanzaro and Mearns developed a measure of NMR which assesses people's expectations that they can change their negative moods—and provides a tool to gain episodic control.

These factors are contained in the NMR measure. Table 4.1 reports example items for general, cognitive, and behavioral NMR.

Catanzaro and Mearns found that the greater a person's NMR score, the less they tend to experience depression and sadness. In addition, Cantazaro and Laurent (2004) found that NMR is negatively linked to avoidance and using alcohol to alleviate negative moods (i.e., alcohol does not relieve depression). The implication for episodic control is clear with regard to mood variation:

Conclusion 4.3: Moods affect how you perceive and process information, including information about other people.

TABLE 4.1 Negative Mood Regulation (NMR) Example Items

General Items

I can usually find a way to cheer up.
Wallowing in it is all I can do (reversed).
I won't be able to enjoy the things I usually enjoy (reversed).

Cognitive Items

I feel okay if I think about more pleasant times.
I can forget about what's upsetting me pretty easily.
Thinking that things will eventually be better won't help me feel any better (reversed).

Behavioral Items

Being with other people will be a drag (reversed).
Doing something nice for someone else will cheer me up.
Going out to dinner with friends will help.

Adapted from Cantazaro and Mears.

Suggestion 4.4: Be mindful and use negative mood regulation with alternative cognitions and rely on people in your social network.

Dual Emotional Instigators: Anger and Depression

Anger

Anger is common. Many people respond to anger *impulsively,* probably with direct fighting tactics of hostility (e.g., a hostile question, a threat, using intimidation; see Table 2.1). Because people often speak impulsively out of anger, they later regret it. Being angry constitutes one of the primary experiences where episodic control is needed.

In a review of the research, Canary, Spitzberg, and Semic (1998) identify other causes of anger:

- *identity management*: a person questions your integrity explicitly or implicitly;
- *aggression*: someone behaves with hostility toward you or someone else;
- *frustration*: someone frustrates you;
- *lack of fairness*: you believe that you are not treated in a fair manner;
- *incompetence*: a person you depend on cannot perform his or her job;
- *relationship threat*: you perceive a third party trying to interfere with your close relationship(s);
- *predisposition*: the reliance on aggression as a *modus operandi*—the predominant strategy for managing conflict.
- *general reaction*: someone mindlessly responds to a situation aggressively.

A plurality of researchers have investigated how challenges to one's identity can anger people. People commonly become angry, and even deadly, when someone questions their identity. Indeed, several researchers have argued that threats to one's identity leads to physical and psychological aggression (e.g., Schönbach, 1990; Spitzberg, 2010). Also, identity management can be central to training people how to manage conflict in the workplace (e.g., Jones & Brinkert, 2008, offer training strategies for identity management).

Expression of anger through direct fighting does not help people to vent their anger and become calm (Canary et al., 1998). Rather, direct fighting tactics often make the anger worse by prompting a reciprocation of direct and indirect fighting (Canary et al., 1998). Anger expression constitutes a critical event where people can exercise episodic control through strategic communication. Elevated anger diminishes your ability to think strategically. For example, one of the authors was flying after a presentation, squished in a middle seat. The person in the aisle seat pushed his arm off the armrest they shared to expand his personal space. Dan was angry but paused a moment to re-group. Then he used the negotiation tactic of *external problem description* by offering to buy this man a drink. We then both enjoyed the flight in good conversation. Strategic conflict allowed for episodic control of anger.

> *Conclusion 4.4: Causes of anger vary and indictment of a person's identity management can be the most severe.*

> *Suggestion 4.5: Be mindful that causes of anger vary and can have negative implications for a person's identity management.*

Strategies to Manage Anger

People's strategic communication in response to anger varies. Using the dimensions of threat and directness, Guerrero (1994) identified four general strategic responses to emotions: *distributive-aggression* behaviors include tactics that are both direct and threatening. *Integrative-assertive* references behaviors that are direct and non-threatening; these behaviors focus on the needs of the other person and are constructive. *Passive-aggression* uses indirect but still threatening behaviors; people are unwilling or unable to express their strong negative feelings but do so in such a way that they cannot be reproached. Finally, *Nonassertive-Denial* refers to indirect behaviors that are non-threatening and even self-protective. Of course, these strategies coincide with those presented in Chapter 2 and are useful for thinking how to act in response to emotions.

Guerrero, Farinelli, and McEwan (2008) found, for example, that people who are treated fairly are more likely to rely on integrative-assertion in response to relationship conflict. People who are treated unfairly rely more on distributive-aggression tactics. The take-away from Guerrero and colleagues' work is to rely on integrative-assertion tactics during interpersonal conflict.

Without using mindfulness, people can escalate from anger to rage (Retsinger, 1991), emotional flooding (Gottman, 1994), and increased negative arousal and excitement (Zillman, 1988, 1990). Zillman (1990) argues that our arousal levels reach a point where anger short-circuits rational thinking. That is, the portion of our brains that provide "executive functions" (i.e., the frontal cortex) is overridden by mere impulses to respond in anger. Such impulsive responses to anger typically produce intense direct fighting tactics that lead to more intense anger (Martin, Anderson, & Horvath, 1996). However, people who possess knowledge about anger and its expression can decide on a strategy and tactics to manage anger more effectively (Stern, 1999).

Responsible expression of emotion (especially anger) provides several benefits. Responsible expression provides feedback about our emotions and allows us to relieve inner tension and to avoid negative secondary emotions such as depression. Our expression of emotion also tells other people that something has happened that we care about; we express our needs and can interact more effectively with others (Mongrain & Vettese, 2003). Expressing anger through assertive-integrative behaviors increases relationship satisfaction and perceptions of communication competence (Guerrero, 1994). Using distributive-aggression (direct fighting) tactics can even help the other person look better, although everyone involved might know that the other person is clearly wrong.

> *Conclusion 4.5: People who act impulsively in anger and use direct fighting tactics reduce their episodic control and will likely regret their behavior.*
>
> *Suggestion 4.6: At the onset of anger, pause for a moment to respond mindfully, and then select a communication strategy that addresses your source of anger.*

Another way to manage anger is to control your paralanguage—especially the rate and volume of speech. Expressing anger using rapid and loud speech increases your own negative physiological arousal; so, you make yourself even angrier. Your negative arousal tells your brain that you are in trouble. Conversely, expressing anger using calm, slow, and soft paralanguage helps to reduce physiological effects and levels of anger (Siegman & Snow, 1997). Reduction in anger represents an effective way for you to obtain episodic control, and it will likely reduce the other person's anger as well.

Consider how airline pilots communicate to passengers when the plane is approaching turbulence. Airline pilots do not scream, "People, I cannot *believe* what I am seeing! You had better get back to your seats! Oh yeah, and make sure you are buckled up . . . God, that storm is big!" Can you imagine the panic that would follow such a message? Instead, airline pilots are trained to convey a sense that all is right in the sky, and they communicate in low tones and in a calm, slow manner: "Ladies and gentlemen, we are going to hit a few bumps. So, I am turning on the seatbelt sign and am asking you to return to your seat. Sorry for the inconvenience, but we should be through this in a few minutes."

Neither total suppression nor unrestrained expression of anger at the other person reflects a smart strategic approach. Averill (1993) advised that people have a right to express their anger when they are faced with intentional hurtful actions or unintentional ones that can be corrected. Tavris (1989) and Averill (1993) agree that your anger should be directed at the source of your anger; that the response to anger should not be over-reactive, and that you should not take your anger out on a third party.

Sometimes, the only way to avoid aggression is for parties to stop their conflict interaction temporarily with a period of silence and/or for them to physically leave the conflict site. Providing breaks in conflict interaction can help people gain episodic control. Both actions allow people time to cool off and calm down (but it does not work for everyone). Such periods of silence work if neither person is in reality "stonewalling," by ignoring the partner in a hostile way. Once people have allowed their emotions to return to their baseline, they return to the conflict interaction with a greater chance they will remain controlled (Zillman, 1990).

If the other person exhibits strong negative arousal, it is counter-productive to confront the person at that time. That person is probably too defensive and his/her emotional responses have already risen above their usual level of containment (Donohue & Kolt, 1992). If people become highly aroused or excited, they experience cognitive deficits in their brains' executive functions. They cannot process rational argument at that point (Zillman, 1993). Again, for episodic control, it might be smart to disengage for a period of time; you yield only temporarily, fully intending to continue the discussion when the person has calmed down and can function normally. The above material leads us to suggest:

> *Conclusion 4.6: Be mindful that anger can short-circuit the brain's executive functions and lead to impulsive, self-destructive behavior.*
>
> *Suggestion 4.7: To maintain episodic control, speak softly and slowly when angry.*
>
> *Suggestion 4.8: Express anger at the person who instigated that anger in proportion to the action that led to your anger (do not overreact).*
>
> *Suggestion 4.9: Avoid conflict (or insert breaks) when anger has overridden either person's ability to engage in mindful strategic communication.*

Depression

Approximately 10% of the U.S. population suffers from depression in any given year (Duggan, 2007). General symptoms of depression include self-devaluation, sadness, weight loss, lack of sleep, fatigue, feelings of worthlessness, general negativity, negativity toward the partner, inappropriate disclosures, and so on (Duggan, 2007; Segrin, 1990). In brief, depressed people suffer from deficits in their self-esteem and social skills that manifest in overall negativity and incompetent conflict strategies and tactics.

Being in a relationship involving a depressed person entails less satisfaction and more anger/resentment than being in a normative relationship (e.g., Hinchliffe, Hooper, & Roberts, 1978). Moreover, depressed people engage in more ruminating thoughts than most people, with increased rumination leading to increased depression, and more negativity toward the problem being ruminated. That depression challenges people to gain episodic control appears obvious. However, how one attains episodic control does not easily address the challenge, because people in depressed relationships likely experience dilemmas regarding how to manage depression.

According to Inconsistent Nurturing Control (Duggan & LaPoire, 2006) the partners of depressed people want to nurture the partner and control the path of depression so the partner gets well. Yet these objectives are inconsistent because the partner wants the depressed person to remain dependent for affection but yearns for times when the depressed person is happy. The depressed person meanwhile enjoys the benefits that come with partner nurturing but wants to live in a more rewarding emotional state (Duggan, 2007). Given these inconsistent desires, repeated cycles of nurturing and control occur where each partner relies on tactics that reflect these incompatible goals. Clearly, depression confounds efforts at episodic control through a complex interplay of mixed intentions.

Obviously, depression has a major role in conflict management. Segrin (1990) noted that depressed people in general engage in more direct fighting and less negotiation, as one might expect. One study illustrates the kind of findings in the research: Henne, Buysse, and Van Oost (2007) reported that

> couples with a depressed [partner] report significantly higher levels of depressive symptoms, ambivalent and avoidant attachment, man-demand/woman-withdraw and woman-demand/man-withdraw interactions, mutual avoidance and causal attributions, and lower levels of marital adjustment and constructive communication, independent of whether the individuals are [depressed] or partners [of depressed people], and male or female . . . (p. 503)

Also, sex differences occur in how people respond to depression and that specific conflict tactics connect with both husband and wife depression. For example, Du Rocher Schudlich, Papp, and Cummings (2004) found that dysphoria (minor experiences of depression) brought about more use of both partners' angry and depressing messages; and the wife's depression brought about more use of depressing messages. "These particularly harmful strategies included verbal hostility, defensiveness, withdrawal, and insults, as well as more displays of negative affect (anger and sadness)" (Du Rocher Schudlich et al., p. 180). These findings regarding changes in one's depression were discovered *after* levels of marital satisfaction and the partner's depression levels were controlled. Such findings despite controls indicate that the link between one person's depression and couple conflict behaviors are clear and "not simply an artifact of co-occurring marital satisfaction" (p. 180).

Although female depression is more common than male depression, it appears that male depression might create more damage. Du Rocher Schudlich et al. found that depression in the husband had greater influence on conflict messages than did that of the wife. The larger effect for husband depression occurred in conflicts about minor issues as well as major issues. In a different study involving depressed husbands and wives, Proulx, Buehler, and Helms (2009) found that the husband's general hostility toward his wife substantially increased the wife's symptoms of depression. However, hostility in the wife did not significantly affect the husband's depressive symptoms. Further analyses found that both partners' warm behaviors change the negative effect of hostility on the wife's depression.

Managing Depression

How people maintain or retrieve episodic control in a depressive relationship initially appears a daunting task. However, Segrin's "social skills deficit vulnerability model" provides a few suggests. In a word, he argues that people become depressed when they lack social skills and must face stressful events alone. Depressed people lack the social support and resources that their counterparts enjoy. In such stressful circumstances then, depressed people fail and receive confirmation that they cannot perform and are not worthy. As Segrin noted, "It is, therefore, the combination of poor social skills and negative life events that are thought to produce depressive distress" (pp. 394–5).

The social skills deficit vulnerability model suggests that they and their partners should seek control over situations that are stressful. Knowing that depressed people are particularly vulnerable during stressful times might suggest that stressful periods require more support and assurance from partners than in other periods. This is at least one potential strategy for gaining and maintaining episodic control.

In terms of relational quality, it appears that reframing the issue can change the ability of one to achieve episodic control. Henne et al. (2007) found that the link between depression and marital quality depended on how people explained the cause of their conflicts. If the conflicts were seen as temporary and no one's fault, then marital adjustment was higher than if the partner or self caused the conflict. As Henne et al. concluded, "the association between depressive symptoms and marital adjustment is conditional on the values of causal attributions" (Henne et al., 2007, p. 505). Given this research on depression and conflict, the following conclusions and strategies are offered:

> *Conclusion 4.7: Depression is an ongoing, sad, self-defeating, and negative experience that is often reflected in a deficit of social skills, hostile conflict, and reduced relational quality.*

> *Conclusion 4.8: Helping depressed people is difficult given an inconsistency of nurturing and controlling motives for relational partners and the negative attributions that depressed people often entertain.*

> *Suggestion 4.10: Provide social support to depressed people, especially when they face stressful situations (such as conflict).*

> *Suggestion 4.11: Help depressed people see alternative attributions to their conflicts, when they attempt to hold someone at fault or view the problem as stable over time.*

Stress

Stress as Bidirectional

Stress is a double-barreled threat in conflict situations because it can be both a source of conflict and the result of conflict. Conflicts with other people are rated as most distressing in terms of both immediate and enduring effects. Bolger, Delongis, Kessler, and Shilling (1989) asked romantic partners to report daily work and non-work stressors and mood, and they found that interpersonal conflict was the most upsetting of all daily stressors. Interpersonal conflicts were the only source of stress to which people did not adjust over time.

Stress primes people for conflict. Lazarus and Folkman (1984) conceptualized stress as "a relationship between the person and the environment that is appraised by the person as taxing or exceeding his or her resources and as endangering well being" (p. 19). Stress results from experiencing demands that seem greater than we can meet, a fear attached to a lack of performance, and/or frustration that we cannot reach our goals (Schafer, Wickrama, & Keith, 1998).

Stress results when we are faced with an overly demanding task, at the workplace, home, and even in leisure activities. The high degree of effort required to work toward completing this task creates negative arousal and ultimately interferes with our ability to complete the task (Keeley-Dyreson, Burgoon, & Bailey, 1991). The frequency, intensity, and duration of these demands, as well as our physiological and psychological responses, affect the level of stress we experience (DeLongis, Flokman, & Lazarus, 1988).

Stress can inhibit strategic behavior that allows for episodic control. For example, stress reduces the amount of thought capacity available to interpret situations because stress causes people to focus on unrelated ideas (Mandler, 1993). Likewise, high stress causes people to divide their attention between the situation and their anxiety; highly anxious people have difficulty in focusing their cognitive efforts on the current task, issue, or problem (Dobson & Markham, 1992). For example, consider the simple question, "What would you like for dinner?" This neutral question could be carelessly interpreted as a *challenge* if one is stressed ("I can't think about that now!") or a *favor* if one is in a positive mood ("Thanks for asking. Do you want to cook tonight?").

One common source of stress is the workplace. In addition to problems that co-workers present, workplace stress can result from noise, changes in work, workload, environment, and other variables (Holt, 1993; Repetti, 1993). A serious reaction to workplace stress is *burnout*. Burnout is not the same as ordinary job stress, which is experienced by most people. Rather, burnout involves emotional exhaustion, depersonalization, and diminished personal accomplishment, although stressed-out people are generally highly motivated and begin their jobs with high expectations. Burnout begins when people realize that reality differs from their expectations (Pines, 1993) and that they might lack what it takes to do everything.

Workplace stress does not stay in the workplace. Stress transfers from one situation to another—a "spillover" (Repetti, 1994; Repetti & Wood, 1997). In her study of male air traffic controllers, Repetti found that fathers experienced negative spillover that was evident in both their expression of anger and their disciplining of their children. She also found that withdrawal is the predominant coping behavior, and she theorized that the fathers use withdrawal to give themselves time to return to their normal emotional state before they spend much time interacting with their children. You might have noticed a similar tendency when coming home after a day at work or school, all you want to do is "chill" and avoid talking with anyone.

In a study of mothers, Repetti and Wood again found that work stress led to emotional and indirect fighting at home. Also, they found that negative reactions to stress, including impatience and irritability, occurred among mothers with high anxiety and with Type A personalities, much as what was found for the male air traffic controllers. Type A people may be most vulnerable to workplace stress and are more likely to experience negative reactions.

The effects of stress are wide reaching. High levels of stress interfere with thought processes, so people with elevated levels of stress experience decreases in their complexity of thought. People are then less likely to control aggression because they lose sight of the negative consequences (Zillmann, 1990). They also experience increases in selectivity of attention, which distracts from understanding what the other person says, and in overall perceptual accuracy (Keeley-Dyreson et al., 1990). As a result, overly stressed people tend not to devote enough attention to the situation, and they overlook information that would help them see what occurred. Aivazyan, Zaitsev, Vadim, Khramelashvili, and Golano (1988) found that people who showed large increases in blood pressure during psychological stress also had more interpersonal conflicts. Other research found a connection between stress levels and health problems, including flu, sore throat, headaches, backaches (DeLongis et al., 1998), and degeneration of the immune system (e.g., time needed for sores and inflammations to heal; Kiecolt-Glaser, Gouin, & Hantsoo, 2010).

BOX 4.1 STUDENT STORY

Juggling Tables

by

Danielle Pasteur

I work as a food server in a restaurant and waiting tables through most of my college career has presented me with many instances of conflict, whether it be between strangers or acquaintances. I was involved in a conflict a few days ago while I was waiting tables during the dinner rush. I had a full section of tables and when it is that busy, it is difficult to give 100% perfect service to very high demanding tables. The people who were involved in the conflict were myself, a customer at one of my tables and a customer at another one of my tables.

Specifically, the conflict began when I delivered food to table #42. The man at that table requested a spoon so his wife could eat her soup. I said I would get it for him and on my way to get the spoon, I had to approach table #40 to get a drink order since they had been sitting there for a few minutes and I had not gotten to them yet and they were staring at me knowing I was their food server. The couple at table 40 gave me their drink order and proceeded to give me their entire food order as well. Though they said they were ready, they were chock full of questions about the menu. It is my job to help customers through the menu (it is quite an expensive one and people understandably like to know what they are paying for), and I answered their questions as quickly and thoroughly as possible.

In the meantime, the man at table 42 stood up and approached me while I was at table 40 and angrily said in a huff, he wanted his spoon. I told him I would be right with him. At this, table 40 began to take an even slower time to decide what they wanted to eat, insistent that they did not want another minute and they wanted to order right then. This whole time I'm feeling very angry and stressed out. I finally broke away from table 40 and got table 42's spoon. The conflict did not end here.

The people at table 40 were rude and condescending to me the remainder of their visit. They tipped me to the point of a personal insult, even though I was nice and they got their food and bottles of wine promptly. The man at table 42 had had very much to drink and at the end of their visit when they requested their bill, despite the fact they had flawless service (besides the spoon) through a three course meal and two bottles of wine, they warned me to be fast with the check because of "that whole spoon thing."

I was angry, hurt, and annoyed. Even the next morning when I woke up I remembered how the men at tables 42 and 40 made me feel belittled and unappreciated. Although this conflict seems like it is very petty and meaningless, it really means a lot. Waiting tables is what I do to support myself through college. The tips people give me are what I have to feed myself and pay my rent. When someone waves that around in my face because of a "spoon incident" or tips me next to nothing for something beyond my control, it is almost abusive. I get so angry at those people I feel pure hate stirring for them. Most people that eat at my restaurant are rather well off and are used to being pampered all the time. Most look at a waitress and think of us as servants and nothings. Little do they know, I'm getting my college education so I can be something one day and never have to clean up after rich jerks like them ever, ever again! As you can tell, this frustration is a little pent up and affects me very deeply.

Before this conflict, my state of mind was good-natured and quite calm. As the conflict was occurring, I felt stressed-out and my anger was rising. After the conflict, the anger lingered and hate for those people began to develop. A conflict like this is tough because I cannot stand up for myself or speak my mind to the person, as they do to me. Part of my job is just taking it. Otherwise, I could lose my job. It is hard to keep all that inside and only absorb it.

From experiencing this encounter, I have learned that people dining at restaurant feel that they are the only people in the whole restaurant. I think more of myself because it is not easy to just let a person be rude to you and not say anything back. In the end, it's the stronger person that did not throw the insults. If I would've chewed the people out like I wanted to, that might've just made me feel worse in the end. My beliefs about the nature of people didn't change as much as made me more aware. It takes a conscience effort to care about other people, especially strangers who are used to having it all, like the rich, don't like to wait for anybody. In the future I will again try to remain calm and not try to take it as personally.

Discussion Questions

1. In what ways did Danielle's stress affect her performance?
2. How might she have prepared for the effects of stress on her emotions?
3. Do you ever experience a similar dilemma?

Coping with Stress

People vary in their ability to handle stress. People who have a low sense of coherence, a stress resistance construct, experience more stress, more anxiety, and more anger than do people with moderate or high levels of coherence. People with low levels of coherence experience stress in this manner because they are less likely to believe that they have the resources to cope. People with higher levels of stress resistance are confident that they can cope because they enjoy family support, an adaptive personality, positive ideas about how they can manage stress, perceptions of personal control, and self-efficacy (Holahan & Moos, 1990).

Your appraisals of stressful situations also affect the levels of stress you experience (Lazarus & Folkman, 1984). People use cognitive appraisals to evaluate the connection between an event and themselves. How people appraise the event influences how they react to the situation. For example, if we label a situation as a threat, we will experience more stress than if we label a situation as a request. For requests, we have some sense that we can deal with the situation, so we set about determining what resources we have to deal with the situation (Tomaka, Blascovich, Kelsey, & Leitten, 1993). For instance, when someone questions an idea you hold ("What support do you have for this argument?"), you could appraise it as a threat to your status or you could appraise it as a request for evidence you need to support an idea, which could benefit your final product. Managing stress effectively requires some element of personal control, and reframing the situations in terms of positive appraisals could help. We need to believe that we can influence the situation or our reaction to it. Sillars and Parry (1982) observed that communication becomes more constrained, less complex, and less reflective as stress levels increase. People who resist stress are able to maintain their health during periods of stress, to communicate in a more flexible manner, and avoid the biases to which less resistant people fall victim (Sillars & Parry, 1982). Moreover, people who change their appraisals of their stress will also change the feelings they experience when reacting to stress, much as reappraising works for changing moods (Burleson & Goldsmith, 1998).

People need a sense of coherence and structure to view the world as a predictable place where efforts are rewarded. We want to find meaning in what appears to be an incomprehensible situation (Stoyva & Carlson, 1993). Stress becomes most rampant when we lose this sense of control. We then feel overwhelmed and helpless, so our anxiety, frustration, and other negative emotions increase to set the stage for ill-advised strategies for managing conflict. One strategy for episodic control involves how you can reframe the source of stress as an event you can do something about. Covey (Seven Lessons) argues that people should prioritize their tasks according to what is important in addition to what is urgent. Giving priority to important activities would enable you to remove unimportant commitments. The research regarding stress leads to the following:

> *Conclusion 4.9: Be mindful that stress is bidirectional—it can instigate interpersonal conflicts, and interpersonal conflicts can increase stress.*
>
> *Suggestion 4.12: Increase your episodic control by (a) re-appraising the causes of your stress, and by (b) re-examining the importance of each task to determine which stay and which go.*

Environmental Instigators

Environmental characteristics can also help provide the basic arousal needed to move from that experience into anger. Noise, defined as unpleasant and unwanted sounds, affects our level of arousal and mood. We are especially affected by loud noises (Graig, 1993). Tavris (1989) points out that loud sounds are arousing and increase the likelihood of anger. But the anger occurs when we are provoked; it is not caused by the noise itself. For example, you would not take personally the loud construction project across the street that wakes you early each and every morning. But you could easily take personally your roommate's habit of slamming the door each time she comes home late, your stepson's banging on the drums when he is grounded, or your supervisor's slamming her hand down on the table to emphasize a point.

Crowds constitute another arousing environmental factor. As with noise, crowds by themselves do not produce anger, but they increase our level of arousal and make it more likely that we will become angry if we are provoked. An important consideration in people's reactions is how they perceive the crowd. If we feel crowded by the people around us, our arousal level increases because we feel that our freedom and control are restricted; we may also feel a sense of fear (Tavris, 1989). Additionally, we may find that the unwanted touch from strangers that occurs easily in crowds can lead to negative physical and emotional reactions (Graig, 1993). These feelings can become over-stimulating and lead to sensory overload, which then leads to higher levels of arousal (Goldberger, 1993).

Another environmental source of anger is traffic. Driving requires alertness and adaptation. However, drivers too often feel that other drivers are interfering with their progress, which increases stress (Novaco, Stokols, & Milanesi, 1990). In other words, we experience frustration from what we perceive as behaviors that block our ability to pursue a goal, even it only means a lane change. Moreover, aggressive driving increases with congestion (Shinar, 1998). Also, drivers tend to interpret the behavior of other drivers as intentional, rude, and insulting while at the same time they see their own aggressive driving as justified and in response to someone else's bad driving (Canary et al., 2002). These reactions are exacerbated by anonymity; we have no idea who is in the other car, and other drivers have no idea who we are. Ultimately, we depersonalize the other driver and the car into one object rather than seeing the car as an object containing a person.

Conclusion 4.10: Several environmental factors can instigate conflict, and most people do not link their conflict readiness to environmental factors.

Suggestion 4.13: Don't allow the environment to cause a negative reaction toward other people.

In summary, many conflict instigators exist. Conflict does not always occur only when someone opposes your goal attempts. Conflict instigation can arise due to alcohol use, moods, emotions, stress, and environmental factors. Being mindful of these instigators of conflict should help you considerably to appraise the onset of conflict and gain episodic control.

5

INTERPERSONAL TRANSGRESSIONS

The previous chapter focused on alcohol, moods, anger, and environmental factors that have affect strategic conflict over time. This chapter concerns transgressions and ongoing relational abuse. These two instigators of conflict represent two extreme contexts wherein the use strategic communication is critical. We begin our discussion by examining how transgressions occur and responses to transgressions.

Interpersonal Transgressions

Perhaps fewer situations require strategic conflict management more than when someone commits a transgression against a partner. Transgressions can cause conflict even though not all conflict involves transgressions (Metts, 1994). Transgressions unfortunately are frequent. For example, Leary (2001) found that all his participants said their partners had violated one or more important relationship rule. Additionally, transgressions affect relationships negatively because the victim perceives that the partner no longer values the relationship as much as s/he once did (Finkel, Rusbult, Kumashiro, & Hannon, 2002). Understanding what transgressions are, the effects they have on conflict and relationships, and ways people handle them provides additional knowledge that can increase your adaptability and effectiveness in handling interpersonal conflict.

The Nature of Transgressions

Transgressions refer to behaviors that disrupt the stability of a relationship because they violate rules for appropriate relationship conduct (Metts, 1994). These rules can be either implicit or explicit; both types assume that people in a relationship have some degree of understanding of the purpose and activities of their relationship (Roloff & Cloven, 1994). Metts added that rules fall into two categories. *Social rules* are rather general, but they still prescribe choices related to behavior, attributions, and interpretations of a partner's behavior. Violations of these prescriptive rules often lead to negative consequences for the rule violator (e.g., interrupting, yelling obscenities, mocking a person). *Relationship rules* connect more specifically to rules adopted within a specific relationship (e.g., rules regarding monogamy, schedules, etc.). Partners develop these rules as part of the ongoing process of developing their relationship.

Serious violations of rules can lead to the end of the relationship even the first time they occur (Roloff & Cloven, 1994), whereas less serious violations can be handled in ways that save and perhaps solidify the relationship. *Seriousness* depends on several factors (Fitness, 2001; Metts, 1994), which include whether: (1) the violation includes public humiliation; (2) both people see the legitimacy of the reaction to a violation; (3) implications for them and for the relationship occur because of the transgression; and (4) the type of the transgression.

Types of Transgressions

Transgressions exist on a continuum from annoying (e.g., your son lying about not having an extra scoop of ice cream) to those serious enough to threaten the existence of the relationship (e.g., your partner lying about not going out with a former lover) (Jones, Moore, Schratter, & Negel, 2001). They can be actions that people do that are blameworthy (e.g., drinking and driving) or a *lack* of action that needed to be done (e.g., forgetting your mother's birthday) (Metts, 1994). Transgressions can be intentional or unintentional. Following the ideas of attribution theory (Chapter 9), intentional transgressions are perceived as more negative (Emmers-Sommer, 2003), and the victim's perception of negativity is greater than the perpetrator's (Kowalski, Walker, Wilkenson, Queen, & Sharpe, 2003). Metts (1994) adds that intentional transgressions are frequently committed as efforts to end the relationship. In romantic involvements, the most frequently identified transgressions are sexual infidelity, emotional infidelity, and deception. In all close relationships rejection, hurt, jealousy, and betrayal are also common types, with infidelity and betrayal being the most devastating in romantic involvements (Jones et al., 2001; Emmers & Canary, 1996).

In response to the related term *unfaithfulness*, Metts (1994) found that transgressions included violating a confidence, violating the privacy of the relationship, forgetting or changing plans, forgetting special occasions, emotional attachment to a former partner, having sex with a former partner, not reciprocating statements of affection, lack of trust, breaking a significant promise, physical abuse, lack of support in times of need, unfair comparison with former relationship. In a study on friendship, Argyle and Henderson (1984) found that violation of one of nine rules would likely cause the end of the friendship. These friendship rules are: not being critical of other relationships, keeping confidences and confiding, accepting other friends, not criticizing publicly, trusting, helping when needed, defending friend when absent, and providing emotional support, and showing positive regard. These lists are certainly not exhaustive, but they indicate the types of rules, both implicit and explicit, that if violated would constitute transgressions.

Consequences of Transgressions

Violations of both social and relational rules lead to a variety of consequences for the relationship. Transgressions have such negative effects on relationships because they are perceived as devaluing the relationship; victims feel that the transgressors no longer value them and/or the relationships as they had previously. Transgressions such as betrayal, deception, and infidelity violate the expectations for continued trust and commitment (Jones et al., 2001). Betrayals also upset the power balance in a relationship and consequently cause "victims" to feel less powerful and to think that the "perpetrators" have put themselves much higher than the partner and their valued association. Victims then respond in ways designed to restore the power balance (Fitness, 2001).

When people experience transgressions, they react in a variety of ways. Guerrero and Andersen (1998) found the following communicative responses to jealousy in the perception of unfaithfulness:

- *distributive communication*: all four of direct fighting categories;
- *active distancing*: both of the indirect fighting categories;
- *counter jealousy*: trying to make the other person jealous in return;
- *guilt induction*: making the partner feel low for the transgression;
- *violence toward the transgressor*: hitting, shoving, and more severe acts of violence, such as threatening with a weapon, using a weapon; and
- *violence toward objects*: punching a wall, throwing things.

In addition to the above reactions to transgressions, people might offer *accounts* or excuses, justifications, denial, refusal, and concessions (including full apologies) for their behavior. We cover accounts for various types of transgression in the following chapters. At this point, we indicate that generally admissions of wrongdoing, promises not to engage in the transgression again, and offers of remediation are much more effective than denial of the transgression, refusal of the partner to confront us, and weak excuses that the transgression was out of the perpetrator's control (e.g., "I was drunk, so I didn't know that I slept with her. Besides you are the one I love").

If we experience anger toward the transgressor, we are likely to confront him or her (Fitness, 2001); because of our righteous indignation we want to seek revenge (Fincham & Beach, 2002). People sometimes believe that revenge will help restore the power balance that has shifted in the direction of the transgressor (Fitness, 2001). If people experience hate, they tend to withdraw in order to avoid interaction with the perpetrator. The third reaction, jealousy, is more complex and can lead to fear of losing the partner, depression, and/or anger (Guerrero & LaValley, 2006).

Hoyt and colleagues (2005) view transgression responses similarly but from a perspective grounded in understandings of forgiveness. They relate victims' responses to three interpersonal motivations that reflect three motivations of forgiveness. They label these motivations as increased motivation to avoid the perpetrators, increased motivation to avenge the hurt, and decreased goodwill or less motivation to be benevolent toward perpetrators. The greater these motivations, the less likely victims are to forgive the transgression.

Whatever their reactions, victims of transgressions feel increased vulnerability (Vangelisti, 2001). Victims find themselves watching the relationship partner more closely because they fear future transgressions (Jones et al., 2001). They also feel hurt, a unique emotion caused by relational transgressions that damage victims' basic understandings of themselves, their partners, and the relationship. The sense that the perpetrator no longer values the relationship also contributes to the degree of hurt they experience (Feeney, 2005). Victims also perceive threats to their self-esteem and their general well-being from these rule violations (Fitness, 2001).

Using an alternative approach, Roloff and Cloven (1994) consider dealing with transgressions from the perspective of relationship maintenance, which they define as "the individual or joint approaches intimates take to limit the relational harm that may result from prior or future conflicts and transgressions" (p. 27). They present five strategies people can use to deal with transgressions in close relationships. First, people can engage in *retribution* by punishing the perpetrator. Second, *reformulation* allows victims to change their understanding of the rules of the relationship so that the behavior is no longer seen as a transgression. Third, *prevention* involves taking action to stop future violations of the broken rule. Fourth, people can *minimize the behavior* so they see the behavior differently by eliminating the negative parts. Finally, they can use *relational justification* to focus on reasons they have for staying in the relationship. Using relational justification shifts people's attention from the transgression to the benefits they perceive they gain from the relationship. These strategies might change the behavior of the perpetrator so transgressions become less hurtful and likely in the future.

Interpersonal transgressions lead to conflict that involves hurt feelings, resentment, and attributions of blame (Hoyt et al., 2005). How victims react to transgressions affects how the conflict progresses. If victims feel hurt and angry, they may seek revenge. If they pursue this action, their behavior then turns the perpetrator into a victim. That person then desires revenge and, if s/he follows through, the partner is then a victim again. This reciprocal behavior establishes an increasing pattern of conflict that can eventually spiral out of control (Kowalski et al., 2003).

Victims do not react in a vacuum, however; the transgressor's actions *after* the transgression can also affect the future of the relationship. Transgressors can experience guilt, especially if the transgression affects their partners in ways that threaten vital emotional bonds (Jones et al., 1995). Transgressors who unintentionally hurt their partners tend to experience more guilt than those who have greater intention (Mongeau & Hale, 1990). Guilt and remorse may then lead to apologies, to convey regret, help manage the situation, and lead to forgiveness by the victim (Fitness, 2001; see also Chapter 15). Sincere apologies might help because they convey regret, help control the partners' attributions of intent and cause, and demonstrate concern for the future (Metts, 1994).

Types of communication transgressors use to seek forgiveness also affect how the victims view the relationship after a transgression (see Chapter 15). Kelley and Waldron (2005) identified five types. We list them here.

- First, *explicit acknowledgement* includes apology and statements of remorse. These statements convey that the victim has no responsibility for what occurred and may legitimize victims' initial negative responses. This type of communication is used extensively.
- *Nonverbal assurances*: these behaviors help convey the sincerity of the perpetrators' regret and are also used extensively.
- *Explanation*, the third type of communication, is used to reduce uncertainty and to help victims make sense of what occurred.
- *Compensation* refers to efforts that involve persistence, efforts by the transgressors to follow the requests of the victims, and the use of resources to somehow "pay back" the victims. These behaviors provide the type of effort victims may need to see to believe the perpetrators' statements of remorse and to believe they want to save the relationship.
- *Humor*, the fifth type, was not reported very often. Although humorous comments may have some effect to lighten the mood and help reframe the transgression, they may also be viewed as a failure to acknowledge fully the seriousness of what occurred.

Kelley and Waldron conclude that these types of communication affect what happens after a transgression. Also, transgressors react differently depending on the type of transgression they committed. If transgressors violate a social rule, they more likely experience embarrassment; if they violate a relational rule, they more likely experience guilt. If transgressors experience embarrassment, they then need to take steps to repair their own face. If, however, they experience guilt, they need to repair the face of their partners and their relationships (Emmers-Sommer, 2003).

Peoples' efforts to manage transgressions, however, are affected by their perceptions of what happened (Chapter 9). Both victims and perpetrators present biased, self-serving interpretations of what occurred (Kearns & Fincham, 2005).

Not surprisingly, perpetrators tend to downplay their responsibility and to see their behavior as caused by factors that are external to elements of their personality (e.g., unreliable, a sleeze). Conversely, victims, tend to exaggerate the severity of the transgression and indicate not understanding the perpetrators' motives (Kearns & Fincham, 2005). Additionally, perpetrators tend to justify their behavior, overlook the negative effects on their victims, view themselves more positively than does the victim, and see their relationship as suffering less damage (Cameron, Ross, & Holmes, 2002).

Transgressions do not automatically destroy relationships; people can limit the damage and decide to repair the harm done to the relationship. If a victim's initial reaction involves hurt and detachment, then time, the behavior of the transgressors, and effort by both people can lead to repair rather than termination. Of course, an important factor concerns the victim's commitment to the relationship. If victims are generally satisfied and committed to the relationship, they will interpret the behavior in the most positive way possible under the circumstances; the transgression becomes the impetus to become more mindful of their relationship and of their desire to remain in it (Roloff, Soule, & Carey, 2001). Additionally, the violation of an implicit rule may lead to discussion that reveals that the two people had different expectations regarding that part of the relationship. Therefore, the partners can discuss, reevaluate the legitimacy and importance of the rule, and then state the rule explicitly in a way that reflects their reconsideration of it (Metts, 1994).

Paramount in managing transgressions is whether one forgives the perpetrator (see Chapter 15 for a more developed discussion of forgiveness). The desire to forgive is most often the opposite of one's initial response to a transgression. People's first reaction is to punish the transgressor and to reinforce the rules of the relationship; forgiveness, in contrast, releases the desire for revenge and allows the victim to heal and move on. The desire to forgive is related to one's level of commitment, the victim's desire to continue in the relationship. High levels of commitment influence people to forgive to maintain what they have and value (Finkel et al., 2002).

Forgiveness connects to characteristics of the transgression, primarily the type and the severity (Waldron & Kelley, 2005). Waldron and Kelley identified several types of forgiveness. *Conditional forgiveness* concerns how victims set conditions under which they will forgive the perpetrator and work to rebuild damaged trust and respect. This response, though, often reflects a weakened relationship; people possibly choose this response to temporarily salvage a relationship even though complete repair does not appear likely.

Waldron and Kelley also identified four other types of forgiveness messages. *Explicit statements* of forgiveness are the most obvious ("Do not worry about this—I forgive you"). *Discussion* of the transgression is not a form of forgiveness, but it helps lay the groundwork for future forgiveness once victims understand more what happened ("I understand that you did not know I am committed to you. If we are going anywhere, then we need to make a commitment [to each other] now").

In an indirect manner, people can convey their forgiveness. *Minimizing* messages represents attempts to reduce the impact of the transgression ("I know you were drunk, and that's why you hurt me"). Finally, people can engage in nonverbal forgiveness, through head nods, eye contact and other behaviors. Be aware that nonverbal communication of forgiveness is the least direct and most ambiguous (Waldron & Kelley, 2005).

> *Conclusion 5.1: People tolerate a partner's transgression to the extent they are committed to the relationship.*
>
> *Conclusion 5.2: Direct communication of transgressions include explicit statements, discussion of what occurred, and conditional forgiveness; minimizing the severity of the transgressions and nonverbal signs of forgiveness are indirect forms of forgiveness communication.*
>
> *Suggestion 5.1: To the extent the relationship is important to you, clarify what you think are severe transgressions.*
>
> *Suggestion 5.2: Decide to forgive or not to forgive. If you forgive, then express your forgiveness directly and clearly, negotiate future behaviors, and reduce rumination as much as possible.*

6

ACCOUNTS

People sometimes fail each other. As Chapter 5 mentioned, people might not do something they should have done or engage in a behavior that they should not have done. Once these transgressions or failure events occur, the person on the receiving end probably wants to hear an account of some form. An *account* is a message that makes sense of why you acted poorly or did not act well. As this special topic chapter shows, the type of account you provide affects whether or not you can reconcile with the people you fail.

The Account Process

Accounts are messages designed to repair the damage people do to each other (Knapp, Stafford, & Daly, 1987). Simple accounts work for situations in which the hurt was minor. In more serious situations more complex versions of accounts are usually needed to help reduce anger and prevent aggression by the victim (Ohbuchi, Kameda, & Agarie, 1989).

The account process is rather consistent. According to Schönbach (1990), the account process includes four basic steps. The first step is the transgression or *failure event* in which a person is judged to be responsible for a negative, reproachable behavior. During the second step, *reproach*, the offended person may react from being slightly miffed to being extremely upset; the degree of reproach a person presents reflects the intensity of the reaction to the failure event. But when reproaching others, a person must also consider that the strength of the reproach can influence the offender's reaction. People are more likely to provide accounts when the offended person responds assertively rather than aggressively and constructively rather than destructively (Exline, Deshea, & Holeman, 2007).

The third step occurs when the offender *provides an* account. As we elaborate, you can offer various kinds of accounts. In the final step, the offended person evaluates the account and reaches conclusions about the event, the person, and the account. This *evaluation* may lead to the end of the conflict through acceptance of the account, or it may lead to escalation of the conflict because the person rejects the account (Schönbach, 1990). Schönbach noted that such escalations of conflict likely involve issues related to identity management and self-presentation, because the discussion topic can change from why a failure event occurred to why the person's account is not believable ("You don't believe there was an accident on the freeway? Are you calling me a liar?"). As the following section suggests, certain types of accounts are more successful than others.

Types of Accounts

Because all transgressions are not the same, they cannot all be explained in the same way. According to McLaughlin, Cody, and French (1990), types of accounts include excuse, justification, refusal, silence, concession, and apology. If a person structures an effective account but chooses the wrong type, the offended person could still reject the account. For illustration purposes, we will use the following failure event: a student does not submit the term paper by the deadline and does not want to be punished. Consider the various accounts available.

First, you can offer an *excuse*. Using an excuse, you admit that the event occurred and admit it was harmful, but you deny responsibility for the event. That is, some other "force" brought about the event, not you. The purpose of this type of account is to put distance between yourself and the event. The most common excuse involves illness in the family. And although we realize that tragedies sometime happen at the most inopportune times, it amazes us how many grandparents die the last week of class. Or the computer crashed and "ate the paper." Or the alarm clock broke, so you slept in too late to finish the paper. Or nature called, so you had to go for a hike. The point is you try to persuade the other person that you should not be held responsible for the failure event (and you add that you really are an "A" student, so the excuse is legitimate). If the excuse offered isn't believable, doesn't indicate that behavior in the future will be different, or doesn't convey respect for the offended person, the outcome of offering the account can be negative. The offended person may refuse to accept the excuse or make unfavorable judgments about the person (Tyler & Feldman, 2007).

Using a *justification* allows a person to accept responsibility but deny that what happened was serious or unwarranted. The person wants to downplay the seriousness of what happened or that the consequences are in fact better when examined more carefully. So you might tell your instructor that the paper is now a better product (you wanted to double-check your facts) or that you did not want to disappoint the instructor so you took longer. And when the instructor asks why the paper does not meet the page requirement, you say "I know you don't want to read fluff."

A *refusal* challenges the accuser's right to ask for an account, refuses to offer an explanation, denies the event occurred, or denies involvement (Schönbach, 1990). For example, you might tell your instructor that you are surprised to be questioned about turning in a late paper, or that you had in fact submitted the paper on time and that the instructor lost it. In a related manner, *silence* simply allows the person to avoid talking about what happened (e.g., when asked why the paper is late, you look down and say nothing).

Fourth, you could offer a *concession*, which would mean that you simply admit you turned in the paper late ("Yes, I know it is late"). Use of a concession allows a person to admit doing something that may have offended the other person, but it fails to include specific statements about what occurred that convey regret and responsibility. Although concessions are not complete, they can in many situations, especially ones in which the offense was not serious, inhibit aggression in the offended partner (Ohbuchi et al., 1989).

Finally, you could use an apology. When people know that they have hurt others and that they are responsible for their behavior, they should choose an *apology* to explain their behavior. Not all apologies are the same. They range from rather simple to much more complex; the type should match the seriousness of the behavior. For example, for a minor offense for which you are responsible, you may choose a simple apology that includes the first three parts of an apology: (1) a statement of the intent to apologize, (2) expression of remorse, and (3) some offer of restitution or compensation ("I know the paper is late, and I want to apologize. I am truly sorry. I will show you on the Final Exam that I really do care about this class").

The more severe the event and the more clearly a person is responsible for it, the more s/he should choose a more complex apology and include all parts of an apology. In addition to the first three parts listed above, a complete apology includes (4) statements indicating understanding of the negativity of the behavior and (5) requests for forgiveness. Apologies with these multiple parts are more likely to include what the offended person wants and needs to hear; the content of the apology affects how well it will work (Fehr & Gelfand, 2010). To illustrate this, we need to change the example: If you purposely lie by omission to your partner, your apology might sound like this: "I didn't tell you about my date with my ex-boyfriend. I am sorry, really. I know that trust is critical to our relationship, and I jeopardized that trust. I plan to show you every day how important you are to me. Please forgive me for not telling you." Of course, your own words and their execution would be different (no doubt including some interruptions by the partner).

But simply saying the right words is insufficient; for any type of apology to be viewed as sincere, the person must appear to be repentant, seem to need no further punishment, and appear to be worthy of forgiveness (Schlenker & Barby, 1981). When you understand the five parts of a full apology, you quickly realize that the words "I apologize" (or "Sorry" or "My Bad") do not constitute anything more than a *perfunctory apology*, one that would be appropriate only for a very minor offense and one for which you hold only very limited responsibility (e.g., bumping into someone walking across campus). These brief words may be the beginning of an apology for a more serious offense, but if nothing else follows, you have provided a pseudo-apology—especially if the words lack sincerity Consider how, after a squabble between siblings, a parent may demand that the two apologize to each other. Each sibling looks at the floor and mutters "I'm sorry" with no real feeling in an attempt to satisfy the parent and escape from the situation. Interestingly, *people tend to prefer even a coerced apology to receiving no apology whatsoever* (Risen & Gilovich, 2007). That is how much people want to hear some type of concession with a connected apology.

Sometimes *pseudo-apologies* go further as they attempt to sound like real apologies. People will provide a statement that is designed to sound like an apology but is really nothing of the kind. When people want to avoid responsibility for their behavior but realize they need somehow to extricate themselves from a situation in which someone has demanded an account, they might say something like, "I'm sorry you feel that way," or "Wow, I certainly didn't intend for you to be hurt by what I said, and I apologize if you were," which really translates into "I refuse to accept responsibility in a civil manner."

Because each type of account serves a different purpose, the types of account people choose to explain their behavior can affect the response they receive from the people they have offended and how these people view them (McLaughlin et al., 1990). In interpersonal relationships, the preferred account is an apology. When people hurt us, we want them to account for their behavior in a way that conveys their remorse and restores our sense of self and value. An apology tells us that the person regrets what happened and indicates that the behavior is less likely to occur again. Apologies allow people to engage in strategic self-presentation and to explain that their behavior in this particular situation does not represent who they are overall (Schlenker & Weigold, 1989).

From a strategic conflict orientation, sincere apologies are a smart bet. Apologies usually provide a more favorable impression of the offender and less intense aggression in the receiver (Ohbuchi et al., 1989). Schlenker and Darby (1981) noted that when people apologize, they minimize the negative consequences of their behavior.

People might hold an irrational belief that apologies actually make them appear weaker. Instead, for most failure events, apologies help you restore your credibility and reduce the likelihood that the hearer will refuse your account. Again, victims want to hear an apology over other kinds of accounts; victims think that their interpretation of the transgression is accurate and want to restore the balance of power, as discussed in the previous chapter.

An excuse is the next most desired type of explanation in interpersonal situations, if it is isolated. An excuse may not accept responsibility, but it still admits what happened; and in some situations the person really isn't responsible; external factors influenced the events (the electricity really did go out through no fault of the student who misses an exam). However, people do not like to hear excuses from someone who gives multiple excuses (e.g., "Sorry I was late again, but there was a lot of traffic/I could not find a parking space/My alarm didn't go off/My pet is sick/My mind is blank"). Based on the attribution principle of consistency (Chapter 9), we have derived a formula for the effectiveness of any given excuse:

$$\text{Excuse Effectiveness} = \text{Plausibility} \star 1/N^2$$

That is, your success in persuading other people that you should not be held accountable for your poor performance is equal to (1) the plausibility of the story, which is multiplied by (2) the inverse of the number of times that the victim has seen you use an apology in the past, which is (3) squared. So all other things being equal, the first time you offer an excuse to someone its effectiveness equals its plausibility (effectiveness = plausibility $\star 1/1^2$). The second time you give an excuse to that person, the plausibility of the excuse is multiplied by $1/2^2$ (or .25), which reduces its total effectiveness by 75%. The third time you give an excuse, its plausibility is multiplied by $1/3^2$ (.111), which reduces its total effectiveness by 89%, and so forth. In brief, we do not believe excuses from people who have a history of making excuses.

Here is a true story: A former student, "Trevor," asked for an incomplete (i.e., a grade that allows a student to finish after the term without penalty) because his grandmother had died the last week of the fall term; and so Dan gave him an incomplete. Trevor returned the winter term in a different course but then needed an incomplete again because his other grandmother had died. Dan is skeptical but gives the incomplete. But the outermost region of plausibility is breeched when during the spring term Trevor announces that his *other* grandmother had died. To our knowledge, people only have two grandmothers (nothing was said about a "step-grandmother"). And so, Dan finally was able to fail Trevor—a small price to pay for killing more than his share of grandmothers.

People are less pleased to hear a justification if, even though the person takes responsibility, she or he downplays the consequences of their behavior. It appears that our feelings are diminished when someone offers a justification ("It's not that big of a deal, it was only a kiss from my ex-boyfriend!").

Of course, we don't want to hear a refusal or silence when we believe someone has failed or transgressed against us. The failure is only intensified when the person we hold responsible denies our right to ask for an explanation for what happened ("You have no right to ask what happened between us," "That is a reaction I will not dignify with a response"). When we have been hurt, we want the other person to acknowledge our feelings and explain the transgression in a way that helps us understand and move on.

Consider how conflict itself provides opportunities for failure. Imagine that you and a friend get into a conflict about money that you owe, and at some point tempers fray. Your friend tells you that you are "selfish," "self-righteous," and "ignorant." You are very hurt by these remarks and storm out of the apartment. Later, you talk to your friend about those remarks. How would you react to each of these accounts?

1. *Silence*—Your friend gives you a quizzical look and walks into another room.
2. *Refusal*—"I don't owe you an explanation. I simply responded to the comments you made. Let it go."
3. *Justification*—"Yeah, I know I said those things but they're only words. No harm, no foul. We're still close, right, or you wouldn't be here talking to me about this now. Let's just put it behind us."
4. *Excuse*—"I said some things I shouldn't have. But I have been under a lot of stress lately because of work and school, plus I haven't gotten much sleep for the last week."
5. *Apology*—"I am so sorry for those comments I made about your being selfish and so on. I can't believe I said those things. You know I don't think about you that way. I wish I could take away the hurt I caused, but I know I can't. Please know that in the future I will guard as carefully as I can against saying such hurtful things to you."

The type of account isn't all that influences our response. When someone provides an account, we make attributions to determine the credibility of those explanations (Chapter 9). If someone provides an account for their failure that reflects internal, stable, controllable, and consistent causes, we would probably be less inclined to forgive the person because the person could have chosen to act differently ("I know the paper is late, but I had a chance to go to Las Vegas for the week and I couldn't pass that up"). We might also think that the behavior is likely to occur again. If, on the other hand, the explanation conveys that the hurtful behavior was external, unstable, uncontrollable, and inconsistent, we might more readily conclude that the person didn't make a conscious choice to fail us ("I know the paper is late, but someone broke into my house and stole my laptop").

Barriers to Apology

Although people who have been failed would like an apology, offenders are not always ready to apologize when someone calls their behavior into question. One reason, as mentioned, is that they do not want to appear weak. Another reason is that the two people involved in the conflict do not perceive events in the same way (Chapter 8). As a result, the reproached person might view the reproach as inaccurate, extreme, or unfair and choose to refuse to account for their behavior. Men and women tend to hold different perceptions of the severity of offenses. Women tend to have a lower threshold for what constitutes an offense, so they perceive more frequently that they have been offended or that they have committed an offense than men do (Schumann & Ross, 2010). Consider the following exchange. She arrives home 15 minutes late and he perceives a transgression and gives her the silent treatment (an indirect fighting tactic), which naturally offends her.

Turn	Speaker	Message
153	M	I'm not mad about last night, I just want you to accept the fact that some, a lot of it was your fault and say "I'm sorry." That's all I want to hear. And for you to mean it, and say it won't happen again, next time you say "I'm sorry"; it's so hard for you to say. That's all I want you to say is, "I'm sorry, it was my fault."
154	F	Well, it wasn't my fault. (Laughs)
155	M	How was it not your fault is what I'm saying?
156	F	Dave, I'm trying to tell you I came in last night and it was not my fault. I came in, expecting you to say, "Hi, honey"; you don't say dirt to me for fifteen minutes and all of the sudden . . .
157	M	It was like five minutes, if that, and I was watching a game. Just like if you we're watching a sad movie and I come in.
158	F	So what Dave? You always greet me.
159	M	So, so if I didn't greet you maybe you should have seen that something was wrong with me.
160	F	I was too pissed off at my own little world to care about yours.
161	M	Exactly.
162	F	So what?
163	M	So what? So I was pissed off in *my* own world.
164	F	So that made us pissed off at each other. So it's really nobody's fault, is that what you're trying to say?
165	M	No.
166	F	No you still think it's my fault. *God forbid* (sarcastically). Let it go at that.

167	M	Because it always just goes at that. All I want you to say is "I'm sorry dude."
168	F	I'm not saying "I'm sorry" because I didn't . . .
169	M	Because you feel no fault, right?
170	F	Right. Right, I was upset.
171	M	So you're blowing up at me tremendously . . .
172	F	So were you, tremendously yelling at me . . .
173	M	I NEVER YELLED AT YOU!

Additionally, in escalating conflict both people may have behaved inappropriately, so both people view themselves as victims and overlook their role as victimizers (Sillars, 1985). Additionally, some people want to avoid accepting the guilt (defined as feeling bad about a specific event) that they think apologizing implies. In addition, people might fear that they will be punished if they apologize, especially if they think they have a good chance of hiding what happened. Finally, shame (defined as perceiving the self as bad) inhibits acceptance of responsibility; but shame also leads to people's being more likely to become angry or suspicious and to use aggressive behaviors (Exline & Baumeister, 2000).

The reluctance to account for their behavior that people experience when they have hurt others may be based on a variety of feelings. Yet without that effort, the people they have hurt will most likely not want or be able to forgive them. This material leads to the following:

Conclusion 6.1: Failure events (transgressions) often lead to implicit or explicit calls for accounts.

Conclusion 6.2: People most often want to hear an apology over other types of accounts.

Suggestion 6.1: Provide accounts that satisfy the partner's reproach: this most often refers to a sincere apology.

7

SEEKING PERSONAL CONTROL
Personality Differences in Managing Conflict

Individuals differ to be sure. Individuals also share certain personality features in a myriad of ways. Because of this mix and match of sharing, researchers can separate individuals on the basis of their personality similarities and differences. In this manner, researchers can examine individual, personality factors.

According to an interactionist perspective on personality, individual differences emerge as the combination of nature *and* nurture: (1) the individual has certain innate characteristics, that (2) become salient in situations that induce those characteristics. Conflict episodes in particular are catalysts for the emergence of particular, salient personality features and affect people's selection of conflict strategies (Graziano, Jensen–Campbell, & Hair, 1996). In this chapter, we focus on those personality features that are prompted by incompatibilities to affect your strategic conflict.

Critically, personality characteristics do not determine behaviors that emerge in conflict encounters. Rather, people have a lot of influence on how personality factors become manifest before, during, and after conflict. From a developmental view, personalities change over time to the extent that individuals mature (Selman, 1980). For instance, Antonioni (1998) observed that certain personality characteristics can become more connected to conflict behaviors over time.

Many people believe that their personality cannot change. They point out that how they behave reflects the nature of who they are ("That is who I am"). These people are right and wrong. They are right in that their self-talk keeps them fixated on their current self-image, which inhibits maturation. They are also very wrong because people have agency to adapt their personality, although perhaps slowly.

For example, one of our clients managed the itinerary of a large hotel that provided well-to-do guests weekly programs. Every week he gave two to three speeches to approximately 100 guests. He was clear, warm, and energetic. Previous to our arrival, he took a standardized personality measure and learned his score. He had a highly introverted, shy personality. When asked how he gave such extraverted speeches with his introverted personality, he said "I have to—it's part of my job." The idea that people cannot change is simply self-defeating. Based on the possibility of personality development and adaptation, we offer this suggestion:

> *Suggestion 7.1: Be mindful that you can adopt communication behaviors that reflect your personality as well as adapt personality factors that demonstrate strategic conflict.*

In this chapter, we offer conclusions and suggestions regarding how you can greater *personal* control by knowing how salient personality factors affect conflict behaviors. First we discuss two of the *Big Five* personality dimensions that are particularly relevant to conflict communication—agreeableness and neuroticism. In addition to the Big Five, we next examine how *attachment styles* associate with conflict communication strategies. Third, we discuss how *narcissism* interacts with problematic situations to affect conflict behavior. Finally, observations regarding *locus of control* show how people variously believe that conflict processes and outcomes. We do not elaborate on argumentativeness, a factor that was a hot topic in communication in the 1980s–1990s. Argumentativeness has been reviewed elsewhere (Cupach et al., 2010). We do, however, summarize its essential concepts and findings in Box 7.1. Having said that, we now begin our chapter with the Big Five.

The Big Five Personality Factors

Recently, considerable research by psychologists and communication scholars has attempted to uncover the most efficient and inclusive set of personality factors. These researchers have converged on a five-factor model—the 'Big Five' (e.g., Goldberg, 1992). The Big Five traits represent how people vary along five dimensions. These dimensions are Extraversion–Introversion, Neuroticism–Emotional Stability, Agreeableness–Antagonism, Openness–Closedness, and Conscientiousness–Undisciplined. According to various researchers (e.g., Antonioni, 1998; Jensen-Campbell & Graziano, 2001), the Big Five contain the following behavioral characteristics:

> *Extraversion* includes assertive, gregarious, outgoing, and sociable behaviors, whereas *Introversion* involves being timid, quiet, deferential, and shy.
>
> *Agreeableness* refers to being cooperative, warm, understanding, and altruistic, whereas *Antagonism* is reflected in rude, harsh, and impolite behaviors.

Conscientiousness involves disciplined, organized, smart, and reliable behaviors, whereas *Undisciplined* includes being lazy, disorganized, and indecisive.

Neuroticism refers to being anxious, depressed, negative, and insecure, whereas *Emotional Stability* is seen in self-confident, self-contained, and calm behaviors.

Openness represents being open to new ideas, creative, and reflective, whereas *Closedness* refers to conventional, traditional, and practical behaviors.

Although all five factors have some connection to conflict management, research has unveiled two as the most salient—Agreeableness and Neuroticism.

Agreeableness

Some people are generally understanding and cooperative; other people tend toward disagreement. It is no surprise, then, that agreeableness has consistently correlated with direct and cooperative behavior (e.g., Jensen-Campbell, Gleason, Adams, Malcolm, 2003; Lanthier, 2007). For example, Graziano, Jensen-Campbell, and Hair (1996) asked agreeable and antagonistic participants to rate the appropriateness of three conflict strategies in close relationships. Their strategies resemble the Integrative/Distributive/Avoidant messages discussed in Chapter 2. Graziano et al.'s strategies were *negotiation* (involving compromise, letting-up on one's stance, etc.), *power assertion* (physical action, threats, manipulation, and so forth), and *disengagement* (accepting the other's position, wait-and-see, etc.). These authors also observed nonverbal behavior of participants when solving a problem.

Several of Graziano et al.'s findings reveal how agreeable–antagonistic people perceive and interact during conflict. Here are a few of their findings: (1) Regarding perceptions, agreeable people liked their interaction partner, they perceived that their partners were more agreeable, and they viewed the conflict setting as more relaxed; (2) regarding verbal strategies, all participants preferred the use of negotiation over power assertion and disengagement strategies. Agreeable participants, however, were less likely than antagonistic participants to favor power assertive tactics. Also, agreeable people were more likely to see various strategies as appropriate in certain relationships. For example, agreeable participants viewed negotiation as more appropriate in parental, sibling, and roommate relationships than with parents; (3) regarding nonverbal behaviors, agreeable people were more likely to show less defensiveness (with crossed arms), more immediacy (by leaning forward more and smiling), and less distraction (by talking with their hands less).

In a follow-up study involving adolescents, Jensen-Campbell and Graziano (2001) found that self-rated and teacher-rated agreeableness correlated negatively with hypothetical fighting conflict tactics. In a word, Agreeableness (for teachers as well as students) was negatively associated with walking away, use of physical force, and use of threats. Agreeableness was also positively associated with Compromise.

The authors explained how Agreeableness can apply to interpersonal conflict situations: "Conceptually, Extraversion deals with social *impact*, whereas Agreeableness deals with motives for *maintaining positive relations with others*" (Jensen-Campbell & Grazino, 2001, p. 325, italics original). Because agreeable people want to maintain positive relationships with others, they are more likely to engage in positive perceptions, positive attributions of the other person's behavior. These positive perceptions and judgments then lead to constructive conflict strategies (Jensen-Campbell & Grazino, p. 329). As indicated at the beginning of this chapter, being agreeable over time does not occur on its own. Instead, individuals must make efforts to control their thoughts as well as actions (Jensen and Graziano, 2007). It takes mindful effort to be agreeable. Based on the agreeableness research, we offer

> *Conclusion 7.1: Agreeableness predisposes people to maintain a positive attitude toward other people and engage in more negotiation and nonconfrontation tactics.*
>
> *Suggestion 7.2: Be mindful to adopt agreeableness as your ongoing way of managing conflict.*

Neuroticism

In an opposite manner, Neuroticism (vs. Emotional Stability) concerns how people who generally experience negative feelings remain cynical of other people's motives. As Thomsen and Gilbert (1998) observed, "Neuroticism (N) and its component subfactors (e.g., trait anxiety, depression, and anger) correlate with negative affective states" when engaged in conflict (p. 835). That is, Neurotic people experience negative arousal more than emotionally stable people do when faced with interpersonal problems. Their increased negativity leads to negative perceptions of their interaction partners, which behaviors might function to address their negative perceptions, and use of conflict strategies that comport with those perceptions.

Note: The reasons people hold negative attitudes toward, and engage in negative behaviors with other people vary. The reader likely believes that some reasons justify ongoing negativity or that nothing justifies being negative to others. Chronic loneliness, for example, can lead to neurotic tendencies in devaluing other people, being pessimistic of their own relational competence, withdrawing from social interaction, and so forth (Bell, 1985). As with chronic loneliness, narcissists might attribute their negative attitudes to factors that are external to them but stable (e.g., "people cannot be trusted," "nothing really matters"). Regardless, we might never know the reasons or motives behind other people's neuroticism. We do know that narcissism, as with other personality features, can change.

Neurotic people (versus emotionally stable people) are not as functional in managing conflict. As one might anticipate, the development of conflict unfolds in negative but predictable ways. For instance, Lanthier (2007) found that neuroticism was positively linked to the severity of sibling conflicts. Siblings relied on direct fighting tactics (specifically, in the *shows hostility* and *put downs/rejects* categories; Table 2.3) when one of them was neurotic than when they were both emotionally stable.

As one would anticipate, people who are neurotic tend to rely on direct fighting and indirect fighting (Tables 2.3 and 2.4) more than do emotionally stable people to get their way. Antonioni (1999) found that neurotic managers relied on indirect fighting to deal with workplace conflict. Thomsen and Gilbert found an interesting but dysfunctional pattern that neurotics tend to employ: First, they perceive their social situations negatively and so do not trust other people; next, they often complain, criticize, blame the other for the conflict, and use other fighting conflict tactics; finally, when confronted on the issue, neurotic people act defensive, use guilt-inducements, and leave the scene in a "hit and run" manner (Sillars & Wilmot, 1994).

Bolger and Zuckerman (1995) summarized two studies regarding how neuroticism and conflict communication mutually affect each other in stressful situations:

> Bolger and Schilling (1991) found that a differential exposure-reactivity model was the most appropriate. Neuroticism led to greater exposure and reactivity to daily stressors, and both of these processes helped explain why neuroticism was associated with increased distress in daily life. Moreover, Bolger and Schilling found that among daily stressors, interpersonal conflicts with adults were the most important in explaining the neuroticism-distress relationship. (p. 892)

Bolger and Zuckerman found that high neurotic participants engage in more conflicts per week than did low neurotic participants, which verifies the idea that narcissists gravitate toward/cause incompatibilities. They also found that high neurotic participants experience greater negative reactivity in terms of anger and depression as a result of their conflicts than did low neurotic participants. Finally, Bolger and Zuckerman found that high neurotic people use different coping responses including planning problem solving, self-controlling behaviors, and indirect fighting than did low neurotic people. In addition, they found that high neurotic people tend to use more direct fighting (especially *making accusations*; Table 2.3) of the other person's conflict and coping behaviors than did their low neurotic counterparts.

At this point, neurotic readers as well as emotionally stable readers might wonder how to use strategic communication given the high negative arousal that accompanies a negative view of others. Research suggests that neurotic people should adjust their directions of thought. For instance, Harris and Lightsey (2005) found that constructive thinking reduced the impact of neuroticism on individuals' subjective well-being, in particular, on their experience of negative affect. Although neuroticism was strongly associated with negative mood measured one month later, *the ability to think constructively significantly lowered the strength of the association between neuroticism and the experience of negative moods.* One subscale of constructive thinking, "naïve optimism," was particularly effective in changing the neuroticism–negative affect link. Naïve optimism refers to holding beliefs such as "it is best to look on the bright side of life and emphasize positive outcomes over negative outcomes" ("Yes, you were fired; and that gives you the opportunity to look for a better job"). The implication of this research is that thinking in constructive ways can mitigate one's own tendencies to respond in ways that might be self-defeating.

Given the review of neuroticism, we offer the following:

Conclusion 7.2: Neuroticism involves negative attitudes and physiological responses to people, especially during conflict.

Conclusion 7.3: Neurotics gravitate toward incompatibility, which instigates conflicts that verify their negative attitudes and behaviors.

Conclusion 7.4: Creative thinking can help people change their negative predispositions into more emotionally stable tendencies.

Suggestion 7.3: Decide if you want to engage in conflict with negative people who invite conflict.

Suggestion 7.4: Infuse alternative, creative ways of approaching problems when interacting with, or experiencing narcissistic tendencies.

BOX 7.1

Argumentativeness

Primarily during the 1980s and 1990s, Infante, Rancer, and colleagues examined "argumentativeness" (e.g., Infante, 1987; Infante, Chandler, & Rudd, 1989; Infante & Rancer, 1982; Rancer, 1998). *Argumentativeness* refers to the tendency to engage in discussions about controversial issues. It is measured through two factors representing one trait—approaching arguments versus avoiding arguments. However, the dimensionality of the argumentative measure has been recently questioned elsewhere (Levine & Kotowsi, 2010). Regardless, this body of research has direct impact on our understanding of strategic conflict.

Argumentativeness is unrelated to verbal aggressiveness or has a negative correlation with verbally aggressive tendencies (Infante & Wigley, 1986). The idea is that argumentativeness refers to being attracted to verbal debate, whereas aggression does away with rational argument and replaces it with aggressive behavior. Finally, argumentativeness differs across cultures (Nicotera & Robinson, 2010). For example, Rancer found that Americans are more argumentative than Japanese, and American women are more argumentative than Korean women (but there is no significant difference among men). In addition, people with an independent self-construal had higher argumentative scores.

Attachment Styles

Attachment researchers examine how young children form attachments with their caregivers, typically their mothers. Cupach, Canary, and Spitzberg (2010) reviewed how attachment styles affect conflict behaviors (pp. 67–9). We rely on that discussion in this section. Early theoretic work indentified three *attachment styles* that emerge during infancy: *secure, anxious/ambivalent,* and *avoidant* (Ainsworth, Blehar, Waters, & Wall, 1978; Bowlby, 1969; Hazan & Shaver, 1987). These three styles become evident in communication where some disruption occurs in an important relationship, beginning with infancy and developing through adulthood. (In this chapter, we shall refer to all caregivers as "parents.")

The three attachment "styles" reflect the child's confidence in the parent's love and whether the child feels safe when disruption in the relationship occurs. *Secure children* become confident in the caregiver's nurturance and love, and secure children feel little distress when their parents leave them alone. *Anxious/ambivalent children* are unsure about the parent's loving support and they become quite distressed when the parent does not show love. The avoidant child is self-reliant but still wants the parent's attention and admiration. Simpson, Rhodes, and Phillips (1996) summarized these attachment "styles" accordingly:

> Children who have *secure* relationships use their caregivers as a base of comfort and security to regulate and ameliorate distress when they are upset. Children involved in *avoidant* relationships do not seek support from their caregivers. Instead, they control and dissipate negative affect on their own often in a highly self-reliant manner. Children with *anxious/ambivalent* relationships make inconsistent and conflicted attempts to glean emotional support from their caregivers, actions that reflect their underly ing uncertainty about the caregiver's availability and supportiveness. (p. 899)

As mentioned, attachment styles learned early in childhood can affect how we relate to people later in life. According to Simpson, Collings, Tran, and Haydon (2007), early attachment styles affect how children later play with others and perform in grade school. The attachment style formed in grade school continues to develop through adolescence and then adulthood (Simpson et al., 1996). In this vein, Hayashi and Strickland (1998) found that, in adult romantic relationships, the most important predictor of feeling secure is whether the participant had at least one parent who accepted the child, and loved the child, and fostered independence. Approximately 60% of college students self-report being "secure," 25% are "avoidant," and about 15% are "anxious/ambivalent." Still, some modifications in attachment styles occur between infancy and adulthood simply because people's sources for attachment and experiences of close relationships often change (Simpson et al., 2007).

Research on adults shows variation due to attachment styles. Secures tend to be at ease with closeness, trust and depend other people, and can acknowledge distress and seek support (Ognibene & Collins, 1998). Secures view themselves more favorably than do other attachment types, and they tend to see family members and friends as being reliable and trustworthy (Feeney & Noller, 1990). The *anxious/ambivalent* person wants closeness but also fears being abandoned (Collins & Read, 1990). Anxious individuals experience more emotional highs and lows in their relationships, engage in more jealousy, and become more obsessively preoccupied with their partners, when compared to other attachment types. They also tend to seek deep commitment in relationships (Feeney & Noller, 1990). The *avoidant* adult conceals feelings of insecurity. That person tends to fear intimacy, hides his or her distress, and chooses not to depend on other people. Avoidant people often do not trust others, and they prefer self-reliance and emotional distance (Feeney & Noller, 1990). Because avoidant people place less emphasis on relational closeness, it is not surprising that avoidant men display less warmth and support to their partners, even when their partner is discussing a topic important to them (Simpson et al., 1996).

Guerrero (1996) found that styles are tied to people's nonverbal closeness behaviors. For example, dismissive and fearful avoidant people communicate fewer signs of interest and positive emotion toward the interaction partner. If such behaviors were reciprocated, then avoidant people would create and maintain a world in which they saw others as inattentive, negative, and uninterested in them.

Importantly, attachment styles coincide with how we cope with conflict. Conflict makes attachment styles salient because conflicts imply a disconnect or separation from close relationship partners. In brief, secures are more likely to use negotiation conflict strategies in their relationships compared to avoidant and anxious/ambivalent individuals (Pistole, 1989). Moreover, secure individuals do not become as emotionally distraught during conflict interactions and recover physiologically more readily than do non-secure individuals (Powers, Pietromonaco, Gunlicks, & Sayer, 2006). The reason secures are not distressed during conflict is that they believe their partner fundamentally cares for them and that they can work through their distresses successfully. Interestingly, people who are not secure but have a secure partner communicate in positive ways during conflict. In a similar manner, Bippus and Rollin (2003) found that friends of secure people view them using more cooperative, integrative behaviors than do friends of non-secures.

The anxious/ambivalent types are less secure about their attachments in close relationships. Although they hold a positive assessment of their partner, they remain unsure about their own desirability. And this combination plays out in both negative and avoidant conflict behaviors. For instance, Simpson et al. (1996) found that anxious/ambivalent types responded in less positive ways toward their partner, especially when discussing an important conflict issue. Ambivalent women, in particular, engaged in negative conflict behavior and displayed high stress and anxiety, when compared to secure women. However, Pistole (1989) found that anxious/ambivalents were more accommodating to their partners. It is possible that anxious/ambivalent people who want affirmation and affection use signs of anger and other negative behavior to demand attention but also give in to their partner if they believe they are receiving enough attention and affection.

Avoidant individuals attempt to mask any feelings of insecurity. Because they want to appear self-reliant, avoidant people disengage themselves from conflict interaction. Simpson et al. (1996) found that highly avoidant individuals minimize their involvement in conflict interactions, experience less anger and stress during conflict than do anxious/ambivalent people, and they engage in communication that was judged by raters to be of poor quality.

The above literature indicates that attachment styles might have profound effects on how people manage conflicts in their important relationships. However, this literature also reflects an individual difference presumption. More precisely, it would appear critical that the dyad contain at least one person whose attachment style is secure. The logic underlying this assertion is based on the research reviewed above showing that, in comparison to other attachment styles, secure individuals report more stable and satisfying involvements. Moreover, Creasey (2002) reported that one person's attachment style can "moderate the effects of his/her partner's attachment representations" (p. 366). Likewise, Canary, Erickson, Tafoya, and Bachman (2002) found that marriages that contained at least one secure individual were more satisfying, and they involved more constructive conflict behaviors when compared to marriages where neither partner was secure. In a word, conflict behaviors enacted in personal relationships are a function of *both parties'* attachment styles.

Moreover, people who are insecure but have a secure partner tend to respond less negatively to conflict interactions than do people who are insecure and have likeminded insecure partners (Gallo & Smith, 2001). Canary et al. (2002) also found that marriages with at least one secure individual involved more constructive conflict behaviors when compared to marriages where neither partner was secure. That is, relationships that contain at least one secure partner appear better able to promote positive conflict interactions than relationships without at least one secure person. As Creasey (2002) argued, in technical terms: one person's attachment style can "moderate the effects of his/her partner's attachment representations" during interaction (p. 366). In sum, because *both parties'* attachment styles affect conflict behaviors, it would be wise for each individual to assess the role that his or her attachment style plays in affecting conflict behavior.

More recently, scholars have developed a two-dimensional model of attachment orientations (Bartholomew & Horowitz, 1991). Bartholomew and Horowitz's dimensions concern (1) positive versus negative view of self, and (2) positive versus negative view of others. These dimensions cross to create a four category system of attachment styles (e.g., Guerrero & Burgoon, 1996): *Secures* hold positive views of close relational partners and of themselves; *Anxious* individuals maintain positive views of others but negative views of self; *Dismissives* ascribe to negative views of partners but positive views of self; and *Avoidants* hold negative views of both others and self. The idea here is that everyone varies along these four dimensions. Using this two-dimensional model (or even a three-dimensional model; e.g., Gallo & Smith, 2001) provides greater precision in discovering how underlying attachment dimensions relate to interaction behavior (Guerrero, 1996). In synthesizing the above material, we offer the following principle:

> *Conclusion 7.5: Conflict is one area that prompts people's attachment orientations.*
>
> *Conclusion 7.6: Your own attachment style affects how you and others use strategic conflict to return incompatibilities into normative states.*
>
> *Suggestion 7.5: To gain personal control, be mindful of your attachment orientation and how it affects your strategic conflict.*
>
> *Suggestion 7.6: Develop relationships with people who reveal a secure attachment style.*

Narcissism

Once considered a personality disorder, researchers now view narcissism as a trait that varies from person to person. People vary in their level of narcissism, such that narcissism is a personality trait that varies from a baseline of *normal narcissism* upward (Foster, Shira, & Campbell, 2006). Two sections imply how you can obtain *personal control* of narcissism during conflict interactions.

The Look of Narcissism

Conceptually, narcissism constitutes a trait regarding people's thoughts and behaviors that promote their self-esteem and social superiority with little concern for other people (Twenge, Konrath, Foster, Campbell, & Bushman, 2008, p. 877). As a personality trait, narcissism contains several dysfunctional characteristics. These characteristic include (1) belief that they are unique; (2) self-estimated superiority to other people; (3) dreams about gaining power and prestige; (4) need for attention, admiration, and even love from other people; (5) inclinations for showing off; (6) ability to appear charming; (7)) interpersonal behaviors that manipulate and exploit others; (8) inability to empathize with other people; (9) envy of other people's successes and possessions; and (10) arrogance, defensiveness, and aggressiveness (Campbell, Foster, & Finkel, 2002; Popper, 2002).

Researchers sometimes categorize narcissists according to two types: grandiose and vulnerable. *Grandiose narcissism* involves flamboyant, dominant, and aggressive behaviors, which might reflect high self-esteem. *Vulnerable narcissism* involves defensiveness and fragile assertiveness, which reflects low self-esteem and feelings of being ineffectual (Miller & Campbell, 2010). Such distinctions are relatively new, however, and do not lead to a conclusive set of conflict behaviors for each type. Moreover, it is possible for people to have one or both forms of narcissism. For example, Morf and Rhodewalt (2001) indicated how both grandiosity and vulnerability occur in the narcissist: Narcissists possess a grandiose yet vulnerable view of the self. Given this combination, narcissists attempt to achieve

> continuous external self-affirmation. Because narcissists are insensitive to others' concerns and social constraints and view others as inferior, their self-regulatory efforts often are counterproductive and ultimately prevent the positive feedback that they seek—thus undermining the self that they are trying to create and maintain. (p. 177)

Although narcissism has been traditionally discussed as a personality disorder, all people vary in the extent to which they are narcissistic, or *normal narcissism* (Foster et al., 2006). Nevertheless, behaviors that reflect higher narcissism are largely maladaptive to interpersonal settings (e.g., lacking in empathy) (Watson, Trumpeter, O'Leary, Morris, & Chulhane, 2006). The connection of narcissism to conflict management can be witnessed in rather general accounts of related variables.

In personal relationships, as mentioned, narcissism positively associates with dominance and aggression. In comparison to people low in narcissism, highly narcissistic people hold an immature view of love, pursue game-playing love, seek physical intimacy for selfish, instrumental reasons, and engage in infidelity (Campbell et al., 2004; Foster et al., 2006; Le, 2005).

Narcissistic people are quite charming when initiating social involvements. However, narcissists face problems in sustaining positive relationships. According to Miller and Campbell (2010), narcissistic individuals "are likeable in initial interactions with strangers because they are viewed as 'entertaining' and 'confident,' but this likeability decreases and even reverses over a period of several interactions" (pp. 184–5). Behaviors that underlie first impressions of narcissists include "attractiveness, from their flashy and neat attire; interpersonal warmth, from their charming glances at strangers; competence, from their self-assured behavior; and humor, from their witty verbal expressions."

Back and colleagues in fact found that narcissists charm people they have never met before. Specifically, narcissism was positively associated with being flashy, charming facial expressions, and self-assuredness. These behavioral characteristics, in turn, lead to perceptions of the narcissist's popularity. Ironically, "People with a sense of entitlement and a tendency to manipulate and exploit others were liked more" when meeting people for the first time (p. 141). In a word, Back et al. found that behaviors that composed being charming, flashy, and self-confident associated with narcissism. However, that first impression of the narcissist evaporates once people learn more about this charming individual.

Ongoing relationships exceed narcissists' ability to impress and enjoy other people. Recall that the narcissist requires that other people affirm their self-concepts (as unique and special). Close involvements are more difficult to manage because people tire of the narcissist's increased disagreeableness, hostility, and arrogance, in addition to a need for affirmation. In addition, narcissists do not obtain rewards from long-term friends or romantic partners if they do not attempt to present themselves positively.

Accordingly, turbulence with their partners emerges (Miller & Campbell, 2010). In brief, interpersonal conflicts for narcissists stem from their lack of commitment to relational partners, lack of care about other people, and lack of loving others without concern for self (Campbell & Foster, 2002; Le, 2005). Of direct relevance to conflict behaviors concerns the aggressiveness that narcissistic people levy against other people who do not stroke their egos.

Bushman and Baumeister (1998) conducted two interesting and informative experiments that revealed the selfish orientation of the narcissist. In Study 1, they divided participants into one of two experimental groups, measured trait narcissism, and asked participants to write a brief essay regarding abortion. Each person randomly received from a bogus stranger either very positive ratings and a handwritten comment on their essays ("No suggestions, great essay") or very negative ratings and a negative handwritten comment ("This is one of the worst essays I have read!"). Participants could then punish the person who supposedly evaluated them. As expected, the combination of high narcissism and insult led to very high levels of aggression toward the person who made the experimentally induced insult. Bushman and Baumeister interpreted their findings in terms of the narcissist's perceived threat to their egos: "Thus, our data suggest that aggression by narcissists is an interpersonally meaningful and specific response to ego threat. Narcissists became exceptionally aggressive toward a person who had given them a negative, insulting evaluation" (p. 227). Study 2 validated Study 1 and revealed that narcissistic participants even punished innocent third parties who did not insult the evaluators. Other people naturally did not punish innocent third parties.

Trends in Narcissism

College student narcissism has likely increased over the past 50 years. Twenge et al. (2008)'s meta-analysis revealed a 30% increase of narcissism between 1980 and 2006. That is, approximately two thirds of recent college students score above the midpoint that was found in the 1979–85 samples. Figure 7.1 illustrates the increase of college student narcissism over this relatively brief span of time.

One implication of the trends data involves both (1) within-generation problems because new generations have increased narcissism, and (2) between-generation problems because different generations differ in levels of narcissism. Twenge et al. (2008) argued that the linear increase in narcissism leads to direct negative outcomes for partners, other generations, and (eventually) for the narcissist. Increased preoccupation with self can erode relationships with low-narcissistic partners in the process noted above—through diminished desires to present a positive self to one person over time. In relationships that include two narcissists, competition regarding uniqueness, superiority, and lack of regard for the other would lead to aggressive conflicts. Conflicts can occur between generations as well, as older adults likely view younger adults as acting entitled, selfish, and uncaring for other people. The narcissist would indeed not care about such attributions, leading to a self-serving denial of the older person's right to criticize and (again) aggressive reactions to such criticism.

Research regarding narcissism invites several behavioral prescriptions relevant to conflict management. Here are a few that we deduced:

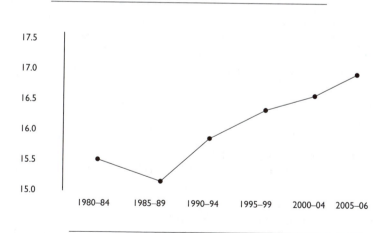

FIGURE 7.1 Average Change in College Student Narcissism 1980–2006

Note: The vertical line represents scores on the Narcissism Personality Inventory.

Adapted From Twenge et al. (2008, p. 883)

Conclusion 7.7: Narcissists believe that they are "unique" and "special." So show your thoughts about their actions (e.g., you are funny; that was nice).

Conclusion 7.8: Narcissists appear charming at first but then aggressive later when their uniqueness and specialness are not reinforced.

Conclusion 7.9: Over time, narcissists tend to have little empathy for others, rely on communicative tactics that emphasize self-presentation objectives rather than those that reference relationship favors (e.g., you will get more money, prestige, and recognition; do this for me, think about others for a change), and use more direct fighting tactics (Table 2.3).

Suggestion 7.7: Be mindful of the beliefs and behaviors that accompany narcissism (e.g., perceived self-superiority, need for attention, inclinations for showing off; charming behaviors; manipulating others, arrogance, and so forth).

Suggestion 7.8: Do not tell narcissists that they are unique or special. They are not alone.

Suggestion 7.9: Be mindful that generational conflicts can arise due to increased trends in narcissism.

Locus of Control

One intriguing individual difference concerns personal views that outcomes of interpersonal problems rely mostly on how conflict outcomes depend on one's own ability and effort versus other people's power or luck. Research reveals that people who believe that productive outcomes of conflict emerge due to their interactive skills and efforts are more likely to work harder to achieve productive outcomes. People who do not believe that their ability and/or effort can affect conflict outcomes tend to engage in behaviors that fail to achieve productive outcomes. We refer to such self-confident orientations as *locus of control*. Under this umbrella term, we refer to related constructs (e.g., self-efficacy).

Locus of Control refers to the extent to which individuals believe that their engagement in particular behaviors will lead to rewarding outcomes (Rotter, 1966). Through social learning, people come to believe that their behaviors can yield different types of rewards (or punishments). They believe in conflict processes and their ability to hang in there. For *personal control*, they use tactics to their advantage. If people do believe that their behavior causes their own rewards and punishments, they adopt behaviors in concert with an *internal locus-of-control*. "Internals" believe that their successes and failures are due to their own motivations, abilities, and effort. To reiterate, internals hold faith in processes that allow them opportunities to achieve desired goals. One item, for example, in the *Affiliation Locus of Control Scale* reads: "It seems to me that getting along with people is a skill" (Lefcourt, Martin, Fick, & Saleh, 1985).

On the other hand, individuals with an *external locus-of-control* believe that their successes and failures are due to factors outside their control. "Externals" do not believe in their ability in *personal control* to manage interaction processes to achieve desired outcomes. Accordingly, externals more readily give up on strategic conflict processes that can lead to success. Externals also consider that their own motivation for behavior depends on other people, chance, or fate (e.g., "My enjoyment of a social occasion is almost entirely dependent on the personalities of the other people who are there" [Lefcourt, 1979]).

Moreover, people's control orientations vary along different domains of behavior. For instance, an individual could have an internal locus of control for making friends but an external locus of control for her own health outcomes. Research has been clear with regard to how one's locus of control affects interpersonal influence and conflict behaviors (e.g., Barbuto & Moss, 2006; Booth-Butterfield, Anderson, & Booth-Butterfield, 2000; Canary, Cody, & Marston, 1986; Canary, Cunningham, & Cody, 1988; Caughlin & Vangelisti, 2000; Goodstadt & Hjelle, 1973; Lefcourt et al., 1985). This research reveals that people with an internal (vs. external) orientation:

- seek a wide range of goals;
- have confidence in their ability to succeed in obtaining goals;
- employ rational arguments and persuasion to influence outcomes;
- disclose what they want;
- engage in fewer demand–withdraw patterns;
- do not refer to a more powerful role relationship (e.g., as a supervisor);
- are persistent when attempting to influence others;
- resist other people's influence;
- push back against other people's pressure to comply with their wishes;
- do not perceive other people as obstructive;
- problem-solve with partners to plan for the future;
- avoid ingratiating other people;
- do not threaten other people.

These behaviors might appear as a long list. However, internals do not engage in all of them, only a few of them pop up in different studies. To show how a high locus of control looks in real life, consider the segment of conversation that follows on p. 98.

Note how the female begins the conflict saying she will make him a deal about cooking meals (turns 3.3–3.4). Hers is not a genuine deal as it involves options based on her two goals, and neither are his to negotiate. It appears that her primary goal is for him to go to bible study on Thursday nights (turn 19.4). The woman clearly keeps on track of her goals, and she leverages how he does not want to cook against the fact that he does not want to go to bible study on his only free night. The husband, however, cannot persist, avoid compliance, or problem-solve to watch TV free of obligations on a Thursday. Also, he is out of control by reacting with a loud protest (turn 4.1), which he quickly abandons. She enjoys a high locus of control whereas he bears the burden of a low locus of control (although he does not have to):

Turn	Speaker	Message
1.1	F	Okay number one item.
2.1	M	You first.
3.1	F	Cooking meals;
3.2		Let's just start with cooking meals.
3.3		Okay I'll make you a deal.
3.4		I'll make you a deal on cooking meals.
4.1	M	NO, I AM NOT GONNA STOP WATCHING baseball games just because . . .
5.1	F	I wasn't going to say that. I wasn't going to say that.
5.2		Do you want to solve the cooking meal problem or do we just want to fight about it?
6.1	M	No because . . .
7.1	F	Would you like me to make the meals?
7.2		Then I want something back.
7.3		That's all, I'll make you a deal.
8.1	M	No, I think you just do it because it's your responsibility.
8.2		You've got kids to feed and stuff.
9.1	F	Why do you say that kids to feed thing?
9.2		We have one kid, he's a grown up.
9.3		He can cook for himself.
10.1	M	He is sixteen.
10.2		He cooks for himself all the time.
11.1	F	He doesn't all the time.
11.2		Anyway, we are supposed to discuss our problem so I . . .
12.1	M	At least you could go grocery shopping.
13.1	F	I buy lots of ready to eat things that people don't eat.
14.1	M	Like, what?
14.2		Like corn in a bag.
15.1	F	That is not true.

15.2		There is T.V. dinners in there. There's pot pies. There's burritos. There's plenty of sandwich meat and stuff.
15.3		There's lots of things that people if they take ten minutes they can make their own meal.
15.4		Nobody is starving here.
15.5		I think you just need to see me cook for some reason.
16.1	M	I just, it's just that I grew up eating nice full healthy well-balanced meals.
17.1	F	You don't need full meals anymore, Doug.
17.2		You need little bitty meals.
18.1	M	Don't say my name. This is going to be broadcast on the internet (laughs).
19.1	F	You don't need big meals, you need little meals.
19.2		You need to have salads for dinner, that's it.
19.3		I'll make a salad.
19.4		Here's what I was going to say: I'll cook a meal every night if you go to Thursday night bible study.
20.1	M	Thursday night now.
20.2		Monday, Tuesday, Wednesday, Friday, Saturday, now Thursday too?
21.1	F	Now it's Thursday night bible study.

Some people have a distorted locus of control. Some people believe their successes are due to internal characteristics, whereas their failures are due to external factors (Lefcourt, 1982). These people are known as "defensive internals." Conversely, "defensive externals" believe that their *failures* are due to internal factors, whereas their successes are due to powerful others, chance, or luck. Moreover, too much internality can be unrealistic and can lead to interpersonal problems. For example, people might hold themselves responsible for all their relational troubles, do not see their partner's role in conflicts and are vulnerable to the partner's accusation tactics. Over time, the vulnerable person probably would adopt an extreme external locus of control and remain in the relationship through guilt. Or someone might adopt an extreme external locus of control whereby he or she sees only external factors as causes of all their behaviors—so they believe that positive and negative processes can, for example, be explained by fate, powers in control, chance, and so forth. Individuals need to adjust these behavioral distortions for greater *personal control*.

These findings lead to the following:

Conclusion 7.10: Internals believe that conflict outcomes result from their own ability and effort; externals do not believe in their ability to manage conflict.

Conclusion 7.11: Internals tend to use strategic conflict, because they rely on many different tactics to achieve their goals.

Conclusion 7.12: Distortions in locus of control can occur, such that people overestimate their own influence to bring about outcomes, including conflict outcomes; or they underestimate their influence to bring about outcomes, including conflict outcomes.

Suggestion: 7.10: Be mindful that you can have a very strong influence on the processes and outcomes of conflict.

Suggestion 7.11: To gain personal control, use strategic conflict behaviors that reflect an internal locus of control: seek a wide range of goals; have confidence in your ability to use communication processes for desired outcomes; use problem-solving and rational arguments to negotiate goals; disclose what you want; persist when influencing others; avoid ingratiating other people; and do not threaten other people.

Suggestion 7.12: Adjust your thinking to compensate for distortions in your locus of control, and look again at Suggestion 7.11.

BOX 7.2 STUDENT STORY

Bathroom panties and throwing trash on her bed
by
Tawnie Fisher

Recently, I moved into an apartment with three girls. Kerry was one of my best friends and I know the other two girls, Abby and Jolene, through her. Abby and Kim shared a bathroom, and Jolene and I shared the other. In the beginning of the year, the apartment remained clean, and we shared groceries, etc. . . .

I quickly learned that Jolene was a slob. Since I am a neat freak, I tried many times to ask her politely to pick up her things that were in the common areas of the apartment. Most of the time she would, but with an attitude. The final straw for me was when I went to Texas with the ISU cheerleading team to cheer on the Cyclones.

I came back to find our bathroom in a disgusting state. Jolene had not only left her dirty panties on the floor but also left her used feminine hygiene products not only in the trash but also on the floor of the bathroom. As one can imagine, I was livid. I didn't have time to speak with her about the matter so I left her a note asking her to clean it up. When I got home from classes later that evening I found that she had picked up the bathroom. I was pleased that the matter did not have to go any further. I couldn't have been more wrong!

When I went into my bedroom I found that she had put the trash bin from the bathroom in the middle of my bedroom floor. I couldn't believe it and I really didn't know what to say to her. This was by far the most disgusting and offensive thing anyone has ever done to me. Since she wasn't home I decided to just get even. I took the trash bin up to her bedroom and tore the bag open and emptied it all onto her bed.

Looking back at this situation, I realize that I should have probably handled the situation differently but at the same time I don't regret what I did. I feel that I exhausted talking with her and she obviously felt the same way. We never spoke about what happened but for the rest of the year our bathroom was kept in good shape. I realize that I need to make better decisions when I pick my roommates. People are not always who you think they are, especially in a living situation.

This situation made me lose my faith in people respecting me and my personal feelings. I know now that I have to stand my ground so that people, particularly people I live with, won't walk all over me. If I don't stand up for myself, people will take me for granted and not care about me or my personal effects and beliefs. So what I learned is, in order to gain respect from people I have to not only make my feelings/beliefs known to them but also make sure that they know that I won't be pushed around or walked over.

Discussion Questions

1. Given the material in this chapter, how would you explain this student's personality?
2. Do you think she adjusted her conflict tactics to help her achieve her goals? Would a different strategy have worked? If so, which one—and why do you select it?
3. Is her conclusion about people fair? What would you say to her about this conclusion?
4. What goal(s) of hers were threatened? Why?

8

POWER AND POWER STRATEGIES

Strategic Conflict is also about power. Power represents a fundamental element of every conflict interaction (Coleman, 2001). Directly or indirectly, power provides the basis for people to achieve their instrumental, relational, and self-presentation goals. When a parent and a teenage child argue about curfew, the parent attempts to maintain power as the teenager attempts to gain power. Additionally, people use what power they have to achieve their goals; the parent relying on reward/punishment power and the teenager on expertise power ("all my friends stay out late"). The present chapter describes power and how it can be leveraged to obtain your desired goals.

The Nature of Power

Power contains certain properties. First, it services both good and bad intentions. People use, misuse, or abuse power (Goodyear-Smith & Beutow, 2001). Next, power succeeds as one's ability allows. As with all abilities, people with power may or may not choose to use it; when they do choose to use it, they may be successful or unsuccessful (Huston, 1983). Parents might not use their power in some circumstances because they want their children to learn by making their own choices. Of course, parents can try to use their power to influence their children's behavior, but the children make their own choices too despite their parents' attempted use of power. Third, to use their power, people must perceive that they have power and *incorporate that understanding into their identity* (Powers & Reiser, 2005). Power offers little strategic advantage if the person does not recognize the power s/he has. A newly promoted supervisor must realize the new levels of power that come with the position and the different actions s/he can now take because of increased power. Finally, people need to employ power when it is appropriate to do so and not capriciously (Duetsch, 1973). Overusing one's capacity to reward or punish can backfire when people stop caring about the rewards or punishments (Kelman, 1961).

Scholars in various disciplines have produced alternative definitions of power, but they have concurred on basic concepts that help us to understand power. McDonald (1980) describes such features. For example, McDonald observed that power: (1) includes the ability of a person to achieve his/her goals for an interaction; (2) should be understood as related to a system rather than to an individual; (3) is dynamic, not static; (4) is perceptual and behavioral; (5) involves an "asymmetrical relationship," where one person tends to have his/her way, even though a person's degree of power is situational; and (6) is multidimensional.

Defining power will help how it plays out in conflict. First, from a broad perspective, power is "a relational concept functioning between the person and his or her environment" (Coleman, 2000, p. 111). Power is also evident in a more specific yet inclusive view that defines power as "the capacity to produce intended effects and, in particular, the ability to influence the behavior of another person even in the face of resistance" (Dunbar & Abra, 2010, p. 658). Second, power differs from its sibling, "dominance." According to Dunbar and Abra, *dominance* "refers to context- and relationship-dependent interactional behaviors in which power is made salient and influence is achieved" (p. 658).

A fundamental difference between power and dominance, then, concerns how dominance plays out in interaction with communication behaviors. We will attend to verbal power strategies in a moment. For now, consider how power was nonverbally communicated in Dubar and Burgoon's (2005) study:

> Participants who were more fluent in their speech, who were more argumentative, who were more vocally expressive, who used greater numbers of illustrator gestures, who were more facially pleasant, who were more dynamic in their bodily movements, or who were less anxious were seen as dominant by both third-party raters and the participants themselves. (pp. 677–8)

For instance, the *visual dominance ratio* represents power this way: The more powerful person looks at the other while talking but looks away when the other person is speaking. For a complete description of dominance behaviors, see Burgoon et al. (1998).

Power as Multidimensional

Power is multidimensional. Cromwell and Olson (1975) identified three dimensions of power: power bases, power processes, and power outcomes. First, *power bases* are sources of power; they refer to resources that provide power to people. The amount of power a resource provides is related to the value people assign to it; if others do not value a resource, the person who possesses the resource derives little power from it. Second, *power processes* include behavioral choices people use during an interaction to gain or maintain control, including level of assertiveness, compliance-gaining techniques, and negotiating strategies. Finally, power outcomes focus on what results from the interaction, including who makes the final decision or gains control (McDonald, 1980). When a conflict ends, the person who gains what s/he wants can be viewed as the "winner" or the person who used his/her power to control the interaction and overcome the resistance of the other person. This indicates that the person who ultimately makes the final decision is, at least at that moment, viewed also as being more powerful. Of course, how that person responds to the possession of power and control affects how the other person feels about both the interaction and the person.

Another multidimensional way to view power is to categorize power as manifest, latent, and invisible. *Manifest power* refers to the ways people display their power through their verbal and nonverbal actions and behaviors. During a discussion, the president of a company conveys his/her power through confident posture, a strong speaking style, and effective eye contact. When these nonverbal indicators of power are coupled with clearly stated orders and ideas, the impression of power becomes even stronger and clearer. In contrast, *latent power* is not directly expressed; rather, people with less power understand the power a person has and anticipate the demands or needs of the more powerful person even before the person says or does anything. Excellent administrative assistants are valued for this skill to anticipate their bosses' needs; they build this skill over the years they work for and get to know a supervisor. Last, *invisible power* results from societal or psychological influences that people may be unaware of because they are simply taken for granted. Cultural norms define one group as more powerful than another. Examples include the culturally accepted relative power of men and women or of parents and children, differences in power that are simply accepted by members of the society (Komter, 1989).

Coleman (2000), who refers to power as an ambiguous and abstract idea that has real consequences, explains yet another multidimensional approach that includes four perspectives of power common in the social science research. First, he defines "power over" as a competitive and coercive view of power that conceives of power as a finite resource so that the more power one person has, the less power another person can have. Coleman next explains "power with," proposed by Mary Parker Follett in the 1920s, as power that people share. This type is not coercive or competitive; rather it is collaborative. Coleman (2000) points out that "power with" usually focuses on people seeing conflict as a mutual problem that both people should work to solve. This understanding of power leads people to minimize power differences and work to enhance the power of the other person so they can work together most effectively. The third perspective considers powerlessness and dependence. Coleman explains that when people experience powerlessness, especially for an extended period, they also tend to become dependent on others. These relationships can be positive and rewarding or negative and even abusive. The final perspective is the opposite of the previous one and includes empowerment and independence. People with power have resources to achieve their goals and to act independently.

Power Bases and Compliance-Gaining Tactics

French and Raven (1959) provided perhaps the first and the most widely recognized typology of power bases. *Legitimate power* is based on one's position or role in various contexts. For example, instructors and professors have an institutional and contractual right to create the class syllabus and lectures/presentations. *Reward* power refers to having something of value that other people want. For instance, professors have the final say on grades. Students clearly understand this power and typically respect it. In contrast, *coercive* power refers to one's capacity for exacting punishment or negative consequences that the target fears. Again, the professor can punish students by docking them for lateness or lack of discussion. *Referent* power concerns whether the target admires and perhaps wants to somewhat identify with the communicator. Some professors are admired by students who want to comply when the professor asks for compliance so they can be seen as having similar attributes and/or be liked by the professor. Finally, *expert power* concerns having special understanding in a relevant area. That is, you can offer analyses and perspective. Raven and Kruglanski (1970) identified a sixth base, *information power*. They differentiated this type from expert by explaining that people may or may not be experts in any area, but they have valuable relevant information or data (e.g., technical support for computer systems).

Scholars have connected bases of power into behaviors that persuade other people to comply. That is, bases of power should unfold in message behaviors that reflect those bases. So power is seen in *power strategies* (e.g., Falbo, 1978), *influence strategies* (Cialdini, 1993), *compliance-gaining strategies* (Wilson, 2002), *control behaviors* (Dunbar, 2004), et cetera. From this point of view, then, French and Raven's power bases should be seen in parallel behaviors. For example, legitimate power includes behaviors that cause another person to feel obligated to acknowledge the structure of power. Reward and coercive power both include behaviors that control what the other person has through one's ability to reward or punish. Referent power includes tactics that make another person want acceptance by the communicator. Finally, expert power involves behaviors that convey knowledge or expertise that others value and desire (Hinkin & Schriesheim, 1989).

Marwell and Schimtt (1976) presented a typology of the kinds of compliance-gaining tactics. Table 8.1 reports these different compliance-gaining tactics. Marwell and Schmitt wanted to determine whether power strategies can be separated according to French and Raven's power bases. Their results largely supported the idea that power tactics can emerge in line with underlying bases. For example Pre-Giving, Liking, and Promise grouped into a rewards favor. They offered the son rewards or positive feelings (liking) if the son increased studying. Also,

TABLE 8.1 Marwell and Schmitt's Compliance-Gaining Tactics

1. Promise	Compliance leads to a reward "You offer to increase Dick's allowance if he increases his studying."
2. Threat	Non-compliance leads to a punishment "You threaten to forbid Dick the use of the car if he does not increase his studying."
3. Pos. Expertise	Compliance will be rewarded due to "the nature of things" "You point out to Dick that if he gets good grades he will be able to get into a good college and get a good job."
4. Neg. Expertise	Lack of compliance will be punished because of "the nature of things") "You point out to Dick that if he does not get good grades he will not be able to get into a good college or get a good job."
5. Liking	Place target in a "good frame of mind" so that s/he will comply "You try to be as pleasant as possible to get Dick in the 'right frame of mind' before asking him to study."
6. Pre-Giving	You give your target a reward before requesting compliance "You raise Dick's allowance and tell him you now expect him to study."
7. Aversive Stimulation	You punish the target until s/he agrees to comply "You tell Dick he will not be allowed to drive until he studies more."
8. Debt	Remind the target of what s/he owes you "You point out your sacrifices to pay for Dick's education, so he owes it to you to get good grades to get into a good college."
9. Moral Appeal	Tell target s/he is immoral if s/he does not comply "You tell Dick that it is morally wrong for anyone not to get as good grades as s/he can and that he should study more."
10. Self-Feeling (Positive)	You tell the target they will feel better about him/herself if they comply "You tell Dick he will feel proud if he gets himself to study more."

11. Self-Feeling	Tell target they will feel worse about themselves if they do not comply
(Negative)	"You tell Dick he will feel ashamed of himself if he gets bad grades."
12. Altercasting	Indicate that a person with "good" qualities would comply
(Positive)	"You tell Dick that because he is a mature man he naturally will want to study harder and get good grades."
13. Altercasting	Say that only a person with "bad" qualities would not comply
(Negative)	"You tell Dick that only someone very childish does not study as he should."
14. Altruism	Tell the target that you need compliance very badly, so do it for me
	"You tell Dick that you want very badly for him to get into a good college and that you wish he would study more as a personal favor to you."
15. Esteem (Positive)	People you value will think better of you if you comply
	"You tell Dick that the entire family will be very proud of him if he gets good grades."
16. Esteem	People you value will think worse of you if you do not comply
(Negative)	"You tell Dick that the whole family will be very disappointed in him if he does not get good grades."

Adapted from Marwell & Schmitt (1967).

a punishing factor emerged in the use of the tactics Threat and Aversive Stimulation, which dealt with punishing the son until such time as the son's grades improved. In addition, Positive Expertise correlated with Negative. Other tactics correlated somewhat as French and Raven's typology implies. Since 1967, scholars have offered other several other dimensions and typologies of compliance gaining tactics (for a comprehensive review, see Wilson, 2002).

Two social psychologists from Canada, Bisanz and Rule (1988, 1990; Rule, Bisaznz, & Kohn, 1985), offered their sequence of influence strategies. Their sequence, called the "persuasion schema" stems from research on what people tend to do to obtain compliance from other people. Five separate strategies occur in these five sequences: asking, self-oriented tactics, other-oriented tactics, social principles, and negative tactics. If the first strategy does not work, then the person uses the second, then the third, and so forth.

First, *asking* is how it sounds. You simply ask the person for compliance. For example, imagine you want to obtain a ride to the airport from a friend (an instrumental goal). So you ask, "Will you please give me a ride to the airport?"

A *self-oriented* strategy presents reasons why you need compliance. Self-oriented tactics include stem naturally from the communicator's belief that the friend should have complied with the request. So statements such as "You are the only person I know with a car," or "I really need a ride to get to my job by Monday," or any other statement that calls attention to your needs falls in this category.

Third, *dyad-oriented* tactics stress how the other person or both would benefit. At this stage, the person would say things such as "I will fill your tank with gas," or "I will wash your car when I return," and so forth. If the person is a good friend, you might say, "C'mon, I will take you to breakfast."

Next, *social principles* refers to a strategy that employs normative, rule-based, or altruistic tactics. So, for instance, you might say, "You are a friend, and friends help other friends" (a norm); "We had an agreement to help out each other" (a relational rule); or "Please think of what I need this time" (altruism).

Finally, you could use a *negative* strategy that emphasizes how the other person will be punished somehow, for example, "You will be sorry if you don't help," or "Next time you want to ask a favor from me, think twice."

To sum up, the persuasion schema sequence would resemble the following (using the same information as above):

You: Hey, how about giving me a ride to the airport Sunday?

Friend: No, I can't. Sunday is football day all day.

You: But I don't know anyone else who has a car. And I need to get back to work Monday morning.

Friend: Yeah, well, I can't be responsible for that.

You: OK, I'll tell you what, I'll fill your car with gas, which will save you bookoo bucks.

Friend: That's OK. I'm fine.

You: Wait! I thought we were friends. Help me out here.

Friend: Yeah, well, we're not *that* close.

You: I see. Next time you need a friend look elsewhere. You are nothing to me!

As this sequence demonstrates, asking implies that the person seeking compliance presumes his or her request will be granted—the other person is supposedly going to comply. Given the resistance, you would need to "step down" to self-oriented tactics. Given the assumption that the other person would comply out of his or her own volition, certainly this person only needs to hear your reasons for asking. Failing those, however, you need to "step down" again. At this point, the social actor becomes mindful that *the person doing the favor might need an inducement to comply.* This is perhaps a surprise to you. When the person refuses again, then you want to turn up the pressure for compliance with social forces of norms or altruism and even negative tactics designed to really force the issue by using coercion.

This research has focused on how people typically request compliance for *instrumental goals.* Imagine, however, that you want to have lunch with someone. Note that you would likely stop at asking and certainly would never get to negative tactics. Also, people most likely use the most polite tactics first (asking and self-oriented) before using inducements in showing benefits to the other person. Forcing the other person to comply reflects how much more persuasion is needed, and that compliance is certainly not a given.

This research on compliance-gaining (and compliance-resisting) tactics is both enormous and specific. That is, many strategies and tactics have emerged in the research that overwhelms attempts to synthesize (Wilson's, 2002, book is very comprehensive and specific on this topic). Having said that, we can offer a few conclusions and suggestions:

> *Conclusion 8.1: Power is complex, multidimensional, and reflected in various compliance-gaining strategies and tactics.*
>
> *Conclusion 8.2: Power is fluid, meaning that power can shift between and among conversational parties as their interactions progress and continue over time (over minutes and years).*
>
> *Suggestion 8.1: Be mindful that power is not a simple, single, and static property that someone has; instead, power can be communicated in various verbal and nonverbal ways.*
>
> *Suggestion 8.2: Do not assume that someone will do you favors or provide you resources; for strategic conflict, plan to offer inducements for their compliance based on your power bases.*

One theory regarding how power works is that of Dunbar and her colleagues (Dunbar, 2004; Dunbar & Abra, 2010; Dunbar, Bippus, & Young, 2008; Dunbar & Burgoon, 2005). Dunbar's (2004) propositions are presented in Table 8.2. We point out two predictions directly relevant to strategic conflict. Specifically, Dunbar and colleagues have stated that control behaviors (dominance bids) connect to power bases in an inverted U manner (Propositions 4 & 8). That is, people with high power and people with low power do not need to use many control behaviors; those with high power do not need to say much to get their way, and people with little power fear using control bids because they might suffer negative consequences for doing so. But the people in the middle do engage in control bids because they are relatively equal with each other and, therefore, need to negotiate the power issue. This theory has been largely supported by the literature. Dunbar and Burgoon found a weak inverted U association between power and control behaviors. Dunbar and Abra however found a clearer link as Dyadic Power Theory suggests.

TABLE 8.2 Propositions (P) of Dyadic Power Theory (Dubar, 2004)

P1. Increases in relative authority are related to increases in relative resources.

P2. Increases in relative resources produce increases in relative power.

P3. Increases in relative authority produce increases in relative power.

P4. The relation between perceived relative power and control attempts is curvilinear such that partners who perceive their relative power as extremely high or low will make fewer control attempts, although partners who perceive their relative power as equal or nearly equal will make more control attempts.

P5. An increase in the number of control attempts will produce a greater probability of an increase in the amount of control.

P6. As a partner's perception of his (her) own power relative to that of his (her) partner increases, his (her) counter-control attempts will increase.

P7. Counter-control attempts have a negative effect on control for the initiator of the original control attempt.

P8. The relation between perceived relative power and satisfaction is curvilinear such that partners who perceive their relative power as extremely high or low will report lower levels of satisfaction compared to partners who perceive the relative power differences as small or moderate.

Propositions are quoted exactly as offered throughout Dunbar's (2004) article.

Functional Uses of Power

Power behaviors are dependent on underlying power bases. In other words, the connection between the bases of power and the behaviors that reflect that power must be melded in some fashion. A functional approach would indicate that power bases and behaviors are connected by the beliefs of the target.

French and Raven's Power Bases

Now that we have described the nature of power, we provide the following to assist your understanding of functional ways to strategically utilize power bases. Recall that power is only effective to the extent that people see that power as benefiting them. First, legitimate power must rely on the target's recognition of their position to affect the target's behavior. Although professors have legitimate control, for example, some students will *not* see themselves on the receiving end of that power. Students might believe that they have equal legitimacy to control the class. They might question your right or (even) qualifications to be a professor, and slander your legitimacy of working where you do. If you can see that your legitimate power base is corrupted by this student, you can change your strategy to rely on rewards and punishments to change the student's behavior.

To use the reward/punish power base you need to ask whether you have means control. Students complete assignments made by professors who teach the classes in which they are enrolled, drivers obey state troopers, employees finish projects assigned to them by their supervisors, and children follow rules established by their parents. In all of these situations, people comply because they recognize that the other person has power to make the request from their position and they can be monitored.

Know as well that people who have reward power usually have coercive power; that is, they can enjoy both *reward and coercive power*. Parents can give their children money, access to the family car, new toys, or other objects and activities the children want. Likewise, they can take away the keys to the family car, deny their children permission to go to a party, refuse to spend extra money on them, or punish them in any number of ways. A term that represents threats combined with promises is *thromise*. For example, "you will do well in this position IF you follow my lead" is clearly a threat and simultaneously a promise, which smart students see.

Referent power, though quite influential, is sometimes less obvious because it depends on one's ability to attract others. Stated as the converse of the functional point presented before, you need to behave in ways that will attract your target(s). Referent power exists only when the target wants to be liked or accepted by another or the target wants to be similar to another. Athletes, musicians, and movie stars are hired to appear in commercials because viewers want to be like those public figures. Similarly, attractive and popular high schools students and sorority and fraternity members have referent power over other students who want to be part of the crowd and be popular themselves.

Kellman's Approach

Kellman (1961) offers an effective theory from a functional perspective. He argued that three bases of power connect to how *power strategies succeed according to functions that the power bases serve for the target*—not the communicator. Stated differently, your use of power must somehow involve the needs and wants of people because they interpret messages according to their functional utility. So your compliance-gaining tactics lead to behavior only if the desired behavior meets the *target's* wants and needs (not your own).

Kelman's power bases are compliance, identification, and internalization. *Compliance* refers to rewarding and punishing power; *identification* concerns referent power as described above, and *internalization* concerns persuading the target to adopt a belief. As noted, however, these power bases do not automatically lead to behavior. Such compliance tactics work only when the communicator has "means control," or when the *target desires* the reward (or fears the punishment) and when the target knows that s/he is *somehow being monitored*. If these factors are missing, no incentive for compliance exists (e.g., as long as no report card exists, why study?). Next, identification power works only when the target views the communicator as somehow attractive (e.g., finds the professor ethical or interesting). If the target is not attracted to the communicator and does not care what the communicator thinks about him/her, then referent tactics will backfire (e.g., a complaint about the professors "inappropriate" behavior). Finally, internalization will work only if the target shares the same values as the point being made or shares in the perspective of the communicator. Otherwise, using any tactic that calls on a change in beliefs and related behaviors will be fruitless.

We present the following, inferred from this research:

> *Conclusion 8.3: People can have several power bases or none.*
>
> *Conclusion 8.4: People's influence power relies on the meaningfulness and importance that each power base holds for their conversational partners.*
>
> *Suggestion 8.3: Realize that you have different bases of power, and that you can strategically decide which power base to leverage.*
>
> *Suggestion 8.4: For strategic conflict, use strategies and tactics that connect to power bases deemed important by your conversational partner.*

Power and Conflict Instigation

People with lower power tend to be dependent and discontent; as a result, they find it harder to respond well to conflict with people of higher power (Coleman, 2000). Keltner, Gruenfeld, and Anderson (2003) theorize that low power individuals show more inhibition and approach others less because they perceive increased threat, increased punishment, and increased social constraints. Low power people also are more likely to experience negative moods and emotions and to make more careful, controlled judgments about others.

High power people tend to underestimate and even ignore the power of low power people and groups; they also tend to attempt to dominate the relationship and make it difficult to work with these others (Coleman, 2000). Keltner et al. (2003) propose that high power individuals should experience less inhibition and higher approach behavior. They explain that people with higher power should perceive others based on their role in helping with goal achievement, pay more attention to social reward, and use more simplistic and automatic ways to think about their social environment. Galinsky, Gruenfeld, and Magee (2003) also found that powerful people are more likely to take action that will help them achieve goals and keep power. These people act in ways that are consistent with their goals and objectives. Levels of power, then, clearly affect people's choices about being direct in managing conflict.

Power during Conflict

The effects of power largely remain intact during conflict, though the levels of dominance might change. That is, the interaction can reveal more or less dominance from one person than another. Power changes can occur through one or many conversations. Here is the segment from a couple we introduced in Chapter 2. Notice how the interaction between them changes, where the husband stops being defensive and goes on the offensive (with a dominance bid). The point here is that the ebb and flow of communication allows for changes in dialogue—the power distribution is slower to change.

Consider the conflict interaction below. It continues the conversation of a couple we introduced in the last chapter, AZ couple #26. The woman adopts many conflict behaviors that reflect an internal's conflict tactics. As a result, she appears confident in herself and how she can control the conversation. Note in particular how she persists in her goal of getting her husband to go to church on his only free evening. This segment is rather long as it shows her persistence and his one-down posturing. Interestingly, she indicts his watching television though it appears she watches TV just as much (see his comment in 34.1). We pick up the conflict where we left off in Chapter 7:

Turn	Speaker	Message
20.1	M	Thursday night now.
20.2		Monday, Tuesday, Wednesday, Friday, Saturday, now Thursday too?
21.1	F	Now it's *Thursday* night bible study.
22.1	M	I have too many other things going on.
22.2		It's like I need to kill another night.
23.1	F	What do you have going on besides working and watching sports on T.V.?
24.1	M	I just like to have *some* free time.
25.1	F	That *is* free time.
25.2		That is a *fun* thing to do.
26.1	M	For *you*.
27.1	F	No, for *you*.
28.1	M	Oh so *that's* the deal.
28.2		That's why you are not cooking?
28.3		Because I don't go to Thursday night bible study?
29.1	F	No, I'm just making you a deal that I'll do that.

29.2		I'm not cooking because I'm a full time worker at a job just like you are.
29.3		From seven to five I work.
30.1	M	Now let's talk about watching games.
30.2		I'll watch Diamondbacks games when they are on;
30.3		I'm not watching it tonight.
31.1	F	But are you listening to it?
32.1	M	Well, I was in there working.
33.1	F	Well, whatever.
33.2		It's like *obsessive*.
33.3		You got to watch here . . .
34.1	M	The amount of sports I watch doesn't come to *half* of what television you watch.
35.1	F	And what do I watch?
36.1	M	You watch anything that's on.
36.2		That's what you . . .
37.1	F	I'm *not* really watching it. [interrupting]
38.1	M	You are sitting there staring at it.
39.1	F	I don't really care about it though.
39.2		I can get up and do anything.
40.1	M	What was I saying ?
41.1	F	How *I* watch T.V. a lot.
41.2		I don't think that's true.
42.1	M	You do!
43.1	F	I just sit there.
43.2		I don't *care* about it.
44.1	M	That's *all* you do!
45.1	F	I'm just trying to get tired so I can fall asleep,
45.2		basically . . . you know . . .

If the person initiating a control attempt is powerful, that attempt is usually met by compliance from the less powerful person; if the person initiating a control attempt is less powerful, the attempt is usually met by a counter-attempt from the more powerful partner. Although powerful people may not want to exert their power through control attempts, they can respond in dominant ways when the other person attempts to dominate discussion. Moreover, even though powerful people may not want to dominate interaction, they might still show more signs of dominance if warranted (Dunbar et al., 2008).

Access to bases of power also affects how people conduct conflict. Tedeschi (2001) explains that people high in French and Raven's (1959) power bases, especially when they have power from multiple bases, believe they will succeed when using negotiation and will, in turn, be more persuasive. Teachers and parents can use their legitimate and expert powers to influence their students and children rather than resorting to instrumental threats or punishments. Conversely, people who lack multiple power bases will be more coercive. For instance, Goodstadt and Hjelle (1979) found that low power people were more likely to use Direct Fight tactics if they were temporarily given a superior's role. That is, lower power people believe they can control others through coercion rather than through communication processes.

Persistence makes a big difference. Less powerful people who repeatedly try control attempts are usually more successful than powerless people who give up (Dunbar et al., 2008). In a similar vein, Tedeshi (2001) stated that when powerful people encounter consistent resistance from their less powerful partners in response to their conflict and influence strategies, powerful people tended to reduce their own use of threats. However, when their partners complied, they continued to use coercive behaviors to win the conflict.

Of course, when being persistent, people should be careful to avoid what might be perceived as whining or nagging. With that in mind, children may respectfully ask their parents multiple times for something that is important, clearly making their argument so that the parents eventually understand the importance and change their response. However, to be successful they need to avoid comments and nonverbal behaviors that make their requests sound annoying and pestering. Likewise, employees can present their argument several times until their supervisors eventually understand its strengths so long as they make their arguments clearly and logically and at appropriate intervals.

Levels of power do not always remain consistent throughout a conflict. McDonald (1980) indicates that people can give power to the other person during conflict through behavioral choices—events that increase or decrease power. The more powerful person may ask questions to allow the less powerful person to explain his/her perspective, overlook opportunities to use power to end the interaction, or consider the needs or goals of the less powerful person.

For example, when a student asks permission to submit a paper after the due date, the professor is the more powerful person in the interaction; the professor has legitimate, coercive, reward, and expert power in this situation. As mentioned above, attractive professors can use referent power. As the conflict progresses, the professor may choose to allow the student to argue to convince him to accept the paper rather than simply refuse the request and impose a punishment, actions his position of power would allow. By behaving in this manner, the professor has given the student the opportunity to use information power to win the conflict; he or she has in essence ceded some power to the student.

Power and Conflict Outcomes

Deutsch (1973) noted that frequent use of negative and coercive strategies leads to alienation and resistance from partners. The power base someone chooses to use affects aspects of a relationship including trust, conflict, and satisfaction (Johnson & Evans, 1997). Using "power over" too much may lead to immediate compliance but will not produce commitment. Reliance on competitive approaches to power reduces people's ability to perceive sharing power as a way to increase their own power. Also, the use of coercive strategies reduces the ability to use other types of strategies because people must continue to oversee and enforce their power because others haven't internalized the behavior or formed positive attitudes toward the actor (Coleman, 2000). Children will obey their parents about doing their homework as long as their parents are present to provide punishments for disobedience. But because they have not internalized the belief that this is a positive behavior, once they leave home for college, these young people frequently will ignore these previous expectations and behave as they choose, all too often to their detriment. Clearly, then, coercive strategies may provide short-term compliance, but they do not produce lasting changes.

Conversely, the use of legitimate, expert, information, and referent power produce both public compliance and changes in changes in private beliefs. Therefore, if parents use these types of power to influence their children's behavior, the children will comply in the short term, but they might will also over time internalize the importance of the behavior and be likely to continue it even when the parents are absent. When discussing drug use with their children, using their position as parents (legitimate), being well informed about the consequences of drugs and alcohol use (expert and information), and creating a reasonable argument (information) will allow parents to influence their children's behavior and their beliefs. They should avoid using threats and punishments (coercive) and promising rewards because neither provides long term compliance. Referent power, the one type that produces the most positive outcomes, including interaction and identification with the person, is the trickiest to use because it relies on the receiver, in this case the children, wanting to be like the actor (parents). This type of power develops over time as children need to develop respect for their parents.

Levels of power also affect people's attributions that explain conflict (see Chapter 9 on Interpreting Conflict). In their study focused on attribution of responsibility for arguments, Trentham and Larwood (2001) found that a person's level of power and the type of power the person had affects participant attributions. Overall, participants attributed greater causal *responsibility to the person with more power* in the situation. They also expected the more *powerful person to take steps to* resolve the problem. People with power appear to possess the resources to solve the conflict; they may use those resources to be sure the conflict is managed so that they achieve their goals, but their partners still see this as what they are supposed to do.

Here are our conclusions and suggestions for how power can help your strategic conflict:

> *Conclusion 8.5: Powerless people can persist in order to achieve their goals.*
>
> *Conclusion 8.6: Social actors can use power to develop functional relationships where people share in achieving your goals, including "power with" and "empowerment" forms.*
>
> *Conclusion 8.7: When more powerful people ignore the needs of the other person and dominate conversation, they preclude mutual problem-solving, support, and buy-in to the decision.*
>
> *Suggestion 8.5: To achieve your goals in cases where you feel powerless, persist if it is appropriate to your partner's expectations for specific behaviors.*
>
> *Suggestion 8.6: Rely most on positive bases of power to get your way; avoid coercion as that tends to work against productivity.*
>
> *Suggestion 8.7: To obtain the other person's reasons, mutual support, and buy-in to the conflict outcome, consider the other person's goals and specific objectives for the conversation.*

9

SEEKING ATTRIBUTIONAL CONTROL

Interpreting Conflict

Turn	Speaker	Message
82	M	Are we done [discussing that topic]?
83	W	I guess so.
84	M	Why? We didn't talk about it.
85	W	Yes we do, we . . . I was just saying that we have trouble communicating. That sometimes, like it doesn't matter how you say it, I'm gonna take it wrong because, no matter how I say it you're gonna take it wrong and . . .
86	M	How can we work on that?
87	W	Well "counselor," [sarcastically] I think that we can work on it. What do you mean, "How are we gonna work on it?" [hostile question]
88	M	We just gonna live that way and be frustrated, or are we gonna work on it?

This chapter addresses the question posed by the man in turn 88: Are you going to be frustrated by how *you and your conflict partners interpret* communication during conflict or are you going to work on it? As this chapter shows, the interpretation of conflict defies quick and simple conclusions. Without knowing how complex people are in their conflict interpretations, we cannot conclude anything of value to the reader. So we want to be careful in representing the findings and principles on how people interpret conflict. We refine our review of necessity to provide the foundation for strategic conflict suggestions. First, we want to set the context with regard to people's capability to be objective witnesses of their conflict episodes.

People as Objective Witnesses

Both parties to conflict believe that they fairly well understand the cause of the conflict and who was responsible for it, but both parties likely have very different understandings of what occurred. In some instances, the two versions of what happened are so different that the two people appear to be in two different places, talking about two different sets of issues. Indeed, people sometimes begin a new conflict about what happened during a former conflict; they become convinced the other person is being stubborn, or worse yet, lying about the event. It is probable that each person is telling the truth—the truth as they see it.

In addition, conflict behaviors become meshed and mixed largely without the knowledge of both people using them. For example, consider how people disagree about who "started" the conflict, or who said what in response to the other. Who initiated a conflict is known as a *punctuation problem* (Watzlawick, Beavan, & Jackson, 1967). People hold a very loose grasp on who initiated and changed the progression of a conflict interaction, so they each "punctuate" the conflict differently—most likely in a way that is self-serving and creates its own problem ("You started this by saying you wanted to leave later than planned." "No, you started this by saying I am always late."). The certainty of who started the conflict or who said what when becomes rather comical when one person claims, "If I only had a video camera, you would see that I am right."

As we noted in Chapter 2, people are very selective and biased when it comes to processing information. *People cannot provide an accurate account of what happens in conflict episodes.* As mentioned earlier, people can sense about 7 *million bytes of information each second but can only attend to 1–40 bytes of information per second* (Berscheid & Regan, 2005). People must select the bytes they attend to. Dear reader, for a minute listen to the background noises you have been ignoring and then return to selecting the information you selected before. In recollections of brief conflict interactions, people can recall approximately one third of message sequences an hour following their interactions and only 2% a month later (Sillars, Weisberg, Burggraf, & Zietlow, 1990). And when people view their conflicts on videotape immediately after they occur, their recollections and interpretations of messages that occurred overlap with the other person's recollections and interpretations by a mere 3% at most (Sillars, Roberts, Leonard, & Dun, 2000). Instead, people's recollections and inferences about conflicts are driven by *their own* experiences of the event, largely separated from the goals, interpretations, and behaviors of their conversational partner (Sillars et al., 2000).

To complicate matters, people tend to *underestimate the impact of their own behavior on their own assessments* of the conflict episode and its outcomes (Canary,

Pfleiger, & Cupach, 2008). One reason for underestimating their own behavior is that people cannot perceive their conflict behaviors but they do experience conflict just the same (Storms, 1973). *In a word, people's field of vision is external to them but their field of experience is internal to them.* This external perception/internal experience difference can affect one's confidence in managing conflict as well as one's bias in his or her view of what messages occurred. For example, you cannot really see yourself talk—perhaps you notice your hand movement and glasses frames (if you wear them). Nor can you hear yourself accurately (to hear yourself more accurately, cup your hands behind your ears and talk). So you cannot see the wince on your face, notice how your eyes widen, nor hear the pauses in your responses. Yet other people can see and hear you, because their field of perception is largely focused on you, and that information builds their own field of experience. In brief, people's perceptions and experiences reflect two different phenomena.

How can two people who participate in the same conflict have two opposing versions of the event—and both be telling the truth? Their perceptions are their reality, even though little agreement exists between the two perceptions (Sypher & Sypher, 1984). Differences in perception lead to faulty communication and misunderstanding, thereby setting up opportunities for escalation of a current conflict or for further conflict (Kowalski, Walker, Wilkinson, Queen, & Sharpe, 2003). However, research shows that mutual understanding is not important to relational quality—perceived agreement on the conflict issue appears most important (Buggraf & Sillars, 1985). Examining the perception process and attribution theory can help explain how interpretation of conflict directly affects conflict message behavior choices.

Perception Processes

Interpersonal perception processes are influenced by the information we have about people; our expectations, experiences, behavior, the relationship between us and other people and the social and cultural contexts of the interaction. Our perceptions are often judgments about people that can help us predict and explain their behavior (Hinton, 1993).

Four Stages in Perception Processes

Differences in people's perceptions begin during the first stage of the perception process, *stimulation*. The environment contains more sources of stimulation than anyone could possibly attend to. Through the five senses, people take in approximately 10 million bytes of information a second; however, people can only process between one and 40 bytes of information a second (Berscheid & Ragan, 2005, p. 163). These numbers indicate that people can consciously process only a very tiny fraction of what their senses are receiving (.000,000,001 to .000,000,040).

These numbers clearly show that people are poor sensory data collectors and even poorer computers.

As a result of an inability to process most sensory data, people must focus on particular stimuli and overlook others. Not surprisingly, two people in an inter-action—even a calm one—pay attention to different perceptual data points that each person identifies as relevant. This is the first stage of information percep-tion—the *selection* of information. During conflict situations, people's selectiv-ity increases; the greater the intensity, the more selective people become (Sillars et al., 2000). People also select and process certain messages and not others because of subjective factors, including mood and preconceptions they bring to the cur-rent situation (Chapter 4).

During *organization*, the second stage, people must somehow manage their selected information. Without this stage, people would have to deal with myriad separate pieces of information about an interaction. Scripts (expectations for how events will unfold), schemata (expectations about people), and rules (prescriptions for appropriate behavior) allow people to group bytes of information into fewer and more manageable categories (Hinton, 1993). We elaborate a bit on schemata because they are particularly relevant to conflict communication.

People use various schemata as means to guide and interpret behavior (Fiske & Taylor, 1984). One type, "role schemata" refers to the behaviors one would expect from a person given their role relationship to you. For example, people holding a *traditional* view of the doctor–patient relationship believe that com-munication should come primarily from the physician and that physician advice should not be questioned. Yet people holding a *consumer* schemata treat their physician as a peer, asking questions and requiring answers. Likewise, schemata people have for marriage and conflict in marriage influences how they handle interactions including conflict (Solomon, Knobloch, & Fitzpatrick, 2004).

Interpretation and *evaluation* of information constitute the third stage of percep-tion. People attempt to understand the information they have organized. Both processes are inherently subjective and reflect past experiences as well as present moods and emotions. At this stage, people decide if an event is good or bad, strange or familiar, and other judgments. Because people have noticed different information, they will also interpret and evaluate people and events differently. In the next section of this chapter, we develop this stage more fully in terms of attribution theory.

The fourth stage is committing the information to *memory*. Our schematas and scripts as well as our interpretations and evaluations influence how we store infor-mation. These factors influence what information is stored and how it is stored (fairly objectively or fairly subjectively). People file in memory information that fits their existing ideas and forget what doesn't fit (Hinton, 1993).

During the final stage, *recall*, we access the information we have stored in our memory. However, recall does not simply pluck a whole memory from storage; rather, people must reconstruct the information into a meaningful idea. As people rebuild their ideas, they cannot recall information equally easily. They readily recall information that coincides with their schema; but they don't readily recall information that is inconsistent with their schema.

Unfortunately, people's recall of interaction content is unreliable at best. Research that compares transcripts of people's conversations to people's recall of those same conversations shows that people on average cannot recall approximately 90% of their conversation within an hour after it occurred and they forget over 95% of what was said a month later (Stafford, Burggraf, & Sharkey, 1987). People do recall more important interaction episodes. They recall about 33% of what was said in a conflict interaction within an hour after it occurred (Sillars et al., 1990). Still, a large majority of interaction content (67%) is immediately forgotten. So although people might believe that they have excellent conversational memory and will stubbornly argue that they know exactly what happened during an argument, they are probably deluded. More accurately, after interaction people's recall affects their conceptions of the other person and how they reconstruct the event.

As an example, let us look at how people's schemata operate in families. Examining different schemata that people hold for families, Fitzpatrick and Ritchie (1994; Koerner & Fitzpactick, 2002, 2006) used two dimensions: *conversational orientation* (i.e., high vs. low value for openness of communication) and *conformity orientation* (i.e., the extent to which family members share beliefs). Families that have high conversational orientation and high conformity orientation are *consensual families*, where members negotiate the tension between openness and obedience, and where children are expected to share their thoughts but conform at the end of the day. Families with high conversational orientation but low conformity orientation are *pluralistic,* wherein open sharing of ideas is encouraged and children can affect family outcomes. Families with low conversation orientation but high conformity orientation are *protective families*, and children are expected to obey their parents and they find little use for communication. Families with low conversation and conformity orientation are *laissez-faire families*, and here children receive little direction from parents and learn how to behave from people outside the family. As one might anticipate, this research shows that a high conversational orientation is associated with positive, support-seeking conflict behaviors; and a high conformity orientation associates with avoiding the conflict or negative conflict messages. However, the schemata change the general influences of these dimensions.

Koerner and Fitzpatrick (2002) found that people with a *consensual* schemata reported greater use of aggression and confrontation during conflicts with romantic partners. Consensual schemata suggest that one should conform but at the same time be vocal, indicating that disagreement should be avoided but when it arises then one should engage in competitive verbal and nonverbal behavior (Koerner & Fitzpatrick, 2002). In a contrary manner, people with a *pluralistic* schemata reported that they engaged in conflict and did so in a cooperative manner. This finding makes sense; people with a schemata that values openness and deviation would come from a family that sees conflict as natural to relationships and communication as a means of negotiating alternative realities. People with a *protective* schemata (i.e., low conversation/high conformity) reported greater than average levels of negative behaviors and negative complementary behaviors (e.g., avoiding the partner, resisting the partner). As Koerner and Fitzpatrick said, "This pattern is consistent with persons who have learned that conflict is negative and to avoid it if possible" (p. 248). Finally, people with a *laissez-faire* schemata reported more avoidance but less resistance to the partner. As you can surmise, people with low tolerance for openness or conformity would have little need to talk about problems or to continue resisting the partner when confronted.

As people move through the stages of the process, their perceptions likely become increasingly different. People begin perceiving different sets of information, even though some points overlap. They then organize information differently. These differences increase when people interpret and evaluate their versions of the event. By the time they store their versions in memory, they believe that their versions of the conflict are accurate. Finally, reconstructing the conflict during recall omits most information and adds further changes, until the two versions held by the two conflict parties appear so different that each person wonders how and why the other person explains the event so badly. *The extent to which you insist that your version is accurate constitutes the extent to which you are wrong.* Instead of being the purveyor of accuracy, in truth you hold only one highly selective, schematically affected, and poorly recalled idea of what happened. This discussion leads to the following principle.

> *Conclusion 9.1: People hold different views of conflict that appear valid to them but are entirely subjective.*
>
> *Suggestion 9.1: Interpret conflict wisely: Be mindful that people hold different views of conflict that are reasonable to them.*

Factors that Further Affect the Accuracy of Perceptions

Although they sometimes do, people usually do not purposely try to create their own version of an event that differs from their partners' version. (To create purposely a version of conflict that is at odds with your partners' version is a form of "crazy-making".) Instead, various selectivity errors, recall, and other factors affect the accuracy of their perceptions.

Paul Simon once wrote, "A man hears what he wants to hear and disregards the rest" (*The Boxer*). This claim has been validated in hundreds of studies on attitude structure and consistency (Eagly & Chaiken, 1993). One common perceptual bias, *perceptual accentuation*, refers to how people select only the information that supports their beliefs and overlook information that contradicts those ideas.

Because conflict parties bring different ideas about the cause of the conflict, other events that have affected the conflict and different meanings for various behaviors, they notice different messages, both verbal and nonverbal (Sillars et al., 2000). During conflict, these differences become even more pronounced as each person identifies information that supports his/her version of events and overlooks information that might challenge that version.

A common tendency in perception is to perceive someone who disagrees with us as biased and to perceive ourselves as objective. Our behavior then influences that person to see us as biased. This perception causes us to become more competitive, action that moves us toward conflict rather than toward resolution. People make quick, immediate assessments of their partners' bias and then decide whether to escalate the conflict (Kennedy & Pronin, 2008). Pronin (2007) refers to this problem as a *bias blind spot*, which interferes with self-awareness and contributes to conflict intensity.

Perceptual errors are also affected by mental shortcuts that people take, or "heuristics." Two common inferential heuristics that people take concern the *availablity heuristic* and the *salience heuristic* (Nisbett & Ross, 1980). The availability heuristic concerns how people do not conduct systematic searches for information. Instead, they seek information that is convenient (e.g., using the web for information versus going to the library for newer books and journals). In terms of conflict, this would mean not researching one's facts as presented and using data that only comes up during conflict, and/or making-up evidence to support one's views. On this last point, the *sleeper effect* shows that people forget the sources of their knowledge but will indicate later that their sources are excellent (e.g., "I read in the newspaper that _____." The salience heuristic refers to how people attend more to information that concerns them, which is often local. Accordingly, people interpret the other person's messages largely as a function of what they themselves want. We elaborate on the goal-related nature of conflict in Chapter 11.

The information people notice and how they process that information is also affected by their level of satisfaction with the relationship they have with the other person in the conflict. Sillars (1985, 2000) found that incompatible couples were more likely than happy couples to distort information and to hold incongruent perceptions. These differences usually reflect their existing ideas about the other person and/or about the relationship. So people in less happy relationships will notice more negative behaviors while overlooking most of the positive ones. In contrast, people in happy relationships notice more positive behaviors and overlook most of the negative ones.

Familiarity can create a false sense of confidence in accuracy. People assume that, because they know the other person so well, they can explain and predict what their partner is experiencing (Sillars, 1998). They also assume that people they are close to agree with them and share their attitudes (Sillars, Smith, & Koerner, 2010). They then extend that certainty into areas in which they might not know the other as well; as a result, they trust the accuracy of their perceptions before they have solid reason to do so (Sillars, 1985). Kluwer, deDreu, and Buunk (1998) found that the self-other bias may be with someone we know rather well. This bias leads us to perceive ourselves as more cooperative, fairer, and generally better than does our conversation partner. Predictably, this bias can lead to stalemates and standoffs.

This certainty motivates people not to question the accuracy of their perceptions; they simply assume their perceptions are right. They fail to notice the ambiguity present in many situations and simply draw conclusions based on faulty inferences rather than facts. Communication is inherently ambiguous and can also be strategically ambiguous, even in very close relationships. Either way, people receive an unclear message and usually decide its meaning. The ambiguity increases the chance for selectivity of information, so people have an incomplete understanding of an event or person. But they are blithely unaware of this problem and proceed to interpret situations such as conflict as if they have a factual and accurate understanding of the event and the other person (Sillars, 1998).

Accurate or not, perceptions are persistent little blighters. Even when people discover new information that challenges their perception, they can stretch their perceptions to include that new information ("I know he helped you with your work, but that only shows how manipulative he is"). Also, negative and abstract perceptions stand up well because they are more difficult to clarify than concrete ones (e.g., perceiving someone as manipulative is validated in both good and bad behaviors). The more concrete perceptions relate to instrumental ideas while the more abstract ones relate to companionate issues (Sillars et al., 1990). For example, who does certain chores around the house provides a relatively clear view than whether your partner shows affection. Although people want to make concrete inferences from a conflict, "given the need to keep pace with interaction these inferences are snap judgments that go unquestioned" (Sillars et al., 2000, p. 483). Accordingly, perceptions related to more abstract concerns will remain ambiguous and untested. People then carry these perceptions into future interactions, where they form the basis for our perceptions of the next conflict, adding an additional layer for potential misunderstanding of the causes and misconduct of conflict.

Perceptual Differences and Conflict

As indicated, parties to conflict can hold perceptions so different that they appear to be dealing with two different conflicts. Moreover, differences in perspective and the inability to recognize the other person's perspective contribute to misunderstanding and lay the groundwork for conflict. Each person brings into the conflict interaction his/her own ideas about the sources of the conflict, the events leading to the conflict, and the meaning of behaviors. Each party to conflict cannot see the same issues or the same events leading to the conflict (Sillars et al., 2000; Sillars, 1998). Moreover, conflict parties have different information about each other's motives, intentions, and behaviors (DeDreu, Natua, & van de Vliert, 1995).

In addition, conflict parties' perceptions of situational details differ (Witteman, 1992). Witteman considered frequency of occurrence, goal mutuality, goal–path uncertainty, attribution of cause to the other person, and negative feelings for the other person. He viewed all as perceptions rather than facts because each person knows only his/her own thoughts; additionally, those thoughts are affected by the biases inherent in the perception process. The perceptions, more than the causes of the conflict characteristics, were related to the conflict style and management of the conflict.

At this juncture, we wish to reiterate that your "field of vision" is largely external to you (Storms, 1973). For example, you do not see your face or even hear your voice accurately when you communicate. You can see your hands gesturing, but that is about it. You hear your voice primarily through the bones in your face and head, which is why you sound so "strange" to yourself when you hear a recording of it. The recording is more accurate than your perceptions of your own behavior. So the other person has much more data regarding your behavior than you. You interpret your behavior as reasonable, making claims to others that "I was very polite and didn't make any snide remarks." However, your partner sees your behavior and notices your eyes looking elsewhere and speaking in a sarcastic voice. Likewise, you tend to focus on the other person while, simultaneously, the other person is focussing on you. Thus, two people who have no clue about what they themselves look or sound like, evaluate each other based largely on information that they have selectively retrieved (Sillars, 2001).

Based on their perceptual biases and fields of vision, each person *punctuates* the interaction event so that s/he is seen as reacting to something the other person said or did (Watzlawick et al., 1967). Indeed, Watzlawick et al. identified the punctuation problem as pivotal to understanding relational dysfunction. Consider the following conversation between the young couple we introduced at the top of this chapter. If you look carefully, you will see that their conflict concerns how to punctuate the event. She faults him for not talking to her when she arrives home, while he denies her punctuation (turns 67–70). Rather, he punctuates his silence as a reaction for not being included, which she discredits (turns 72–75). The conflict then shifts but he pursues the topic, leading to the segment we presented in the beginning of the chapter. Clearly, the punctuation of their conflict is biased.

Turn	Speaker	Message
67	W	[We have problems communicating] 'cause I think you say things like last night when I came home, and I was really mad at Amy, and you didn't say anything to me when I walked in the house—

68	M	[sarcastically] Which I never do.
69	W	Yes you DO. You always say something to me when I walk in the house—
70	M	[sarcastically] Right. Right. I never am silent.
71	W	Right.
72	M	So, I wasn't included. I was a little annoyed.
73	W	But I didn't do anything. I was home what, 15 minutes after I told you I was going to be. Is that right?
74	M	Yeah. But I worked all day and I was a little annoyed that you weren't home!
75	W	[sarcastically] Oh, I'm sorry you had to wait 15 minutes! When I got home you were watching the basketball game—*that's* a little annoying.
76	M	I was a little worried about you, but not much. I figured you were just drunk.
77	W	Tom! It's *not* typical.
78	M	It's typical that you're going to go to your friends and do that.
79	W	Okay, and the third [conflict topic] . . .
80	M	[sarcastically] All right, *that* was good communication.
81	W	(Laughs)
82	M	Are we done with that one?
83	W	I guess so.
84	M	Why? We didn't talk about it.

We must depend on their perceptions because they provide our only empirical connection to the real world. And because feelings are very real to them, people use them to predict how their partners feel, not realizing that their conversational partner likely experiences different feelings during conflict (Sillars, 2000; Sillars, Pike, Jones, & Murphy, 1984). As indicated, each person provides different information about details of the conflict including the cause of the conflict, focus of the conflict, and the roles each person played during the conflict. As the conflict continues, differences in perception become even stronger, and at some point communication becomes the most difficult (Sillars, 1998). In a word, differences in perception very well might fuel the escalation of conflict because both people simply become unable to understand the other person and what that person says and does (Sillars, Roberts, Dun, & Leonard, 2001).

> *Conclusion 9.2: One person's field of vision radically differs from the other person's field of vision.*
>
> *Suggestion 9.2: Be mindful that during interaction your partner has more data about your behavior than you do, so obtain that information to help your cause.*

Perceptions Vary According to Roles

A series of studies shows how the same person can have alternative perceptions simply by shifting roles. Baumeister, Stillwell, and Wortman (1990) asked participants to write stories about conflict and anger from both of their roles as a victim and as a perpetrator. Baumeister et al. found that the roles altered what happened. Perpetrators tended to present their behavior as directed by meaning and as comprehensible; victims, on the other hand, portrayed perpetrator behaviors as arbitrary or incomprehensible. Perpetrators also saw their behavior as a single instance with no longterm consequences, whereas victims saw ongoing consequences, including hurt and loss. Because participants wrote narratives as both victim and perpetrator, the differences in perception seem to reside in the roles rather than in the individual. And in both roles, participants indicated no understanding that these differences in perception existed. Parents often punish their children to teach them. Children often believe the punishment is a product of anger, not love.

In a study of aversive behaviors (Kowalski, Walker, Wilkenson, Queen, & Sharpe, 2003), participants indicated again that the perceptions of victims and perpetrators differ, but the differences were inconsistent across all types of behaviors. Interpretations of complaining and dependency did not differ between roles, possibly because these behaviors are less directed at the individual and can be both positive and negative. However, victims perceived lying, betrayal, teasing, and arrogance as more negative than did perpetrators. Using their perceptions of the incident, victims then decided how to react to these aversive behaviors, and often they retaliated in kind, turning the perpetrator into a victim and setting up a cycle of reciprocity that has the potential to spiral into ever more aversive and even aggressive behavior (Kowalski et al., 2003).

In an earlier study, Kowalski (2000) focused on one aversive behavior—teasing. Teasing can be positive or negative, good-natured or mean. Because teasing comments are open to interpretation, recipients (victims) may have some difficulty accurately identifying a teaser's (perpetrator's) motives. How people perceive teasing is related to their mood, the reactions of other people present, their past experiences with teasing, and even personality variables. Some people cannot stand to be teased, other people don't mind it, and still others enjoy slicing and dicing their conversational partners in exchanges of repartee.

In Kowalski (2000), perpetrators tended to see teasing as humorous, less annoying, and less damaging than the victims saw it. Victims, who perceived the teasing as very annoying, also thought that the person teasing them viewed them negatively and they perceived the teasing to indicate that the perpetrator didn't value their relationship. Perpetrators also did not seem to grasp the possibility of longer-term negative effects on people's self-esteem. Even though teasers indicated that they were aware of the negative effects of their behaviors, and that they felt guilt about their teasing, they thought the victims' views of teasing were more positive than they actually were. These results indicate that a person's role in the conversation leads to alternative interpretations of and likely has unintended consequences for the conflict parties.

In addition, people rely on their reactions to messages to make sense of them. How many times have you been put down but did not realize it at the moment ("Nice shoes"). Only later do you realize that the compliment was a put down and become angry. Vangelisti (2001) explained that people react to hurtful statements if they perceive they have been hurt. Different appraisals of a situation lead to the experience of different emotions. People can become angry or experience another emotion such as pity ("This poor idiot doesn't know what he is saying"). Lazarus (1993) described cognitive appraisals as subjective evaluations that are influenced by the intensity and quality of one's emotions. In other words, a person's reaction to a situation depends on subjective appraisals.

Perspective Taking

As mentioned, differences in perspective and the inability to recognize the other person's perspective contribute to misunderstanding (Kowalski et al., 2000). Perhaps the one activity that is needed most and used the least in conflict is perspective taking. *Perspective taking* refers to the process of seeing the issue from the other person's point of view, or as one scholar defined it as "the cognitive process of understanding how another person thinks and feels about the situation and why they are behaving as they are" (Sessa, 1996). Perspective taking is one component of *empathy* (the other being emotional contagion—catching the other person's emotion). As you can imagine, perspective taking is a highly sophisticated activity that has been positively associated with various proactive and supportive message behaviors.

Because people's perceptions differ so widely, people benefit from checking their perceptions and from thinking about how their partners might perceive the interaction. This meta-perception should lead to greater understanding, which Sillars (1985) defined as the ability to take the other person's perspective and to view the situation as s/he does. This effort to create understanding may help reduce differences in perception and attributions and thereby help create more satisfying relationships (Sillars et al., 1990). But people seldom consider the other person; they rarely have a good understanding of another person's perspective until they make a conscious effort to gain information about how that person views what is occurring (Sillars, 1998). Our own thoughts are, of course, clearer and more elaborate to us, so being aware of what others might be thinking causes us to seek more information to achieve some sense of balance between the two thought processes (Cloven & Roloff, 1990). Also, more similar perspectives and mutual focus on self and other lead to more constructive conflict (Sillars et al., 2001).

Recognizing the perspective of another person is a skill, one that develops over the early years of one's life into adulthood (Selman, 1980). Some people become quite adept at taking the perspective of other people; they come to appreciate how conflicts are a natural part of an interdependent association between two people and that people are not always consistent with their own attitudes (Selman, 1980). However, other people never develop perspective-taking skills; they continue to view themselves as victims of conflict that they never intended and cannot understand when someone does not behave in accordance with their attitudes (Selman, 1980). Appreciating the complexity of people and relationships allows us to seek more information and adjust to it.

BOX 8.2   STUDENT STORY

Kids Kids Everywhere
by
Ben Brossmann

They're in movie theaters, they're in restaurants, they're in colleges, they're everywhere! A new breed of parent has assumed permission to tote their cranky kids with them to nearly every establishment around. Don't get me wrong, I love kids, but when has it become appropriate to bring a teething child to a restaurant? to a party? to class? Parents are showing up in record numbers accompanied by their brat packs expecting the childless to approve, and most of us don't.

About a month ago, I was stuck in coach on a non-stop flight from Phoenix to New York. I was sandwiched between a pair of self-absorbed moms and their lap-sitting two-year-olds. The airline attendant saw me before take-off and gave me a look of pity; I smiled back to acknowledge her kind attention to my oncoming agony. I knew this was going to be the longest six hours of my life.

Once the cabin pressure was adjusted after takeoff, it all began. One kid cries and they all start to cry. Ten minutes into the flight, all of the other passengers were unnerved by screams from cranky kids. I took a baby count—the total was 16. If I were to cry like that and throw tantrums, they would land the plane and site me for breaking some FAA rule.

The most disenchanting aspect about these two soccer moms was the fact that not once did they apologize. Instead of at least acknowledging the fact that they indeed were inappropriate in slinging their sickly little brats into a seat fit for one they just smiled at me! *Smiled!* As if accept this! Mid-flight I needed to use the restroom but to get into the aisle one of the moms would have to let me out. The scowl I got from her made me feel as if I was asking her for an unbelievable favor.

Discussion Questions

1. Do you agree with Ben that small children are "everywhere?"
2. In what way did Ben's framing of the situation affect his mood?
3. Do you think the flight attendant sympathized with Ben, or is it possible that her smile reflected a different attitude?
4. In what ways might perspective-taking have helped Ben change his view of "self-absorbed" moms?
5. What other perceptual and attributional errors can you find in this story?

Perspective taking requires motivation and sophisticated thinking; it takes time and energy to integrate the other's thoughts into our own. Unfortunately, we assume that the other person's thoughts, feelings, expectations, and intentions reflect exactly those of the other person (Sessa, 1996). This behavior is so common that we do not realize that we do it (Sillars, 1998). And during conflict, people tend to become less willing and able to engage in complex thought processes; instead, they have mostly negative thoughts, overlook alternative explanations for behavior, and are minimally aware of the interdependence that leads to reciprocal actions (Sillars et al., 2000). Furthermore, because people's own thoughts and feelings are strong, they naturally attend to them with little consideration of the thoughts and feelings of the other person. Moreover, people use their own feelings as a basis for guessing what their partners might feel (Sillars, 1985; Sillars et al., 2001).

Perspective taking during conflict offers multiple benefits. First, considering both people's views helps to provide a more circumspect understanding of what is occurring. We are not limited by our own ideas and interpretations; we can begin to see that the other person has processed different information and reached some different conclusions about what happened. Because we have more information about the other person and the event, we can engage in a broader array of collaborative message behavior. Taking the perspective of the other person also helps us think about the other person as well as about ourselves, so we can deal with the conflict with consideration for the other person (Sillars et al., 2001). We also use this information to focus more on differences so that our conflict discussion remains more on task rather than devolving into personal attacks (Sessa, 1996). When interpreting the social world, perception is reality. The above material leads to the next principle:

> *Principle 9.3: Perspective-taking helps people understand their conflict because it requires consideration of the other person's thoughts and feelings.*
>
> *Suggestion 9.3: Engage in perspective-taking early in the conflict episode so that you can obtain information about the other person's views on the topic.*

Dimensions of Attribution Regarding Causes of Conflict

After people form their perceptions of events, they then want to know why these events occurred and/or why people engaged in certain actions. To help them understand, people make attributions, a higher order cognitive process that provides explanation for events and behaviors (Weiner, 1986). Attributions are relevant to conflict because negative relational events tend to lead to more attributions about the partner and his/her behavior (Holtzworth & Jacobson, 1985). Naturally, when people become hurt and angry, they want to figure out why their "loving" partner would treat them in such a negative manner.

Dimensions of Attributions

Attributions that people make for the cause of the conflict and the other person's behavior contain various properties, or dimensions. One dimension is whether the behavior was *internal* (related to personal factors) or *external* (related to situational factors). Internal attributions lead us to think that the behavior was caused by some personal characteristic. In contrast, external attributions allow us to think that what occurred was not usual because it was caused by characteristics of the situation. Making external attributions, rather than internal attributions, for negative events and behaviors tends to be more functional for both parties (Zillmann, 1993). For example, we decide that our partner yelled at us because of pressures at work rather than because s/he is a mean person. Or we believe that a co-worker's failure to show up for work is due to an emergency rather than laziness. One study illustrates how attributing the conflict as the other person's fault leads to increased competitiveness.

Sillars (1980) examined how roommates' attributions for who was to blame for a conflict affected their own behavior. He found that roommates were more likely to use integrative strategies when they attributed cooperation to the other person and more responsibility of the conflict to themselves. Also, when they attributed more responsibility to themselves, they saw the behavior as less stable and were more likely to use integrative strategies. In contrast, when participants attributed more responsibility to their roommates, they saw the cause of conflict as more stable, were less likely to use cooperative conflict tactics, and were more likely to use competitive conflict tactics. During conflict, we evaluate how much *control* the person had. If people determine they had control over their behavior, they tend to react more strongly (Betancourt & Blair, 1992). We do not tend to hold people responsible for behavior they did not perform, although we do consider that they should have predicted how their behavior would affect us, and what we want (Fincham, Bradbury, & Grych, 1990). For instance, we are more likely to be patient with elderly people slowly walking in a crosswalk than with teenagers who take just as long without a clue about the people waiting to drive.

People derive internal or external attributions depending on whether the behavior is seen as intentional (Fincham & Bradbury, 1987; Jones & Davis, 1965). For instance, one of the first assessments we make of a hurtful message is whether the person meant to be hurtful. When we think people know that their behavior will have hurtful consequences, that they thought about the behavior in advance, and that they chose to perform the behavior, then clearly they intended to hurt us (Vagelisti, 2001). We then tend to respond emotionally and in ways that might have damaging effects. For instance, Vangelisti and Young (2000) found that, when people interpreted hurtful behavior or comments as intentional, they distanced themselves from the other person. Moreover, the distancing occurred with unintentional behavior only if people also attributed the behavior as internal (a personal trait) or if they felt the behavior disregarded them.

In addition to the dimension of internality, attributions reflect the *consistency* of the event or behavior (Kelley, 1973). That is, we determine whether the event is stable over time or an unstable isolated event. We consider whether the person has behaved this way with us before or if we have seen him/her behave this way with other people. For example, arriving to work late *again* can be explained by stable features of the person (e.g., laziness, unreliability) rather than a lack of parking spaces that day.

A third dimension of attributions concerns how a cause contains *global* implications or whether the cause is specific to the conflict. If, for example, you attribute the cause of your partner yelling at you because she or he is mean, then that attribution also explains why he does not tip waiters and waitresses, doesn't stop for pedestrians, and doesn't like dogs. However, again, if you attribute the cause of your partner's yelling to pressures at work, then that attribution does not explain why he doesn't like dogs (or any animal, for that matter). Explanation for his not liking animals must come from somewhere else.

Importantly, these dimensions characterize attributions, and they lead to alternative forms of conflict management. More precisely, internal, stable, and global attributions for conflicts associate with poor problem-solving communication, negative conflict-management communication, weak social support messages, and expression of negative affect (Fincham & Beach, 1999). However, external, unstable, and specific attributions associate with functional problem-solving, positive conflict communication, social support messages, and expression of positive affect (Fincham & Beach, 1999). Given the research on attributions for conflict causes, we offer the following principle:

> *Conclusion 9.4: Attribution inferences: Positive attributions to the causes of and behaviors during conflict involve external, unstable, and specific factors; negative and damaging attributions involve external, unstable, and specific factors.*
>
> *Suggestion 9.4: Attempt to attribute the causes of and behaviors during conflict to external, unstable, and specific factors.*

Attribution Biases

Attributions are seldom accurate. People can operate with only their own take on conflict, so errors in explaining the event repeatedly occur. To begin, we know that a person's self-perception of behavior correlates poorly with how a partner perceives the behavior (Sillars et al., 2000; Sypher & Sypher, 1984). One reason for the lack of correspondence in interpretation resides in the various *attribution biases* that everyone carries.

First, the *actor-observer bias* (or the *fundamental attribution error*) concerns how we tend to rely on internal factors when making inferences about other people's behavior, whereas we tend to see our own behavior as externally caused (Canary & Spitzberg, 1990). We experience the external factors that affect our behavior—for example, being late to work: the late-night at work, the last minute preparation that was needed, the unforeseen errand, and the nightmare traffic. But we cannot experience the other person's external constraints, so we place more weight on internal factors that provide ready-made explanations (e.g., lazy, unreliable). The "ultimate" fundamental attribution error occurs when we infer that the other person's negative behavior is due to internal factors but their positive behaviors are due to external factors ("She did a good job on this report—she must have gotten some help.").

Next, the *self-serving bias* leads us to interpret an event in ways that are more favorable to ourselves and less favorable to the other person (De Dreu et al., 1995), and we see our own behavior more positively than not (Sypher & Sypher, 1984). Combining the actor-observer bias with the self-serving bias we find that people tend to attribute positive conflict behaviors and outcomes to their own internal features, whereas they attribute negative conflict messages and outcomes to their partners (Sillars et al., 2001). Naturally, both people make similar attributional biases for the same situation; both people tend to see their behaviors as positive and the other person's behaviors as less positive.

People also notice the other person's negative behavior more than their positive behavior—this is called the *negativity* bias (Kellermann, 1984). Negative behavior (more than positive behavior) leads to attributions in part because it is unexpected and in part because it appears threatening (Canary & Spitzberg, 1990; Forgas, Bower, & Moylan, 1990). In other words, people tend to think that the other person performed more negative behaviors and fewer positive behaviors; they, in contrast, think the opposite: they performed more positive behaviors and the other person performed more negative ones. This perception of negative behavior can lead to escalation because the negative behavior of one person can lead to reciprocal negative behavior by the other (remember that both people have this bias, so both people will reciprocate negative behavior). This negative behavior then confirms the original negative attribution and in turn can stimulate more hostile behavior. Neither person wants to be the first to compromise, so the conflict escalates (De Dreu et al., 1995).

The *relationship-enhancing bias* indicates that happy couples make internal attributions for positive behaviors and external attributions for negative behaviors. Unhappy couples do the opposite, seeing positive behaviors as due to external forces and therefore not to be repeated but seeing negative behaviors as internal and repeatable (Baucom, Sayers, & Duhe, 1989). Satisfied partners view positive as well as negative behaviors as more positive in intent, motivated by selfless and praiseworthy attitudes (Fincham, Beach, & Nelson, 1987).

Although discrepancies in attribution occur, attribution differences between satisfied partners are greater in dissatisfied relationships. People who attribute their relationship problems to the partners' negative behavior will likely use direct fighting tactics. This behavior confirms the other person's negative attributions and tends to become self-perpetuating as people continue to confirm their attributions. In the worst cases, this cycle becomes a pattern that is hard to break (Sillars, 1985).

Based upon their attributions, people create narratives about their conflicts and their overall relationship. These narratives reflect the variety of attributional biases we have just discussed. These narratives frame interpretations of the other person's behavior and those interpretations lead to additional narratives. People respond to the interpretations as well as the behaviors. Two people can create irreconcilable narratives, which in turn lead to incompatible attributions about causes and communication (Sillars et al., 2001).

Attributional biases are also affected by a person's mood (Forgas, 2001). People's moods affect the information they notice and the processing strategies they use. People in a good mood use simple heuristic processing whereas sad people use more complex processing methods (Forgas, 1995). People also are more likely to recall information that is congruent with their mood. More telling, people are generally unaware of mood influences, and the more confidence they have in their judgments, the more mistaken they are (Forgas, 1998).

Emotion also influences attributions of responsibility. People engage in mood congruent attribution processes. Happy people tend to use external, unstable, and specific causes for conflict. People who are sad tend to attribute the cause to internal, stable, and global factors regarding themselves. The angry person likely believes that the other person is responsible for the conflict. Guilty people tend to perceive themselves as the cause of whatever happened (Keltner, Ellsworth, & Edwards, 1993). Additionally, happy people tend to make more optimistic and understanding judgments, but people in negative moods tend to make more pessimistic and self-defeating judgments (Forgas, 1994). The self-serving bias occurs for people in neutral moods (Forgas et al., 1990). Affect is most influential when people are in situations that make it difficult for them to find a way to process the information. As a result, they begin to focus on irrelevant information, and the role of mood is magnified. Irrelevant information becomes more salient (Kitayama, 1991).

The point to this material concerns how explanations that we give to events are quite biased, and these biases are the product of another irrational factor—mood.

Conclusion 9.5: Attribution errors distort explanations for conflict events and behaviors are distorted by them, so you should adjust your attributions to reduce the errors in your own attributions.

Suggestion 9.5: Realize that your attributions are vulnerable to errors. To obtain attribution control *adjust your thoughts to strategic conflict to minimize these errors.*

Suggestion 9.6: "Preattribute annoying events and information about such events— to the extent possible—to motives and circumstances that make the induction of annoyance appear unintentional and nondeliberate, and . . . reattribute annoying events and information about such events in the same manner" (Zillman, 1993, p. 382; emphasis original).

Perception and attribution constitute the bases of conflict management. Conflict requires that people recall and interpret complex and ambiguous information. Fincham and Bradbury's (1987) Attribution Efficacy Model claims that during conflict in close relationships, people ask two questions: What caused the conflict? and How can the conflict be solved? In our efforts to answer these questions we try to determine blame from among possible sources such as ourselves, our partners, the relationship, the external environment, God's will, chance, luck, fate or whatever. When we blame ourselves, we consider causes that are external to ourselves, unstable, and specific to one isolated conflict. When we blame our partners, we use causes that contain intention, stability, control, and general influences (Doherty, 1981). How we assign blame then directly affects us and not the other person. Our responses also affect our choices for strategic communication during conflict (Fincham & Bradbury, 1987).

This leads to our final suggestion for this chapter:

Conclusion 9.6: People tend to believe falsely that their attributions of conflict influence how the other person should behave.

Suggestion 9.7: Be mindful that your attributions directly affect your own conflict strategies first but can have only indirect effects on your partner.

10

INTERCULTURAL CONFLICT

As the world continues to shrink, one will likely encounter people from different cultures. Open travel between national borders, foreign trade, and other opportunities suggest that intercultural contact has become the norm and not an exception (Ting-Toomey, 2010). This chapter examines how features of culture correspond to intercultural conflict.

Culture refers to "a system of knowledge, meanings, and symbolic actions that is shared by the majority of the people in a society" (Ting-Toomey, 1994). Culture works to develop individual and community identities, as well as communicative behaviors, rites, and rituals among group members. Cultural members do not all share the same view of their culture (Keesing, 1974). Likewise, people have their own view of their culture. When people from different cultures interact, conflict likely emerges if neither person recognizes the other person's cultural identity and beliefs. *Intercultural conflict* concerns perceived or actual incompatibility of cultural values, situational norms, goals, face orientations, scarce resources, processes, and/or outcomes in a face-to-face (or mediated) context (Ting-Toomey & Oetzel, 2001). This chapter discusses how conflict varies according to cultural variability factors.

Before we discuss intercultural factors that affect conflict, an observation should be made: Many researchers examine the role of culture by using nations. Instead of measuring if people differ on features of culture, researchers often assume that different nations represent cultural differences (e.g., Americans are competitive, whereas Koreans are cooperative). However, such is not necessarily the case. For example, Gudykunst, Matsumoto, Ting-Toomey, Nishida, Kim, and Heyman (1996) found that Japanese and South Korean participants differed from participants who lived outside Asia. They also found that Australians used communication styles similar to Americans, who live thousands of miles away. But Australians were quite different from their Asian neighbors. In other words, location is not equal to culture.

We now know that using the nation to represent culture provides an indirect and sometimes crude estimate of cultural variation. Using meta-analyses to summarize the research, Oyserman, Coon, and Kemmelmeir (2002) found that underlying dimensions of culture explain behavior much more powerfully than differences between nations. This chapter will comment on how dimensions of culture can help explain intercultural conflicts.

Cultural Dimensions Tied to Conflict

For the past 50 years, researchers have examined dimensions on which cultures differ or are similar (see the Oyserman et al. review on individualism/collectivism). These dimensions represent *cultural variability*. For some time, researchers of intercultural conflict highlighted the dimensions of individualism–collectivism, power distance, and self-construal (Ting-Toomey & Takai, 2006). Given its dominance in the research, we discuss these three dimensions with a focus on individualism–collectivism. Then we discuss conflict management differences tied to cultural variation.

Individualism versus Collectivism

Researchers of the individualistic–collectivist dimension examine how much cultural members value individual rights and resources over group members' rights and resources. For example, *individualistic cultures* place a primary emphasis on the self; the individual takes precedence over the needs, desires, and goals of a group. The "I" is emphasized over the "we." High individualistic values are found in the United States, Australia, Great Britain, Canada, the Netherlands, and New Zealand. *Collectivist cultures*, however, focus more on the in-group collective than the needs of the individual (Triandis, 1995). In these cultures the "we" is emphasized over the "I." China, Japan, Taiwan, Mexico, Indonesia, Columbia, Venezuela, Panama, Ecuador, and Guatemala represent collectivist cultures. As Triandis argued, different orientations toward individuals and groups yield different ways of handling and engaging in conflict. (Note to reader: the above two sentences show how cultural dimensions can be equated with different nations—as discussed above.)

Two examples illustrate how people from the same culture can differ in their views of the role of the U.S. national government. The opinions are taken from the *Salt Lake City Tribune* (June 24, 2011, p. 2):

> *A collectivist view:*
>
> In fact, the purpose of government is to do collectively what we could not do as individuals. By pooling our resources, we can assemble a military for

our mutual protection, build roads to facilitate commerce, pursue research to achieve better living, . . . and accomplish many other common goals. (Dana Carroll)

An individualistic view:

As for the idea of "common welfare," there is no such thing. A society is only made up of individuals—there is nothing greater than that. Take away an individual's right life and property and you've eliminated everything of value. The smallest minority on earth is the individual, and you cannot sacrifice one individual's rights to benefit the majority. (Amy Sandoval)

These statements reveal individualistic versus collectivistic views, and they show that the views within one nation can differ.

Power Distance

Although people can exhibit individualistic and collectivistic values, Hofstede (2001) argued that cultures also display power distances aligning with their individualist or collectivist values. Power distance refers to "the degree to which inequities in power are viewed as natural and inherent in the individuals in a culture" (Gudykunst & Ting-Toomey, 1996). High power distance cultures view power as vital and necessary to society. In high power distance societies, social hierarchies and status differences clearly emerge. In low power distance cultures, people are seen as equals and inequities in power stem from different roles (e.g., supervisor, father).

As with individualism and collectivism, power distance occurs through interaction and is reflected in corporate cultures (Carl, Gupta, & Javidan, 2004). In this case, power distance refers to the way corporate cultures approach power. Large power distance corporations groom unequal power distributions and desire feedback from experts or other high-status individuals. Small power distance corporate cultures strive for symmetrical relations, equal power distributions, and opportunities for individuals to share information.

Placing the individualism–collectivism dimension on a horizontal axis and large/small power distances at 90 degrees on a vertical axis yields four primary approaches: impartial, status–achievement, benevolent, and communal (Ting-Toomey & Oetzel, 2001; Ting-Toomey & Takai, 2006). Figure 10.1 illustrates how power differences overlap with individualist–collectivistic cultures. In addition, these four approaches can identify how corporations can be portrayed.

The *impartial approach* combines individualistic values and small power distance. This approach values personal freedom and equal treatment (Smith, Dugan, Peterson, & Leung, 1998) and can be found in Denmark, the Netherlands, Sweden,

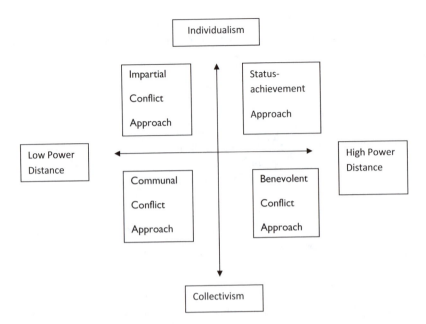

FIGURE 10.1   The Intersection of Power and Individualism

Note: From Ting-Toomey & Oetzel (2001).

and Norway (Hofstede, 2001). This approach indicates that direct and straightforward messages reflect how people (e.g., management vs. worker) can confront the other person because status is not a big deal. The *status-achievement approach* merges individualistic values and large power distance. People highlight the importance of personal freedom, but power inequalities must endure so the company can run efficiently. This approach is reportedly common in France and the United States (Storti, 2001; Ting-Toomey & Oetzel, 2001). The *benevolent approach* combines collectivist and large power distance, and it stresses obligation to others and power inequalities. This approach occurs in many countries, including Latin and South American nations (e.g., Mexico, Venezuela, Brazil, Chile), most Asian nations (e.g., India, Japan, China, South Korea), most Arab nations (e.g., Egypt, Saudi Arabia, Jordan), and most African nations (e.g., Nigeria, Uganda) (Hofstede, 2001). Finally, the *communal approach*, which is the least common of the four approaches, combines collectivist and small power distance. This approach emphasizes interdependence and equality. Hofstede reported that Costa Rica is the only country to fit this approach.

Understanding the individualism–collectivism dimension remains important to the extent that people rely on these dimensions to guide their behaviors. In general, individualistic people tend to use words to convey their ideas and feelings, so they choose direct words, developed explanations, precise usage, and exaggerated stories (Gudykunst et al., 1996). People in collectivistic cultures rely on context for meaning, so they select indirect language and listen; they show sensitivity, less openness, fewer words, but more words that state appreciation for the identity management of group members (Gudykunst et al., 1996; Oetzel, 2005).

The use of low-context versus high-context communication helps one understand the role communication plays in individualist and collectivist cultures. A low-context style of communication refers to a reliance on explicit language to make one's ideas clear. Information is shared and expressed to manage conflict and fill in missing contextual information (Hall, 1976). In addition, low-context communicators use overt expressions, focus on the sender, and prefer direct strategies (Ting-Toomey, 1985). Low-context communication occurs within individualistic cultures, such as the U.S., Norway, and Germany. On the other hand, high-context communication offers minimal explicit language, so message receivers must glean relevant information from the context of the interaction (Hall, 1976). High-context communication utilizes an indirect negotiation mode and subtle nonverbal cues. High-context communication occurs in many collectivist countries, such as China, Japan, and Mexico. The above material leads to the first principle regarding cultural variability:

> *Conclusion 10.1: People in different cultures prefer to communicate directly or indirectly to represent their cultural values.*
>
> *Suggestion 10.1: Be mindful of the possibility that people from other cultures communicate (in)directly and in ways given the value of their situational cues.*

Individualistic versus Collectivistic Cultural Differences in Conflict

For years, researchers reported that individualism–collectivism affects interpersonal conflict in predictable ways. The general hypothesis is that people in individualistic societies prefer confrontational procedures, whereas people in collectivistic cultures prefer harmony-enhancing procedures for managing conflict. So, for example, one would expect cultural differences in communication directness. Indeed, Ohbuchi and Takahashi (1994) found that participants from Japan (ostensibly a collectivistic culture) used avoidance and indirect bilateral strategies (such as suggesting, appeasing and impression management) more often than did participants from the United States; whereas Americans preferred negotiation and direct fighting (e.g., threat, coercion) strategies more often in interpersonal conflict situations (p. 1357).

Yet (as mentioned), comparisons between nations provide only an indirect measure of underlying cultural dimensions. In fact, several findings based on national differences do not support the hypothesis that individualistic people are more direct, clear, and competitive than collectivistic people. Trubinsky, Ting-Toomey, and Lin (1991) found that, as they predicted, Taiwanese used obliging and avoiding styles more than did Americans. However, Taiwanese also used integrative and compromising styles more than Americans, contrary to expectations. And contrary to expectations, Oetzel, Ting-Toomey, Yokochi, Matsumoto, and Takaki (2000) found that Americans preferred integrative facework behaviors more than did Japanese, and Japanese participants viewed dominance as more effective than did Americans.

Importantly as well, comparing people from one nation to those from another, regarding particular conflict strategies, does not test people's overall preferences for one strategy (e.g., cooperative tactics) over another strategy (e.g., competitive tactics). Gabrieldis, Stephan, Ybarra, Pearson, and Villareal (1997) found that Mexican (vs. American) participants preferred collaboration and accommodation, as one might anticipate based on the individualism–collectivism dimension. However, participants from both cultures preferred cooperative tactics over competitive ones, and participants from both cultures were similar in direct fighting tactics.

Cai and Fink (2002) tested the hypothesis that people across cultures prefer cooperative to competitive conflict against the hypothesis based on individualism–collectivism (i.e., individualistic people are more direct, assertive, and confrontive). Cai and Fink did not find evidence for the influence of individualism–collectivism on conflict behavior. Instead, they found that, regardless of individualism–collectivism, respondents preferred negotiation, then obliging and avoiding, and finally compromising and dominating conflicts styles. Moreover, Cai and Fink's findings indicate that individualists preferred avoiding more than collectivists did, but no cultural difference was found regarding direct fighting (see Ishida et al., 2005, for similar findings). So individual preferences for conflict strategies across nations are similar, although cultural differences in conflict behaviors due to individualism–collectivism might occur. That is, people across cultures appear to first rely on cooperative conflict tactics, then avoidance, and then competitive tactics (Cai & Fink, 2002; Ishida et al., 2005). This leads to the next principle regarding cultural variability and conflict management.

Conclusion 10.2: People across cultures tend to use cooperative conflict tactics, then avoidant tactics, and finally competitive conflict tactics.

Suggestion 10.2: Rely on negotiation and nonconfrontation when in conflict with people across cultures.

Individual and Cultural Characteristics

Although group-based cultural patterns (e.g., individualism–collectivism) are important to understanding low- and high-context communication, individuals within cultures develop personality tendencies toward conflict. In particular, a person's conception of self in relation to others provides a powerful means to understand how individual beliefs combine with culture to affect conflict behavior. More precisely, *self-construal* references an individual's self-image that is composed of both an independent self and an interdependent self (Markus & Kitayama, 1991, 1998).

The *independent construal of self* emphasizes that each individual is unique, with specific feelings, motivations, and thoughts. Independents believe s/he can control more outcomes in various situations (Markus & Kitayama, 1991). On the other hand, the *interdependent construal of self* emphasizes in-group connections, which includes recognizing where one belongs with respect to other people (Markus & Kitayama, 1991). Although people can adopt both dimensions of self-construal, one's culture tends to place an emphasis on adopting an independent or an interdependent self. As one might anticipate, individualistic cultures promote its members to adopt an independent self-construal, whereas collectivistic cultures cultivate an interdependent self-construal. In this vein, Gudykunst, Matsumoto, Ting-Toomey et al. (1996) found that independent self-construals coincide with elements of individualistic cultures, whereas interdependent self-construals complement collectivistic cultures.

When one's culture matches one's self-construal, predictable conflict behaviors emerge. Individualists with independent self-construals differ from collectivists with interdependent self-construals (Oetzel & Ting-Toomey, 2006; Oetzel et al., 2001; Ting-Toomey, 2000; Ting-Toomey & Takia, 2006). Here are a few of those differences:

- Individualists tend to adopt an *outcome-oriented* model of conflict, where they emphasize solutions to problems. Collectivists adopt a more *process-oriented* view of conflict, where parties remain sensitive to each others' need for a positive public image (or "positive face") and need for autonomy (or "negative face").

- Individualists see conflict as a challenge to their personal goals. Collectivists tend to view conflict as a potential threat to face and to in-group versus out-group membership.

- Individualists focus on individual pride and self-esteem, individual emotions, and a sense of autonomy and power. Collectivists emphasize saving face, group harmony, and reciprocity of emotions, favors, and obligations.

- Individualists tend to manage the problem openly and directly, such that the issue under discussion takes precedence over the other person's face needs. Collectivists try to manage problems in subtle and indirect ways so that *both* parties' needs for integrity and autonomy are preserved.

- Individualists can become frustrated if conflicts are not managed openly and directly. Collectivists see conflict as a threat if substantive issues are discussed before face needs are properly managed.

- Individualists tend to use more competitive conflict strategies and tactics that reflect their desires to solve problems in a clear, direct, and open manner. Collectivists prefer indirect means of confrontation (e.g., hinting, avoidance).

- Individualists tend to view conflict as productive if they reach their goals using communication behavior that meets the other person's expectations. Collectivists tend to view conflict as productive if both parties can claim they have won.

At the same time, however, not all self-construals match the underlying characteristics of one's culture (Markus & Kitayama, 1991). People from an individualistic culture can adopt an interdependent self-construal, and people from collectivistic cultures might adopt an independent self-construal. How such mismatches affect conflict can only be estimated from the research. It appears likely that independent and interdependent self-construals *filter* (or "mediate") the effects of the larger culture on interpersonal conflicts (Oetzel, 2005). Such filtering indicates that attitudes, beliefs, and values tied to cultural variations directly affect one's self-construal; then, individual self-construal directly affects alternative behavioral choices (Kim et al., 1996).

Why such culture/individual mismatches occur can be traced to several reasons, including the following two: (1) people adopt identities primarily based on their close social networks and relationships (friends, family, etc.), whose values can differ from a majority of other cultural members; and (2) developmental changes lead people to modify their identities, including self-construals (e.g., a Chinese exchange student becomes more self-reliant during years of study in the US).

Differences Due to Self-construal

Independent and interdependent self-construals affect one's communication (Kim & Leung, 2000). Oetzel and Ting-Toomey (2003) reported that independent self-construal associates primarily with "self-face concern" and competing conflict strategies. Interdependent self-construal associates with "other-face concern" and use of avoiding and integrating conflict strategies. *Self-face concern* involves protecting one's own identity when one's own image is threatened during a conflict episode. *Other-face concern* focuses on protecting and accommodating the other conflict party's identity during a conflict episode. A third face concern, *mutual-face concern*, represents efforts to protect both parties' images and the image of the relationship (Oetzel, Ting-Toomey, Masumoto et al., 2001).

Thus, independent self-construal tends to be indicative of individualist cultures where low-context communication and self-face concern are emphasized. According to Ting-Toomey (1994), independents with self-face concern appear to select dominating conflict styles more than do interdependents. Conflict for this style of communicator arises due to incompatible personalities, goals, or beliefs. Interdependent self-construal, on the other hand, represents collectivist cultures that emphasize high-context communication, other-face concern, and mutual-face concern. High-context, interdependent communicators during conflict are more likely than independents to use third-party help when trying to resolve conflict (Ting-Toomey, Oetzel, & Yee-Jung, 2001). Similarly, interdependents focusing on other-face concerns are more likely to use avoiding and integrating conflict styles than their independent counterparts (Oetzel & Ting-Toomey, 2003; Oetzel et al., 2001). As an additional note, Ting-Toomey (2010) found that biconstrual individuals (i.e., people who highlight both independent and interdependent selves) tend to have more diverse strategic conflict tactics than do independent, interdependent, and ambivalent (low on both independent and interdependent selves) people.

The above findings might suggest (and several researchers argue) that people from collectivistic cultures are more cooperative in their conflict management behaviors versus people from individualistic cultures. Also, people from both kinds of cultures report that they *rely first on negotiation conflict tactics*, then avoidant conflict tactics, and then direct fighting tactics (Cai & Fink, 2002).

In summary, research indicates that cultural variability and self-construals combine to affect conflict behaviors. The dimensions of individualism–collectivism, power hierarchy, and low-context versus high-context communication reflect cultural variability. More directly relevant to conflict, independent and interdependent self-construals affect conflict tactic choices that people make. Overall, however, people across cultures use cooperative, then avoidant, and then competitive conflict strategies and tactics. Interdependent people do focus more on mutual face needs when managing conflict. The following section reviews a theory that specifically explains how and why face needs are met.

Conflict Face Negotiation Theory

Conflict face negotiation theory links cultural values to face-saving and conflict styles (for a detailed review of this theory see Ting-Toomey, 2005). As previously mentioned, the ways people deal with conflict are influenced by their cultural backgrounds and personality tendencies. According to Oetzel and Ting-Toomey (2003), face negotiation theory holds that:

> (a) people in all cultures try to maintain and negotiate face in all communication situations; (b) the concept of face becomes especially problematic in uncertainty situations (such as embarrassment and conflict situations) when the situated identities of the communicators are called into question; (c) cultural variability, individual-level variables, and situational variables influence cultural members' selection of one set of face concerns over others (such as self-oriented face-saving vs. other-oriented face-saving); and (d) subsequently, face concerns influence the use of various facework and conflict strategies in intergroup and interpersonal encounters. (p. 600)

In addition, this theory proposes three key features of intercultural conflict—knowledge, mindfulness, communication skills—that result in being a competent communicator (Ting-Toomey, 2005). The first component, *culture-sensitive knowledge*, encourages individuals to develop an in-depth understanding of cultures other than their own and to try to adapt from an ethnocentric to an ethnorelative lens. For example, although many Americans do not know the capital of Canada, many Canadians not only know the capital of the US, but they know the name of its president, vice-president and other important facts.

Being *ethnocentric* involves viewing one's own cultural way of communicating as the best, thereby believing that other cultural members' communication habits are improper, incorrect, or inferior to one's own. For instance, Americans visiting France often complain about the rude French. Actually, the French convey their politeness explicitly, for example, by saying *merci* (thank you) before and after ordering food. On the other hand, Americans convey politeness implicitly and nonverbally, but they do not consistently say "please" or "thank you." Instead, Americans appear ruder to the French as they visit restaurants and demand their food ("I'll have the pommes frites") without saying please or thank you. *Ethnorelativism*, on the other hand, involves understanding that people behave and communicate differently due to their cultural values, and that no one way is better than another (Bennett & Bennett, 2004).

> *Conclusion 10.3: People often judge other cultures according to their own cultural attitudes, beliefs, values, and behaviors.*
>
> *Suggestion 10.3: Lose the ethnocentric lenses when interacting with a member of a different culture. For better vision, rely on ethnorelative lenses.*

The second feature is *mindfulness*, which involves the willingness to attend to one's own cultural and personal assumptions and beliefs while attending to the other communicator's cultural and personal assumptions and beliefs (LeBaron, 2003; Ting-Toomey, 1999). As we argued in Chapter 1, being mindful of one's behavior leads to more productive interactions and conflict outcomes. Being mindful is not simply being aware of one's habits; it also involves recognizing the norms for appropriate behavior and lessons to be learned from other cultures.

> *Suggestion 10.4: Be mindful that your communication, especially during conflict, might reflect an instinctual response that is inappropriate to other cultural norms.*

The final component of *face negotiation theory* concerns *constructive communication skills*, which refers to a person's ability to be appropriate and effective when engaging in conflict. This also involves being able to adapt one's skills during intercultural conflict when necessary. Skills include a consideration of face-saving concerns, reframing the conflict, and collaborative dialogue (Ting-Toomey, 2004). Additionally, Ting-Toomey (1994) offers several skills for the individualist engaging a collectivist culture during conflict: be mindful of face-maintenance assumptions, attempt to be positive and proactive, appreciate quiet observation, practice deep listening skills, release the conflict if the other party does not want to discuss it, and respect a collectivist-interdependent approach to managing conflict. For collectivists engaging in conflict with an individualist, Ting-Toomey (1994) offers the following strategies: be mindful of individualist assumptions, focus on resolving substantive issues, try not to take the conflict personally, assert and express emotions, provide verbal feedback, practice active listening skills, and respect an individualist's approach to handing conflict (for a more detailed review of these skills see Ting-Toomey, 1994). This material leads to the fifth and final principle in this chapter:

Suggestion 10.5: Practice strategic conflict skills viewed from the other person's cultural point of view.

11

SEEKING GOAL CONTROL
Goal Achievement and Defense

People are goal-oriented. Goals include: losing weight before a big event, attending a university, buying a car, et cetera. As well, people interact with other people to obtain what they want or to retain what they have. Interpersonal goals include getting a friend to go out, persuading your partner to commitment, defending yourself against ridicule, and so forth. Naturally, goals we seek often do not coincide with what other people want. When interpersonal goals are not compatible, then interaction partners have conflict. As Chapter 1 noted, many researchers believe that incompatible goals or perception of incompatibility between people defines interpersonal conflict (Putnam, 2006). Even if one does not define conflict in terms of incompatible goals, then one must at least acknowledge that incompatible goals constitute an important source of interpersonal conflict (Bergmann & Volkema, 1994).

To understand conflict, the reader needs to learn about goals. Many communication scholars have linked interpersonal goals to communication behavior (Wilson, 2002). Such effort has meant that we had to first identify a set of representative goals that people pursue everyday and then tie those goals to communication behavior. This chapter discusses those efforts, and it reveals the nature of people as well as strategic conflict.

Conflict implies valued goals are at stake. Moreover, conflict situations become complex because each person tends to want more than one goal and so eyes the important goals differently (Clark & Delia, 1979; Dillard, Segrin, & Harden, 1989). What you value is not the same as what other people value. To obtain a pragmatic understanding of conflict messages, one must know about the nature of goals. Then one can understand how goals affect conflict strategies.

The Nature of Interpersonal Goals

A goal is defined as something that people want to achieve or obtain at some point in the future (Dillard, 1990a; Pervin, 1989b). In addition, goals contain cognitive and emotional elements that affect how people behave toward each other. Lack of goal compatibility can test the tolerance of people whose goal is blocked by another person. Once this occurs, people act to achieve or to safeguard their goals.

Goals Lead to Action

Goals can be understood as the beginning of a sequence that includes plans and actions or what Dillard identifies as goal–plan–actions (GPA) (Dillard 1990a, 1990b). Plans follow goals and determine what behaviors should be used. Once a goal is obtained or not, then people use that experience in further pursuit of goals, which again leads to communication and so forth. Put differently, a person's thoughts and desires for a goal motivate action, which is then directed toward the future and the achievement of other desired goals (Locke & Latham, 1990).

Goals Are Dynamic

People's goals before an interaction may not be the same as goals they have as an interaction progresses (Sanders, 1991). Hocker and Wilmot (1991) label goals as prospective, transactive, and retrospective to represent the various times at which they are formed. *Prospective goals* refer to the goals you have before an interaction; *transactive goals* emerge during interaction; and *retrospective goals* refer to how people can reframe to make sense of what occurred during the interaction. For example, you may begin a goal of convincing a friend to help you move furniture, but when you learn that your friend is having difficulties with an important project due the next day, you may change your goal to helping your friend complete the project on schedule. When looking back on the day you might tell yourself that you really did not want to move the furniture and mostly wanted to spend time with your friend. After all, the furniture can wait.

Differences among Goals

Goals differ in several important ways. First, they differ in the degree of challenge they present; more difficult goals require higher levels of effort, attention, time, knowledge, and skill to achieve (Locke & Latham, 1990). Challenging but attainable goals generally lead to more positive results. But when people face difficult goals that are not clearly attainable, they have problems working to find integrative ways to solve problems (Huber & Neale, 1987).

Second, goals differ in their timing. Some goals appear to require urgent action, whereas other goals are less urgent and could remain a goal for life (Canary, Cody,

& Manusov, 2008). Naturally, people focus more on their urgent goals (e.g., spending your money this summer on travelling) than long-term goals (e.g., saving money for a new car next year). Other people can flip their goal priorities, so the long-term goals become more of a catalyst for behavior than immediate satisfaction (you decide to save your money for a car).

Finally, goals differ in their abstractness (Cody, Canary, & Smith, 1994). Some goals, labeled *supraordinate*, include many events but are too general to offer much insight regarding concrete behaviors (e.g., "I want to have fun"). *Basic-level* goals differentiate people's behavior in through participants' relationship with regard to (1) the role relationship of other people involved, and (2) a more concrete objective. A basic-level goal that falls under the supraordinate goal of being likeable could be "I want my friend to share an activity with me." This basic-level goal specifies a role relationship (friend) and the behavior (share activity). People are most aware of this type of goal and can remember this goal ("My friend Dave and I went out") (Austin & Vancouver, 1996). Again, role relationships and objectives define the basic-level goal. The most specific goal type, *subordinate goals*, do not generalize to other situations because they are unique to the people involved and the behavior that occurs (e.g., "I want my friend Carol to go shopping with me this Saturday"). It is impossible to make generalizations from people's subordinate goals. Thus, scholars have examined basic-level goals.

Goal Importance and Commitment

People's willingness to achieve any goal is influenced by the importance they attach to each goal and the commitment they feel toward it. As people evaluate the importance of their goals, they also prioritize them (Austin & Vancouver, 1996). Because people weigh their goals according to situational factors such as the roles of the participants, the setting in which the interaction occurs, and the relational history of the participants, people tend to prioritize goals differently (Tracy, 1984). The importance people attach to their goals also influences their commitment to the goals. The more important a goal is, the more likely a person is to engage in actions to achieve that goal (Dillard, 1990a), and the more willing s/he is to continue to expend effort to achieve that goal (Austin & Vancouver, 1996).

Goals, Planning, and Plans

Once people recognize their goals, they take the next step in the goal–plan–action sequence (Dillard, 1990a)—creating plans that will direct people to engage in the actions necessary to achieve their goals. Without planning and plans, people are poorly equipped to pursue and achieve their goals. People often do not have a clear focus on what they want, so they act without thinking and lack the flexibility provided by initial and alternative plans. People plan *proactive goals* in advance, and so they refine their goals and how they will strategically approach other people. However, *reactive goals* tend to take people by surprise (Canary, Cunningham, & Cody, 1988; Sillars & Weisberg, 1987) when they are confronted and have little or no time to plan behavior to achieve or retain their goals (Cody et al., 1994).

Waldron (1997) explains three types of planning that are conceptually similar to the idea of proactive and reactive goals. *Pre-conversational planning* establishes plans before the interaction occurs. Conversely, *conversational planning* represents how the plans are used during an interaction or real-time planning of the moves during a conversation. Unlike the first two types, which focus on the individual, *interactive planning* considers planning as a process of mutual construction and coordination of plans.

People need to act if their plans are to mean something. Various external and internal forces influence whether to act (Pervin, 1989b). People might not always enact a goal–plan–action sequence successfully because of several factors, including: other's, conflicting goals they have, the characteristics of the situation, and/or lack of ability (Berger, 1997). When people do translate their plans into actions, goals and plans remain dynamic as you have experienced many times. Plans often do not work and so people need back-up plans or move to a different objective. As people pursue multiple goals simultaneously, their goals may change in strength, importance, and even content during the course of the interaction (Berger, 1997).

Content and Function of Goals

Goals can be categorized according to their content (instrumental, relational, and self-presentation) and their function in an interaction (primary versus secondary goals). Clark and Delia (1979) present a now generally recognized categorization of goals based on content. The three basic types are *instrumental*, *relational*, and *self-presentation*.

Instrumental goals refer to getting resources or favors from someone else (Roloff, 1987). Another person's resources can include money, material objects (such as clothes), expertise, social networks, and so forth. Favors refer to obtaining permission or effort (e.g., to borrow money from a roommate, to use a friend's car, to get permission from your partner to have a party). U.S. college students pursue instrumental goals the most (Dillard et al., 1989). So they engage other people initially to obtain a resource and favor. This is not to say that U.S. citizens are clueless regarding other goals—only that instrumental goals are more often the primary source for action.

Relational goals involve achieving, maintaining, and de-escalating a relationship (Clark & Delia, 1979). When relational goals are strong, we focus on the relationship with our family, friends, and lovers, and want to act in ways to protect the relationship. The more people focus on relational issues during a conflict, the more likely they choose constructive communication behaviors (Sanderson & Karetsky, 2002).

Self-presentation goals involve presenting a particular image to the partner, and that image reflects who we are as people—our identity. Although they might lie beneath our recognition, self-presentation goals are critically vital to us; we want to manage interactions in ways that allow us to present our desired image and maintain a sense of self-worth (Clark & Delia, 1979). Common self-presentations include being perceived as knowledgeable, likeable, and relevant to some degree. Other people might want to appear as powerful (to intimidate people to gain their compliance) or powerless (to get pity from other people and thereby gain their compliance).

People tend to act very strongly when their self-presentation goals are challenged, such that people will forget what the conflict was initially about (Schlenker & Weigold, 1989; Schönbach, 1994). For instance, one of us recalls a situation where one couple agreed to sell their million-dollar home to another couple. However, the deal almost collapsed because of a $75 toaster that was attached to a kitchen shelf; both parties wanted it. The toaster became a pivotal issue and a "matter of principle" to both parties. After a few frustrating days, the realtor understood a very simple truth: the issue was that both sides wanted to be treated with respect, regardless of their goal to get the toaster. To resolve the conflict, the realtor purchased a similar toaster and installed it. Both clients then happily proceeded with the sale.

A few lessons about strategic conflict can be derived from this story: (1) people should be sensitive to each other's self-presentation; (2) conflict escalates when one's identity management is questioned; (3) the smallest of conflicts can be seen as criticism of one's identity; (4) people can become quite antagonistic when their self-presentations are the source of conflict, and their identity is on the line; and (5) instrumental goals in conflict can morph into relational and self-presentation goals, without people recognizing the shift.

Self-presentation goals relate to the concept of impression management because people make choices about how to present themselves; and such choices reflect what the person believes is accurate about his/herself or what that person knows is inaccurate but needed. For instance, some teachers talk about how much money they could have made if they only had pursued a different career. Yet, much of the time that argument lacks any real evidence (O'Sullivan, 2000). Impression management implies that people need to know the effects of pursuing their goals in social interaction. To do so, people should also assess the goals as represented in the other person's behaviors (Pervin, 1989a). Most people give the impression that they are knowledgeable and likeable, respectable and socially interesting.

Conclusion 11.1: People create plans to achieve their instrumental, relational, and self-presentation goals.

Suggestion 11.1: Be clear about three of your goals and create at least one plan of action.

Suggestion 11.2: Be mindful of other people's self-presentation goals.

A second view categorizes goals as either primary or secondary. That is, one goal represents what the person wants most and that primary goal is compatible or incompatible with less important secondary goals. Dillard et al. (1989) define *primary goals* as those that initiate an action and receive most attention. Wilson, Aleman, and Leatham (1998) add that primary goals help both parties in an interaction to understand what is going on.

One aspect of a primary goal is that it largely reflects the reason why two or more people communicate with each other (Samp & Solomon, 1999). Primary goals also signal expectations about both parties' rights, identities, and obligations. However, the primary goal might not always be the most important goal for people in interaction. For instance, one might pursue a primary goal of getting a southeast Asian client to negotiate a contract, but in Southeast Asia the primary objective is not always instrumental: the primary goal there is to maintain face and get to know each other before the instrumental goal is pursued. People in the US can also become angry when the other person disagrees with their self-presentation attempts. For example, a person telling a story to a group wants acceptance but another person sees him as egotistical and says, "Yeah, I've heard that before. It's an old story." The first person would publically "lose face," become angry, and return the criticism with a put-down of the other person.

Primary goals also raise the issue of *secondary goals*. *Secondary goals* set boundaries for the behaviors people should use as they attempt to achieve their primary goals. In other words, secondary goals can constrain the behaviors in which people engage to pursue their primary goals (Dillard et al., 1989; Wilson et al., 1998). For example, DeTurck (1987) found that, when people are concerned about maintaining their valued relationship with their interaction partner, they are less likely to use coercive behaviors to get what they want. Secondary goals "derive directly from more general motivations that are recurrent in a person's life" (p. 20). In essence, primary goals "are secondary goals which have become temporarily dominant" (Dillard et al., 1989, p. 21). For instance, some students want extra time to complete their papers and ask that the professor changes the deadline. Although getting extra time is their primary goal, the secondary goal of showing respect often trumps their primary goal; negative thoughts about the professor are not expressed to his or her face. Knowing your primary and secondary goals indicates you can adjust your communication to meet your goals as well as the other person's goals.

Conclusion 11.2: Secondary goals can alter or complement people's primary goals.

Suggestion 11.3: Become mindful of your primary and secondary goals, to consider how secondary goals constrain or complement your primary goals.

Achieving Goals

Clark and Delia (1979) contend that some aspect of all three goals is present in all communication encounters. Other researchers have supported this claim (e.g., Cody et al., 1994). According to Waldron (1997), researchers dealing with cognitive properties of conversation have confirmed that conversational goals are "multiple and fluid" (p. 205). Instrumental, self-presentation, and relational goals represent three functions of strategic communication that "frame a communication event and that relationship partners expect to achieve as they negotiate definitions and understandings" (Newton & Burgoon, 1990, p. 479).

People can achieve their multiple goals either simultaneously or sequentially within a single interaction (Sanders, 1991). Instrumental goals have received the most attention from argument researchers investigating reasoning and logic, although relational and self-presentation goals affect the focus and processes of conflict interaction. For example, where self-presentation is paramount, admiring someone's business card is important because their business cards represent who they are, their identity. Also, people may focus on their instrumental goals, but their arguments in pursuit of those goals may have unintentional consequences for the relationship. Likewise, identity management (self-presentation) goals may not begin as a focus of an argument, but they become increasingly important as people perceive that their partners are challenging their self-presentation personally (Hample & Cionea, 2010).

During interaction, people seek to achieve both their primary and secondary goals. More than 90% of participants in one study pursued two or more goals during an interaction (Ohbuchi & Tedeschi, 1997). In influence attempts, for example, people want to be effective by achieving their primary goal; at the same time, we want to be appropriate so that we can achieve our secondary goals (Dillard, Palmer, & Kinney, 1995). The goal types sometimes occur individually, but they often overlap. For instance, relational goals and self-presentation goals can merge into one that focuses on saving the other person's face needs. That is, goals can coexist (Hample & Cionea, 2010; Hample & Dallinger, 1992). Waldron (1990) explains that even as an instrumental goal becomes more important, people do not abandon their relational and self-presentation goals. People want to continue to appear to be smart and likeable, though in conflict some people switch strategies to use direct fighting. Also, recall that meeting the other person's expectations positively associates with obtaining goals.

Even in situations where an instrumental goal has no clear connection to secondary goals, relational and self-presentation goals still have influence on the choices people make about ways to achieve their primary goals (Clark & Delia, 1979; Hample & Dellinger, 1992). In fact, your first primary goal might be to know the other person better (relational goal) and then pursue the instrumental goal. People also point their identity management/self-presentation goals as the reasons they would not use certain compliance-gaining strategies (those similar to direct fighting; Wilson, 2002). People want to present themselves consistently as competent and likeable—someone their colleagues, friends, and lovers would find interesting and enjoyable (Honeycutt, Cantrill, Kelly, & Lambkin, 1998).

Dillard and his colleagues (1989) categorize secondary goals as *identity* (related to self-concept), *interaction* (concerned with social appropriateness), *relational resource* (concerned with qualities of the relationship), *personal resource* (concerned with a person's time and physical or even mental assets), and *arousal management* (concerned with maintaining a comfortable level of arousal). These goals "derive directly from more general motivations that are recurrent in a person's life" (p. 20). In essence, primary goals "are secondary goals which have become temporarily dominant" (Dillard et al., 1989, p. 21). As we indicated from the start, we believe that identity management and relational goals (in addition to instrumental goals) are primary goals. Dillard's sample of college students probably focused on instrumental concerns.

Achieving multiple goals can be confusing and complex. Here is one reason why: Highly competent communicators tend to view the world using several dimensions that go beyond surface level explanations. Notice how the concept of of "right versus wrong" can refer only to one categorical dimension with no room in between. Competent communicators understand the concept of right versus wrong. Competent communicators might also believe that "right versus wrong" is multidimensional: in terms of shades of grey, in different cultures, in ethical dilemmas, and in the fact that people's attitudes often do not correspond with their behaviors, in that people can simultaneously be right and wrong (e.g., "I was wrong to steal the milk but my baby needed food"). Highly competent communicators pursue multiple goals and integrate them so as to deal with them simultaneously (Cegala & Waldron, 1992).

In contrast, low-cognition people tend to view the world as a simple place where right and wrong are obvious. Low-cognition people typically focus on instrumental goals, which they see as separated from their relational and self-presentation goals. Low-competence people tend to be self-focused and less able to identify and adjust to their conversational partner's goals (Cegala & Waldron, 1992; Lakey & Canary, 2002). After criticizing a co-worker's ability to perform a task correctly, low-cognition people might not understand why their co-worker does not want to go out after work.

At times, the goals of two people are compatible, so achieving them is not unusually difficult; at other times the goals conflict and create a challenging situation. For example, politeness theory, which focuses on face, the image people choose to present publicly, posits that people want to pursue their own goals; but at the same time, they want or need to consider the face needs of another person, both *positive face* and *negative face*. Positive face refers to people's desire for other people to accept their behaviors as worthy and helpful. Negative face refers to people's desire to be autonomous and free from other people's intrusions (e.g., "we need to discuss this *now*") (Brown & Levinson, 1987). Finally, mutual face refers to the extent to which people want to maintain both people's positive and negative face. As most research indicates, people in eastern cultures are more sensitive to communication involving these three forms of face concern—positive face, negative face, and mutual face—than are people in western cultures (Oetzel et al., 2001; Ting-Toomey, 2010).

Brown and Levinson claim that because other actions and goals can threaten both types of face, people use politeness to achieve goals and protect both types of face for both people. Cupach and Metts (1994) explain that people use politeness to negotiate the difference between indirect statements that could be ineffective and direct statements that could be offensive. Even when making direct and unreasonable requests, people are judged more positively if they communicate politeness (Ohbuchi, Chiba, & Fukushima, 1996). Choosing polite and indirect strategies serves to protect the face of the recipient of a seemingly face-threatening statement.

Politeness theory suggests that people attempt to fashion messages that allow them to achieve their multiple goals rather than pursuing their goals as they had intended and ending in conflict with the other person or their own goals (Brown & Levinson, 1987). Dillard (1997) adds that people want to achieve their instrumental goal while minimizing any negative effects on their relational and self-presentation goals. Altering their approach and viewing the situation differently helps to reconcile the goals of the two people involved in an interaction. O'Keefe and Shepherd (1987) refer to this redefinition of the situation as *integration*. Integration involves the creation of a new context in which the conflict among the goals has been eliminated. However, not all communicators choose this constructive approach to dealing with their dilemma. People have two additional options: They can use *selection*, giving priority to one goal and ignoring others, or *separation*, dealing with the goals individually (O'Keefe & Shepherd). O'Keefe and Shepherd found that people who use integration strategies acquired more favorable ratings of interpersonal success.

Goals and Conflict Communication

Goals and conflict communication are intricately related. Sedikides (1990) stated that communication is the means through which people achieve their interpersonal goals. In turn, goals are important to communicative behavior because they cause people to act (especially in interpersonal conflicts). Minimally, talk is a primary for fulfilling goals (Tracy & Coupland, 1990). According to Sanders (1991), the idea that what actors say and do is influenced by goals is true by definition. In addition, Berger (1997) argues that goals, plans, and planning are interdependent, which relates the interaction of the three concepts to strategic communication.

One way in which goals and communication connect is the influence of interaction goals on the information people observe as well as on the manner in which they process and evaluate it (Lipkus & Rusbult, 1993). For example, basic-level goals, such as defending oneself against criticism, affect people's perceptions of compliance-gaining situations, as well as the strategies they choose (Canary, Cody, & Marston, 1987). The subjectively perceived characteristics of the situation affect the language people choose. Bingham and Burleson (1989) explained that the primary goal activates related knowledge structures and concepts stored in long-term memory; the activation of relevant knowledge structures thereby creates expectations about the interaction. These expectations then influence what features of the interaction are most salient to the communicator. Clearly, different primary goals would produce different messages because goals guide the production and enactment of behaviors and language choices (Berger & DeBattista, 1993).

Critically, goals provide meaning for interaction and an acceptable explanation for why people engage in particular activities and continue to engage in them (Dillard, 1990b). Wiemann and Kelly (1981) presented a view of interpersonal communication that includes *pragmatics*, the idea that communication primarily functions to achieve some purpose. Jacobs and Jackson (1983) propose that people make sense of a message through its relationship to some goal; that is, people initiate and respond to actions because of the goals implied by people's communication. In other words, people can understand someone's behavior by the goal(s) they believe he or she is trying to obtain (e.g., "The professor tells jokes because she wants to be liked").

Cegala and Waldron (1990) found that people using moderately direct messages seemed able to achieve a balance between appropriateness and effectiveness, because they thought about instrumental, relational, and self-presentation goals or both people. Those using direct messages focused on instrumental goals and had few goal-oriented thoughts. People using indirect messages seemed to have to devote most of their attention to designing more elaborate messages to make their point. Finally, Samp and Solomon (1999) contend that the structure of people's messages provides some information about both their primary and secondary goals. Their research revealed that the focal center of a message was related to the primary goal and that the existence of multiple goals encouraged message embellishment.

Goals connect to choices people make about conflict strategies and tactics. By using dyadic data and a dyadic analysis technique Lakey and Canary (2002) found that goals of both people in a conflict connect to both people's behavior; that is, people's strategy choices associate with their own goals *and* their partner's goals. As far as your own goals are concerned, the more you want to achieve your instrumental goal, the more you want to present yourself in a positive way. Importantly, the more you care about the relationship you have with the other person, the more likely you are to choose cooperative conflict strategies. Also, the more you want to present yourself as threatening or intimidating, the more you are likely to promote yourself as powerful and willing to use that power. On the other hand, the more you want to appear in a negative way (e.g., as selfish) and the more you care about the instrumental goals, the more likely you are to choose competitive strategies. Still, your own goals are not the only influence on your choices. You also respond to your partner's goals. The more you think that person cares about the relationship and the less you think they want to present themselves negatively, the more likely you are to choose cooperative, integrative strategies. But if you think someone wants to appear dangerous through threats and the less you think they care about the relationship, the more likely you are to choose distributive strategies (Lakey & Canary, 1997).

Implicit Thoughts about Communication

O'Keefe and associates (O'Keefe, 1988; O'Keefe & McCornack, 1987; O'Keefe & Sheppard, 1987) have argued that people hold different assumptions about the basic purpose of communication. They call these implicit models *Message Design Logics* (MDLs). *Expressive, conventional,* and *rhetorical* constitute three different MDLs.

An *expressive* message design logic holds that the function of communication is to express one's thoughts. Expressive MDLs view communication as the process of conveying meaning. People with an expressive MDL tend to give relatively little thought to what other people think and often say what they think, for example, "That argument is weak." The rationale given for such open communication is that the communicator is "honest," "says what is on his or her mind," and is "frank."

On the other hand, a *conventional* MDL views communication as the primary means to coordinate behavior according to social conventions (e.g., rules). Here the conventional MDL person remains very sensitive to violations of what they consider appropriateness and are uncomfortable when they see a friend break the norms. Thus, the conventional MDL person attempts to discover how to define the situation and act accordingly (e.g., "formal vs. informal"). For instance, adolescents commonly attend to norms that other teenagers hold, for example, how to wear one's hair, getting pierced, selection of clothes, and so forth. The ability to interact with one's friends will appear to depend on the extent one can act cool by enacting relevant norms.

Finally, the *rhetorical* message design logic refers to the belief that communication functions primarily to persuade other people during conversation. Rhetorical MDLs believe that self-expression and social conventions can be profitably used or changed to meet their interpersonal objectives. O'Keefe and colleagues (O'Keefe & McCornack, 1987; O'Keefe & Shepherd, 1987) argue that the rhetorical MDL is superior to the other two types. Our view is that people should understand these different MDLs in operation and choose the one they find most effective and appropriate. That is to say, the reader can decide whether or not to express yourself to others, how to view and follow norms, and how interaction allows the opportunity for change.

Roloff and Janiszewski (1989) add that the more carefully one constructs a message, the more likely the message will overcome obstacles to goal achievement and, therefore, be successful. The interplay of goals and messages is especially relevant to, and evident in, situations in which people have multiple goals. These situations are quite complex and require the use of different types of messages to achieve the various goals. In these situations, cognitive processing affects message production; people who can handle the increased cognitive demands will be able to create and convey messages that reflect their various goals (Cegala & Waldron, 1992; Greene & Lindsey, 1989). According to MDL, people try to create messages that allow them to pursue multiple goals (Tracey & Coupland, 1990).

O'Keefe (1988), in her discussion of goal structure, defined three levels of message complexity that seem to parallel these distinctions. *Minimal messages* occur when communicators have no clear goal, *unifunctional messages* focus on one goal, and *multifunctional messages* are used to pursue multiple goals. Multifunctional messages are designed with attention to all relevant goals, whereas unifunctional messages focus on one goal and ignore the others. To extend this idea, interpersonal goals are generally achieved more effectively through multifunctional messages that convey the actor's goals and consider the needs of the partner (O'Keefe & McCornack, 1987). More specifically, strategies and messages should be chosen that work together to allow people to achieve their instrumental, self-presentation, and relational goals for a particular interaction (Applegate & Leichty, 1984).

Likewise, people's messages reflect their goals and help them to achieve them. Without communication in some form, people would be basically unable to achieve their interpersonal goals. Based on the above, the following principles are warranted:

> *Conclusion 11.3: People attempt to accomplish more than one goal at a time, with certain goals as primary and others are secondary.*
>
> *Conclusion 11.4: Self-presentation conflict can lead to aggression when people's self-presentations (identity management) are directly or indirectly rebuked.*
>
> *Conclusion 11.5: People hold different Message Design Logics; effective communicators know that such differences exist and they choose which MDL is the most effective and appropriate in a given episode.*
>
> *Suggestion 11.4: To achieve goal control through strategic conflict be mindful that your goals can change with information gained from your conversational partner. So be aware of your own goals and how to achieve them.*
>
> *Suggestion 11.5: Be careful to maintain mutual face, so that conflicts about one or both parties' identities do not overshadow conflicts and lead to aggression; rather, underscore your respect for the other person.*
>
> *Suggestion 11.6: For strategic conflict, know that you have a Message Design Logic that leads you to use communication in particular ways.*
>
> *Suggestion 11.7: Adapt your Message Design Logic that is the most effective and appropriate in a given episode for specific individuals.*

Goals and Conflict

Goals and conflict are clearly connected because conflict occurs when people perceive that their partners in some way have goals that clash with their own. Peterson (1989) agrees that conflict is directly related to people's goal-related behavior. When an interaction begins, both people have some sense of what their goals are and how they want the interaction to end; however, their goals often aren't the same, so conflict ensues. When conflict begins, people generally want to achieve their instrumental goals while behaving in ways that will allow them to present themselves in a positive manner and that will maintain or advance a relationship (Spitzberg & Cupach, 1984). Specifically, conflicts are first seen, conveyed, and managed through communication (Canary, Cupach, & Serpe, 2001). Also, as people attempt to achieve their goals for a conflict interaction, they generally want to behave in ways that are perceived as competent. Their multiple goals for interactions move them to action, cause them to plan ways to achieve their goals, and affect their communicative behavior.

One reason conflict situations deteriorate is that people don't expect the conflict. When they are confronted by their partners, people focus on communication designed to defend self from the other person. This goal often leads to direct fighting strategies (Canary, Cunningham, & Cody, 1988). When people must respond quickly, because they are not prepared to be confronted, they have less attention to devote to strategy choice, so they are less likely to be polite (Ohbuchi et al., 1996).

The more intense a conflict becomes, the more emotional and the less orderly and goal-directed people become (Sillars & Weisberg, 1987). As conflicts progress and escalate in negative ways, the focus often shifts from the instrumental goal to the self-presentation goal (Schönbach, 1980). When people think their primary goal is threatened, they place more importance on their self-presentation goal. They may choose to pursue that goal by attacking their partner's self-presentation goal. Both people then become focused on this goal (Turk & Monahan, 1999). This focus on self-presentation goals then interferes with people's ability to address substantive issues. Therefore, people must resolve the identity issues before the argument can continue and be productive.

This shift occurs because people often personalize the conflict and use negative labels for the other person (Hample & Cionea, 2010; Hample & Dallinger, 1990) This unconstructive cycle is too common and causes people to become defensive because they want to protect their preferred image (Donohue & Kolt, 1992). They use messages that include counter-attacks, efforts to strengthen their identity against further attacks, and even seek support of their identity from others who might be present (Schlenker & Weingold, 1989). These negative behaviors often then lead people to bring in relational issues, none of which relate in any way to the original instrumental goals that first motivated the discussion (Donohue & Kolt, 1992).

Conflict is inherently face-threatening, so concern for face is often central to a conflict interaction (Rogan & LaFrance, 2003). Facework can be involved in the shift during a conflict from instrumental goals to self-presentation goals. When face concerns become the primary focus, people tend to use negative strategies and tactics (Wilson & Putnam, 1990). When people perceive that someone has used verbally aggressive messages, they feel attacked and may be likely to retaliate with similar comments in an attempt to regain lost face (Infante et al., 1992). But concerns about their own face are not enough; people must recognize the role of both face protection and face support of their partner (O'Keefe & Shepherd, 1987). Arguments do not continue indefinitely, so people at some point must find ways out of arguments. Facework behaviors, such as agreeing, apologizing, and working to restore the relationship, help restore face and cooperation. The concern for protecting the face of self and other allows people to achieve their instrumental goals while at the same time protecting the relationship and their preferred image (Oetzel, Ting-Toomey, & Yokuchi, 2000). Another alternative, leaving the conflict either physically or psychologically, ends the conflict but doesn't restore face (Benoit & Benoit, 1990).

Conclusion 11.6: People value positive, mutual, and negative face, such that conflict can escalate when any of these is not honored.

Suggestion 11.8: Honor other people's positive face needs and negative face needs, and seek mutual face.

Several researchers have connected people's goals and the conflict behaviors they choose. Canary et al. (1988) found that the type of goal communicators had influenced their use of distributive and integrative conflict tactics. These authors concluded that other researchers should consider this influence of goal types on message choice and the potential effects it might have on studies of situational differences in communication behavior. Ohbuchi and Tedeschi (1997) also found a connection between goals and tactics, especially for social goals (relational and self-presentation). When people care more about their relationship, they prefer conciliatory tactics, but when justice or hostility goals were present and relational goals were absent, they prefer assertive–aggressive tactics. Sanderson and Karetsky (2002) also found that concern about relational goals led to constructive behaviors and away from denying or avoiding. They work through the conflict through problem-solving to maintain their relationship.

People's failure to achieve their goals also affects their communication behaviors. If they are more committed to their goals, when faced with failure to achieve their goals, people will consider changing higher-level characteristics of their communication including content and structure of the message. However, the common tendency is for people to change the lower-level characteristics of their messages, such as volume and rate. So in a conflict, if you think the other person is blocking your efforts to achieve your goals, you will likely simply to repeat your message in a louder, faster, and more intense way than it was previously. These changes likely decrease the possibility that your goals will be achieved (Berger, Knowlton, & Abrahams, 1996).

Sensitivity

If people want to handle conflict competently, they need to consider the multiple goals that both they and their partners have (Applegate, 1990). Being mindful of the goals of interaction partners, as well as of their own goals, should help people avoid sacrificing their secondary goals in their focused pursuit of their primary goal (Cupach & Canary, 2000). People use social and personal knowledge of their partners to include in their own strategic conflict; perceptions of their partners' goals, plans, beliefs, and resources affect their own goals and plans (Read & Millar, 1989). Reconciling conflicting goals is difficult, but people need to obtain information about their partners' goals and plans to help them understand the history and context of the conflict. Doing so will help them deal with conflict in ways that will protect their relationship (Peterson, 1989).

Information-sharing (both giving and receiving) allows the actor to believe that the partner wants or is willing to let him/her achieve his/her goals. Peterson (1989) expressed a similar idea in his concept of social validation. He explains that the process involves the person's knowledge of his/her own goals and plans, the expression of these views to the partner, the accurate reception and perception of this information by the partner, and a response from the partner.

Read and Miller (1989) emphasize the importance of partners' knowing each others' goals; however, they also acknowledge the difficulty of learning what those goals are, because people do not always reveal their goals and are often not willing to discuss them directly with their partners. Likewise, Peterson (1989) indirectly recognizes the difficulty inherent in this process because of the many barriers to effective communication and because of the levels of insight and trust required in social validation.

When people lack clear information about their partners' goals, they attempt to fill in the gaps. In discussing their interpersonalism model, Read and Miller (1989) indicate that because people lack direct revelation of goals from their partners, they often use attributions based on social and individual knowledge to infer the others' goals, with all the inherent biases and other problems involved in such attribution. Yet people continue to infer their partner's goals because managing seemingly incompatible goals is "one of the most difficult and important problems encountered in any relationship" (Peterson, 1989, p. 330).

Attention to a partner and his/her goals reflects both self-presentation and relational goals; people are seen as responsive and sensitive rather than egotistical and self-centered (Tracey, 1984). They are also viewed as more attractive because people are drawn to others who help them achieve their own goals (Lipkus & Rusbult, 1993). Also, when people think others want to help them achieve their goals, they are more likely to find ways to handle conflicts that allow for discussion and more integrative behaviors and solutions (Witteman, 1992). Seeking information about others' goals conveys interest in other people. Information sharing helps people explain their goals; in turn, the questioner develops insight and understanding to use in guiding strategic conflict (Tutzauer & Roloff, 1988).

Information about their partners aids people in forming impressions of their partners and interpreting their statements accurately (Wyer, Swan, & Gruenfeld, 1995). This knowledge can also help people have smoother interactions. After all, misunderstandings can occur when people define the goal for a situation differently (Wilson et al., 1998). Overall, the interdependent nature of the actions required to achieve interpersonal goals necessitates that, to be perceived as competent communicators, people must consider the goals of both participants in an interaction.

In contrast, people who pursue their own goals while ignoring or denying the validity of their partners' goals risk damaging the relationship (Newton & Burgoon, 1990). Additionally, ignoring others' goals could result in people's creating less than optimal plans for achieving their own goals; in the worst situations, ignoring the partner could most likely result in failure to achieve goals (Berger & Kellerman, 1994). Although gaining information about the partner's goals may not be simple or direct, knowing those goals to some extent is necessary for a person to plan strategically to manage the conflict successfully.

Conclusion 11.7: Conflict refers to incompatibility of two goal sets between people, which requires direct and cooperative conflict tactics to solve those incompatibilities.

Suggestion 11.9: Be mindful that two goal sets operate because conflict inherently carries with it disagreement that requires negotiation with the other person; accordingly, rely on negotiation tactics.

12

HEALTH AND CONFLICT

People are largely unaware of the fact that the conflict strategies they decide to use can have a direct effect on their own physical health. But researchers have recently linked conflict to physical health in numerous studies. These studies focus on how predispositions to be hostile and the adoption of competitive conflict tactics affect one's health. In particular, competitive demonstrations of hostility and anger affect the endocrine system, the cardiovascular system, and the immune system; however, more positive communication during conflict does not have a negative effect on one's health (Robles & Kiecolt-Glaser, 2003). Moreover, the bulk of this research casts interpersonal conflict as wellspring of stress that has physiological consequences. The following paragraphs briefly review some of this material (for thorough reviews, see Kiecolt-Glaser, McGuire, Robles, & Glaser, 2002; Kiecolt-Glaser & Newton, 2001; Robles & Kiecolt-Glaser, 2003).

Effects of Conflict on the Cardiovascular System

Although various causes of coronary heart disease exist, the way that people respond to interpersonal conflict has now been clearly identified as one of those causes of heart disease for both clinical and normal populations (Bleil, McCaffery, Muldoon, Sutton-Tyrrell, & Manuck, 2004; Suarez, 2004). For example, the way people manage hostility and anger appears to affect how fatal is coronary artery disease (CAD). Boyle and colleagues (2004) followed patients with CAD for an average of 15 years. They found that CAD patients who responded to others with hostility (as measured by a combination of cynicism, hostile attribution, hostile feelings, and aggressiveness) were much more likely to die than were CAD patients who did not respond with hostile tactics. Similarly, Bleil and colleagues

(2004) found that the tendency to react in anger and the aggressive expression of hostility increased people's levels of carotid artery atherosclerosis (lesions in arteries involving the brain), a leading cause of stroke, heart attacks, and other heart diseases. Importantly, increases in atherosclerosis due to anger and hostility were found after controlling for other physical risk factors, such as age, weight, and amount of smoking. These findings indicate that the competitive expression of anger directly increases people's atherosclerosis. It has been said that smoking a cigarette reduces one's life expectancy by 7–11 minutes; in the same way, each competitive conflict strategy reduces one's life expectancy, depending on how much anger and hostility you show.

Even healthy people who react with hostility experience negative health consequences in terms of cardiovascular reactivity (CVR) (i.e., the extent to which the heart works harder and takes longer to recover). Suarez and colleagues (1993, 1998) examined how women and men reacted to another person's rude behavior. They divided their samples into groups who self-reported high versus low hostility. Then they randomly assigned these people into no harassment versus high harassment groups (where high harassment involved a technician criticizing their performance on a task, and no harassment involved no criticism). Results revealed that highly hostile people in the harassment condition had significant increases in their cardiovascular reactivity (in terms of heart rate, forearm blood flow, and blood pressure), as well as significant increases in their own subjective experience of anger. These effects did not occur for the other groups. Accordingly, this study shows that one's predisposition to encounter other people with anger can damage the individual heart.

Likewise, Siegman and Snow (1997) examined how one's own expression of anger affected cardiovascular reactivity (CVR). In that study, participants recalled recent anger-producing events and were assigned to one of three conditions— no expression of anger (recall experience only), outward expression of anger (speaking loud and fast), or incongruous expression of anger (speaking soft and slow). CVR was higher in the outward expression condition that either the experience only or incongruous condition. In addition, self-rated anger was highest in the outward expression condition (speaking loud and fast when angry) and was lowest in the incongruous condition. Siegman and Snow concluded, "It is the combination or interaction of anger and loud and rapid speech that produces exceedingly high CVR levels" (p. 39). In brief, how you communicate nonverbally when angry also affects your heart.

Effects of Conflict on the Endocrine System

The endocrine system refers to how various ductless glands (such as the pituitary gland) deliver chemicals that tell other organs to perform in particular ways. The Ohio State research team headed by Janice Kiecolt-Glaser (e.g., Kiecolt-Glaser et al., 1993) has shown that hormones that regulate reactions to stress and metabolism are significantly affected by conflict. These researchers found that increases in epinephrine (also known as adrenaline) and norepinephrine occur in healthy newlyweds who engaged in negative problem-solving. Epinephrine and norepinephrine are catecholmines that are largely responsible for the fight-flight syndrome, which involves increases in heart rate, blood pressure, perspiration, and so forth. Also, Kiecolt-Glaser et al. found that other hormones (e.g., ACTH and prolactin) were also affected by negative conflict interaction (i.e., increases in ACTH but decreases in prolactin). Moreover, these effects lasted at least a day (the time period of the study). Likewise, Suarez et al. (1998) found that highly hostile people had significantly higher hormonal scores and longer recovery for norepinephrine, cortisol, and testosterone. Overall, the research shows that engaging in negative conflict—even when one is healthy and is in a happy relationship—significantly alters one's hormones in negative ways. Prolonged changes in hormones, such as the ones mentioned above, through the consistent use of negative conflict tactics likely entail debilitating health effects, such as hypertension, heart disease, and obesity, which in turn can lead to a reduction in the quality of life and eventually to death. However, the calm and positive management of conflict does not affect one's health in negative ways.

Effects of Conflict on the Immunological System

Interpersonal conflict also affects how well the body resists disease. And researchers have examined how the use of negative (vs. positive) conflict tactics leads to the disruption of the immune system. Research has shown that "immune dysregulation may be one core mechanism for a spectrum of conditions associated with aging, including cardiovascular disease, osteoporosis, arthritis, Type 2 diabetes, certain cancers, and frailty and functional decline," as well as the effectiveness of vaccines and wound healing (Kiecolt-Glaser et al., 2002, p. 537). For example, recall the Kiecolt-Glaser et al. (1993) study of healthy and happy newlyweds. They found that negative conflict behaviors in particular lead to decreases in immune functioning, for instance, decreases in natural killer (NK) cell dispersion.

One might wonder whether people already infected with a contagious virus might recover if they react toward others in positive ways. In one study, conflict was linked to whether healthy adults catch a cold once they are infected with a cold virus. Cohen and colleagues (1998) asked participants to self-report events that increased their stress for one month, three months, and six months. Cohen et al. then subjected participants to one of two cold viruses (remember, the participants volunteered!). People with chronic stress (for more than one month) were much more likely to catch a cold than those with low stress. Cohen et al. concluded that "Chronic stressors based on interpersonal conflicts . . . and problems associated with work [e.g., unemployment] were primarily responsible for the associations found in this study" (p. 221). Those with chronic interpersonal conflicts were almost *three times* more likely to catch a cold when infected than were those without conflict but who were also infected.

Kiecolt-Glaser et al. (2002) noted that the immunological system is most affected by the endocrine system and other risk factors (e.g., smoking, age). Accordingly, the model that emerges is that general tendencies to react with hostility combine with the competitive communication of anger (or perceptions of negative conflict) to bring about secretions of hormones that adversely affect the cardiovascular and immune system over time. Consistent with this view, Suarez (2004) first noted that C-Reactive protein has been linked to CVD in both high-risk and low-risk populations. Next, Suarez hypothesized, and found, that healthy people who exhibited anger in a hostile manner had increases in C-Reactive protein beyond any other risk factors. He concluded that the competitive expression of anger can lead to increased C-Reactive protein that, over time, leads to various cardiovascular diseases and stroke.

Directly related to this discussion, Newton and Kiecolt-Glaser (2003) adopted a model (McEwen, 1998) that identifies four ways that communicative processes can negatively affect one's health:

(1) There are "repeated hits" by different stressors. And conflict qualifies as a stressor that often entails many repeated hits (recurring conflict with a particular person, conflicts at work and home, etc.);

(2) Individuals do not change their communication or other behaviors to adapt to these stressors. And people in conflict often behave in the same strategic way to bring about the same negative physiological effects;

(3) People experience a failure to shut-off physiological reactions to the stressors once they are initiated. And because negative conflict requires a longer recovery time for the body to become well again, the body cannot tend to other functions; and

(4) People do not respond well to stressors. Research illustrates that many people simply lack the communication skills needed to react effectively when in conflict. (Newton & Kiecolt-Glaser, p. 413)

In brief, conflict can tax your health *if* you engage in destructive behaviors but not constructive behaviors. And the negative effects of your own hostile conflict tactics on your own physical health are usually not obvious. You might feel an increase in blood pressure and so forth, but you probably have not realized that those signs of arousal are representing damage your body. Given the above research, the following principle clearly is warranted:

> *Conclusion 12.1: The principle of staying alive: people who manage conflict constructively live longer than do people who manage conflict destructively.*

BOX 12.1   STUDENT STORY

No Smoking Allowed
by
Benjamin Myers

While on the ASU debate team my freshman year I had the chance to meet some very intelligent people, including Justin Sloan. We became good friends very quickly. Looking back, in some respects I idealized him and wished to become a debater of the same caliber. In my sophomore year, I began to notice a personality trait of Justin's that I despise in people—he was a bully. Justin was not a bully in the classical sense of the word; he never beat me up and took my lunch money. But he still had ways of exacting punishment on those he viewed as unequal, or using his wit and analytical tools he would degrade other debaters who he felt were not as talented. David, also known as Tex, was a mild mannered kid who was the butt of many of Justin's put downs.

I soon began to realize that I no longer wanted to debate and the reason for this was that the environment had become infectious and I no longer liked myself as a member of that society. As I began to view the debate team from the perspective of an outsider, the intellectual abuse Tex was enduring at the hand of Justin began to greatly upset me. I did not feel it was my place to say anything however. After all, as I mentioned above, Justin had never displayed any aggression directly towards me. That was all about to change.

One afternoon I was over at Justin's apartment where he lived with a good friend of mine named Scott. While Justin and me were still cordial to each other, I began to observe that our friendship was beginning to wane. Scott and I, however, were very close friends and I would often hang out at his and Justin's apartment to enjoy Scott's company. That particular afternoon Scott and me were watching the movie *Rob Roy*, drinking a few beers, having a good time. More insight into my behavior comes from the fact that Scott used to allow people to smoke inside at the old apartment where he and I once lived. However, when they moved into their new apartment Justin unilaterally declared that smoking in the house would no longer be allowed Scott in an effort to appease Justin agreed to not smoke in the house, but would continue to smoke inside when Justin was not around.

The conflict that erupted between Justin and me revolved around the above decree. While watching the movie, Scott said it was acceptable to smoke inside because Justin was not home. Watching *Rob Roy* while drinking a few beers and cursing at the British for being insensitive world conquerers makes me think that perhaps I was looking for a fight. I will admit that I was not in the most positive mindset at the time that Justin stormed into the house, saw that I was smoking inside, and immediately lashed out at me. He went into a diatribe about how I was an "idiot," how I could not even follow "simple instructions" and that I should "get the [expletive] out of my house" if I was not going to respect his wishes. Although I was clearly in the wrong, the manner in which Justin handled the situation infuriated me. My initial reaction to this the verbal onslaught was to go outside in an effort to respect his wishes.

While outside my temper began to flare. I began to think that someone should stand up to Justin and that he should not be allowed to get away with verbally assaulting people any time he wished. I began to recall images of bullies in elementary and middle school and the immediate images of Justin constantly picking on Tex and others around him that he viewed as intellectually inferior. I decided to confront Justin.

I was smoking the remainder of my cigarette when Justin came outside to leave. I shouted out at him, "I hope you're as good with your fists as you are with you mouth [expletive]!" Justin quickly responded by rushing back up the stairs to meet my verbal challenge with his fists. Luckily, Scott jumped in between the two of us and managed to negotiate the ensuing physical conflict successfully. Justin left and, after a few minutes, I resumed a normal breathing pattern.

Discussion Questions

1. What were the critical factors that set the stage for the conflict before Justin got home?
2. Was Justin justified in calling his former friend an "idiot" and telling him to get out if he cannot obey house rules?
3. Why do you think Benjamin go madder and madder when he went outside to smoke?
4. In a few places, the expletives were deleted. But we can imagine what they might have been. Does swearing ever have a functional role in conflict management?
5. Imagine you have conflicts such as this on a routine basis. What effect do you think they would have on your health?

13

ONGOING SERIAL CONFLICT

Often individuals can end conflict disputes relatively quickly (Lloyd, 1987; Vuchinich, 1987); although many conflicts end without clear resolution (Benoit & Benoit, 1987; Gottman, 1999; Johnson & Roloff, 1998; Lloyd, 1987; Trapp & Hoff, 1985; Vuchinich, 1987, 1990). Scholars have defined unresolved conflict differently. Gottman (1999) labeled ongoing *perpetual problems* as "issues with no resolution that the couple has been dealing with for many years" (p. 96). Coleman (2000) used the terms *intractable conflict* to depict conflicts that remain "recalcitrant, intense, deadlocked, and extremely difficult to resolve" (p. 429). Intractable conflict is characterized by hopelessness, pervasiveness, intense emotionality, and complexity (Coleman, 2000, 2003). Coleman and others examine intractable conflict in terms of macro-level contexts, such as intergroup, political, and international conflict. Still, intractable conflict features of hopelessness, intense emotionality, and the like appear quite applicable to interpersonal, family, and work contexts.

Trapp and Hoff (1985) presented a third label, *serial argumentation*, which occurs when an argument extends beyond a single episode and partners repeatedly confront one another regarding the same issue. According to Johnson and Roloff (1998), "a serial argument exists when individuals argue or engage in conflict about the same topic over time, during which they participate in several (at least two) arguments about the topic" (p. 333). Serial arguments can occur for a couple of hours, months, years, and perhaps across a lifetime (Trapp & Hoff, 1985). This chapter focuses primarily on serial arguing because research using this definitional approach focuses predominantly in interpersonal relationships.

Serial arguments most often occur in close relationships. Eleven of 12 (92%) of Trapp and Hoff's (1985) participants reported engaging in arguments that occurred across several episodes. Moreover, almost half of the college students sampled in

Benoit and Benoit's (1987) study described being involved in a serial argument with the same person fairly often. In addition, Johnson and Roloff (1998) discovered that romantic partners disagreed about a single topic an average of 13 times, with partners currently experiencing an average of two ongoing disputes.

Accordingly, we explore the concept of serial arguing within the overall purpose of this book (to find research that lends itself to personal application). This chapter discusses the following in terms of serial arguing: characteristics and determinants, communication patterns, individual and relational implications, and constructive communication.

Characteristics and Determinants of Serial Arguments

Characteristics of Serial Arguments

Serial arguments by nature *extend over time*. Johnson and Roloff (2000a) explain that "the nature of serial arguing inherently implies that individuals have not been able to bring their opinions, values, and behaviors into alignment after a single confrontation" (p. 677). In other words, serial arguments consist of *linked argumentative episodes* (Roloff & Johnson, 2002) that often occur through cycles wherein they flare-up and then return to a latent state (Trapp & Hoff, 1985). Argumentative episodes frequently begin when one partner provokes the other (Vuchinich, 1987). In addition, these episodes are typically short; however they may extend into lengthy disputes (with an average of about five turns).

Second, the crux of serial arguments concerns how they focus on a single issue. Johnson and Roloff (1998) found three common *issues of focus* in serial arguments. These include expectancy violations, different relational perspectives, or different value/belief systems. Thirty-three percent of Johnson and Roloff's (1998) participants described violated expectations that detailed relational transgressions, such as lying or failure to follow through on a promise or commitment. Next, 63% of respondents reported differences in perspectives on relationships; these differences focused on issues of relationship exclusivity and the future of the relationship. Finally, 33% detailed conflicting values or beliefs on topics such as religion, politics, social issues, and personal tastes. Although serial arguments focus on the same issue, conflict episodes can vary greatly in content (Roloff & Johnson, 2002). Accordingly, one issue remains at the heart of the matter for every recurring episode, although the content of what people say changes across episodes.

Finally, people who engage in serial arguments have several *goals* they desire to achieve. Bevan, Hale, and Williams (2004) found four major goals and several minor concerns for serial arguments. The most common goal was reaching mutual understanding and resolving the conflict. The second goal was that individuals engage in serial argumentation to fight; that is, they desire to argue and rouse the partner. To increase relational progression or ensure the continuation of the relationship was the third major goal. The fourth goal revolved around demonstrating dominance and control. Minor goals included expressing positivity, expressing negative emotions, winning at all costs, achieving personal benefits, derogating the partner, and changing the partner. As is evident from this research, most of these goals are destructive, indicating that individuals involved in serial arguing more often than not hold self-centered or negative objectives.

Understanding the characteristics of serial arguing can help individuals reduce frequency of episodes and potentially resolve the conflict entirely. In addition, the prevalence of negative goals indicates that destructive communication strategies will most likely be utilized. This has serious implications for both individuals and relationships. Thus, people should understand the determinants of serial argumentation.

Determinants of Serial Arguments

Serial arguing often involves a cascade effect of determinants, where one episode or communicative element influences the next episode and communicative element and so forth. Johnson and Roloff (1998) conducted research to understand this cascade further. These researchers found that *antecedent conditions*, or when individuals focus on the nature of the issue, begins the ongoing conflict. Next, considering the issue leads to *primary processes*; this refers to the decision to confront the other person and to the act of arguing. The option to confront the other may occur immediately following the initial disagreeable behavior or time may be taken in order to prepare. Once the confrontation begins, arguing often ensues. This two-step process is followed by the *secondary processes*, which occur during dormant periods of the serial argument. Johnson and Roloff present three secondary processes: (1) predictability of conditions; (2) the extent to which individuals dwell on what was said during each episode; and (3) the number of arguments. In other words, when individuals do not confront the partner they begin to believe they can predict what will happen, they mull over what has been said, and they believe the number of arguments about this topic will continue. Such rumination leads to the final step of consequence conditions. *Consequence conditions* involve coping strategies individuals use to maintain their relationships. Two choices emerge as the most dominant: avoidance and disengaging behavior.

As this cascade effect demonstrates, resolution does not occur in any of these steps (Johnson & Roloff, 1998). When partners experience this cascade process, they reduce their ability to resolve the conflict (Johnson & Roloff, 1998). Moreover, Trapp and Hoff (1985) held that such a cascade model applies to all interpersonal relationships. That is, personal relationships are not exempt from enduring serial arguments. In addition, this cascade can cause individuals to fall into destructive patterns of communication that can adversely affect the relationship. Thus, the next section explores these patterns of communication.

Destructive Patterns of Communication in Serial Arguing

Individuals who engage in serial arguing often fall into destructive patterns of communication. Johnson and Roloff (2000b) found that it is common for the same person to initiate the argument, whereas the partner consistently resists. This pattern has been referred to as the *demand–withdraw pattern* when one partner desires a change in the status quo and therefore makes a demand while the other partner continually withdraws or avoids the issues (as specified in Chapter 2; Eldridge & Christensen, 2002). The initiator role, as defined by Johnson and Roloff (2000b), "assumes that the individual has chosen to engage the partner over some action (as opposed to silent endurance)" (p. 4).

This confrontation typically begins through the use of direct fighting tactics arising from feelings of anger (Malis & Roloff, 2006a). This specific sort of anger arises because people tend to wait to confront their partners until the problem reaches a level they can no longer deal with (Newell & Stutman, 1991) or when multiple provocations occur (Baumeister, Stillwell, & Wortman, 1990). Because the *initiator* chooses when to engage the partner, this person can have the opportunity to plan the time, the place, and how to begin the argument. Thus, initiators can prepare their arguments (Stutman & Newell, 1990). The individual who is unaware that the conversation partner has a plan, or does not realize the extent to which the behavior distresses the initiator, occupies the role of *resistor*.

Prior to the initial confrontation, the "resistor" finds him or herself in an uncontrollable situation as she or he cannot gauge the initiator's anger (Baumeister et al., 1990). Due to an inability to gauge the other person's anger, the resistor often does not see a need to change and may withdraw from the situation when the initiator demands (presuming time is needed to think about a response). Although resisters might recognize that their withdrawal from the situation preempts resolution (Johnson & Roloff, 2000b), resisters likely do so to avoid the initiator's demands.

Demand–withdraw patterns can lead to *counter-complaint* patterns whereby the resistor tires of the initiator's demands and begins to shift the roles by countering with a grievance of his or her own. Johnson and Roloff (2000a) found that this pattern involves couples engaging in *mutual hostility*. Hostile behaviors occur when both partners threaten, hurl insults, blame, or criticize. Similar to demand–withdraw patterns, the resolvability of the serial argument once counter-complaining begins decreases and relational harm increases (Johnson & Roloff, 1998; Johnson & Roloff, 2000a). Thus, neither pattern of demand–withdraw or counter-complaining is an effective approach to serial arguing.

Consider again Couple 26's encounter, where (as noted in Chapter 2) the demand–withdraw roles switch and lead to rather negative, sarcastic tactics on both partners' parts. Following the wife's demand that he cook, the husband switches from his withdraw role to a demand role uses a *hostile imperative* that the wife should shop for more food, which the wife *rejects* and states that a lot of food is not eaten. Then the husband increases his antagonism by using *sarcasm* (turn 14), *hostile questioning* and *disgust* (turn 16), and then *hostile interruption* (turn 18). In the next few turns, the wife clarifies what the refrigerator holds and concludes that "no one is starving here." In this manner, a second segment of demand–withdraw occurs:

F9.1 Why do you say that kids to feed thing?
  9.2 We have one kid;
  9.3 he's a grown-up.
  9.4 He can cook for himself.

M10.1 He is sixteen.
  10.2: He's cooking for himself act all the time.

F11.1: He <u>doesn't</u> all the time.
  11.2 Anyway, I mean, we are supposed to discuss our problem so I . . .

As the reader can imagine, this conflict continues. But in the next turn the husband reverses his role to demand something from the wife (turn 12.1), which is an interesting ploy. Caughlin and Vangelisti's research (1999, 2000) suggests this switching of roles—in the same interaction, both partners can demand:

M12: [interrupting wife at turn 11.2] At least you could, um, go grocery shopping.

F13: I buy *lots* of ready to eat things . . .

M14: yeah [sarcastically]

F15: that people don't eat.

M16.1: Like WHAT? [loudly]
  16.2 Like, like corn in a <u>baaaag</u> (in disgust).

F17.1: That's not true!
  17.2 There is T.V. dinners in there.
  17.3 There's pot pies.
  17.4 There's . . .

M18: [interrupting] Burritos.

F19.1: Burritos.
  19.2 There's plenty of sandwich meat and, and stuff.
  19.3 There's lot of things if people would take 10 minutes they can make their own meal.
  19.4 Nobody is starving here.

As indicated in Chapter 2, the wife resumes the demand role, entering it with *presumptive remark* in 19.5 about the husband's motive (Table 2.3), to which he replies defensively, citing how he was raised, to which she responds with *sarcasm and put-downs* (Table 2.3) about the husband's girth:

F19.5   I think you just need to see me cook for some reason.

M20:   I just, it's just that I grew up eating nice, full, healthy, well-balanced meals.

F21:   You don't need full meals anymore, Bob—you need *little bitty meals.*

M22:   Don't say my name. This is going to be broadcast on the internet.

F23.1: (laughing) You don't need big meals—you need *little* meals.
F23.2: You need to have *salads* for dinner.
F23.3: That's it. I'll make a salad.

Johnson and Roloff (2000a) explicate one other communication pattern that arises during serial arguing. More often than not the issue of a serial argument remains the same, but the content changes; however, couples may fall into a pattern where the content of an episode recurs. Repetition of content does not affect perceived resolvability or relational harm, but individuals should recognize them, particularly repeated content couples with a demand–withdraw or counter-complaining pattern.

> *Conclusion 13.1: The cascade process of serial arguments reduces the possibility of resolution and increases the use of destructive patterns of conflict such as demand–withdraw and counter-complaining.*
>
> *Suggestion 13.1: In serial arguments, avoid engaging in indirect fighting and direct fighting tactics of demand–withdraw and counter-complaining patterns.*

Effects on Individuals and Relationships

Serial arguing can cost all parties involved in the conflict, as separate entities and as a whole. In comparison to arguments resolved in a single episode, greater potential exists for damage due to the cyclical nature of serial arguing (Bevan et al., 2004). Additionally, serial argumentation appears to possess more negative features (Johnson & Roloff, 1998, 2000a) than other forms of interpersonal conflict (Canary, Brossmann, Brossmann, & Weger, 1995). Thus, serial arguing threatens individual and relational well-being.

Individual Well-Being

Conflicts that extend beyond a single argument episode have adverse effects on a person's mood state (Bolger, DeLongis, Kessler, & Schilling, 1989). Specifically, serial arguing leads individuals to higher stress levels, intrusive thoughts, hyperarousal, avoidance, and a decrease in daily activities due to emotional problems (Malis, 2006). More importantly, individuals who mull over the conflict after each episode are more likely to experience health problems, anxiety, stress, intrusion, hyperarousal, avoidance, pain, depression, and less desire to engage in daily activities. These health and mental well-being issues will likely increase if a resolution is not met (Malis, 2006).

Characteristics of serial arguing, such as frequency of argumentative episodes and perceived resolvability, have been studied to understand their impact on individuals' well-being. *Perceived resolvability* refers to whether one believes that the conflict can be readily resolved to both partners' satisfaction. Although the number of arguments does not correlate to personal well-being (Johnson & Roloff, 1998; Malis & Roloff, 2006a), perceived resolvability significantly and inversely correlates with well-being. This means that the more an individual perceives the conflict to be resolvable, the less stress, thought avoidance, intrusiveness, and hyperarousal that person experiences (Malis & Roloff, 2006a). Thus, the less likely an individual believes the conflict can be resolved, the greater the stress levels and stress-related problems such as eating problems, anxiety, and hyperarousal (Malis & Roloff, 2006b).

Couples who engage in the demand–withdraw pattern experience ill effects on their minds and bodies as well. According to Malis (2006), initiators of serial arguing more likely ruminate over the conflict than do resistors. Rumination then can lead to greater experiences of health problems, stress, pain, and intrusive thoughts and feelings regarding the conflict episode. Moreover, Malis and Roloff (2006a) found that initiators experience negative post-confrontational outcomes including attempts to avoid thoughts and feelings regarding the conflict and disruption of everyday activities due to declines in physical health. In other words, initiators are more likely than resistors to experience greater negative psychological and physical problems. Resistors, on the other hand, experience fewer physical and mental health problems (Malis, 2006). Interestingly, those who withdraw when confronted attempt to control their own well-being and are successful, while simultaneously their withdrawal behavior contributes to their partners' (the initiators') stress (Malis & Roloff, 2006a). Thus, it appears to be more beneficial to be the person withdrawing in the argument as opposed to the initiator.

Roloff and Reznik (2008) examined individual well-being when partners engage in counter-complaining or mutual hostility. They found that hostility was linked to eight physical and mental well-being indicators. Direct fighting tactics, *shows hostility* in particular, are negatively connected to stress, hyper-arousal, high anxiety, avoidance when thinking about conflict, sleeping problems, physical pain, engaging in fewer daily activities due to emotional problems, and engaging in fewer daily activities due to physical health problems. Furthermore, Malis (2006) observed that mutual hostility led to bad moods and intrusive thoughts. Unfortunately, use of hostile counter-complaining cannot easily be overcome by the presence of constructive communication habits, thereby making counter-complaining a very hurtful pattern of behavior that leads to mental and physical troubles (Roloff & Reznik, 2008).

> *Conclusion 13.2: In serial arguments,* demand-withdraw *and* shows hostility *tactics can readily escalate into more intense reciprocation and complementary direct fighting.*
>
> *Suggestion 13.2: To prevent hostility in serial arguments, avoid a negative resumption of serial arguments; instead rely on negotiation disclosure tactics (Table 2.1).*

Relational Well-Being

The recurring nature of serial arguing harms relationships. Serial arguments also affect relational quality. More specifically, serial argument connects negatively with each partner's perception that the conflict issue can be resolved (Johnson & Roloff, 1998). In other words, if an individual perceives the conflict as not being resolvable, the greater the relational harm as witnessed by decreases in relational satisfaction, commitment, and overall relational quality.

Johnson and Roloff (1998) also observed serial arguing regarding violated expectations (e.g., a person should not betray or lie to a friend), and such expectations can lead to a decrease in relational quality. Furthermore, the more individuals do not think the issue is resolvable, the more they believe they can predict details of the serial argument, including: what would be said, the amount of time mulling, and the number of additional arguments (Johnson & Roloff, 1998, 2000a). Recalling the cascade effect of serial arguing, predictability, which is a primary process, can lead to rumination, which is a secondary process. This effect continues into negative patterns of communication.

Individuals involved in serial arguing frequently engage in prolonged thought regarding the conflict, which indicate negative outcomes for the relationship. According to Cloven and Roloff (1991), individuals who ruminate about the dispute and do not engage the partner in communication focus more on their own perspective, enhance problem severity, and hold their partners responsible for the conflict. Accordingly, individuals grow to believe that they hold the correct position and see the problem as worse than it actually is. Moreover, individuals rutted in serial arguments tend to shift blame, accept minimal responsibility for the problem, and hold their partner accountable for the conflict. Thus, minor disputes can grow into larger issues if mulling persists and, if severe enough, this secondary process can lead to consequential outcomes, which include destructive patterns of thinking and communication.

Both demand–withdraw and hostile counter-complaining represent dysfunctional patterns of communication that yield nothing productive for either side. Both patterns negatively correlate with perceived resolvability and positively correlate with relational harm (Johnson & Roloff, 1998). That is, both destructive patterns lead individuals to believe the issue cannot be resolved, which (in turn) leads to resentment and relational demise. Partners involved in these patterns experience decreases in relational satisfaction, quality, and commitment (Johnson & Roloff, 1998).

Research has supported three common communication patterns couples engage in when dealing with serial arguing. The first pattern involves repeating the complaint, which leads to a complaint-response pattern. The second pattern concerns mutual hostility. Typically, both partners begin assertively and then shift to more hostile behaviors when their assertive attempts fail. The third pattern occurs when individuals offer assurances, such as expressing commitment and affection. The use of social support is a prominent maintenance behavior (Chapter 3). Johnson and Roloff's (2000a) research shows how these patterns influenced relational quality and perceived resolvability of the conflict.

Johnson and Roloff (2000a) sought to understand how individuals then respond to the above patterns and how coping strategies relate to resolvability and relational quality. The first strategy involves *making optimistic comparisons*, where partners evaluate the current relationship relative to its past or other relationships. The second strategy involves *selective ignoring*, where partners attend to positive elements of the relationship and ignore the bad parts. The third strategy involves *taking a resigned impotent stance*, such that any personal responsibility for dealing with the problem is denied.

They found that patterns of confirming behavior associate with perceived resolvability and lower relational harm. Also, the more couples engage in mutual hostility the more damage occurs to their relationship. Mutual hostility, however, was unrelated to perceived resolvability. Use of repetitious content negatively associate with perceived resolvability, but (in this sample) was not correlated with relational harm.

Frequent negotiation (Table 2.1) can attenuate the negative effects of rumination (Cloven & Roloff, 1991). Frequent negotiation tactics, such as problem-solving, mitigate problem severity and blaming the other person. Using relationally enhancing behaviors as well, which include statements of commitment, intimacy, and closeness, negatively correlates with content repetition and hostility (Johnson & Roloff, 2000a). Relationally confirming behavior, while engaging in the conflict episode and making optimistic comparisons between conflict episodes, positively associates with perceived resolvability (Johnson & Roloff, 1998, 2000a). Also, Negotiating tactics are inversely related to relational harm (Johnson & Roloff, 2000b).

Conclusion 13.3: Negotiation conflict tactics combined with relational enhancing messages positively associate with perceived resolvability and relational quality.

Suggestion 13.3: Be mindful that, except in cases of intractable conflict, serial arguments can eventually be resolved; avoid rumination.

Suggestion 13.4: Use negotiation conflict tactics in conjunction with messages posi-tively associate with perceived resolvability and relational quality.

Using constructive communication has implications for individual and rela-tional well-being as well. Individuals who cope with the conflict episode by main-taining optimism experience decreases in the following: physical health problem, worrying, stress, intrusive thoughts, hyperarousal, decline in daily activities, and a bad mood (Malis, 2006). Additionally, individuals using constructive communi-cation habits including expressing feelings and offering solutions experience less hyperarousal and avoidance (Roloff & Reznik, 2008). Finally, individuals who focus on the positive aspects of their relationships and use the positive behav-iors mentioned are more likely to reduce post-episodic stress including intrusive thoughts, hyperarousal, sleeping problems, anxiety, and eating problems (Malis & Roloff, 2006b). Clearly, remaining positive and constructive during conflict has benefits for individual mental and physical health.

One final way to diminish the negative effects of serial arguing on the indi-vidual and relationship is to make the topic taboo (Roloff & Ifert, 1998). By doing this, one or both partners recognize that future conflict regarding this topic is harmful. As Roloff and Ifert (1998) found, making a serial argument a taboo topic should be done silently and indirectly, particularly when the issue can harm the relationship. If the topic, however, is of less importance both partners will be more likely to engage in a discussion on making the topic taboo.

Suggestion 13.5: If one topic overly dominates your discussions over time, declare the topic taboo.

This chapter explored serial arguing within personal relationships. At some point, however, it might be wise to leave the scene. As Roloff (2009) said, "Accept that which you cannot change, and if you cannot accept disagreement, consider terminating the relationship" (p. 342). Thus, the final principle is offered as a general rule of thumb when engaging in conflict, particularly serial arguing.

Suggestion 13.6: Choose your battles wisely.

14

ABUSE, DIVORCE, AND EFFECTS ON CHILDREN

This chapter examines how communication has dramatic effects on people's health and relationships. As the title of the chapter indicates, much of the research shows that certain conflict strategies can lead to damaging (and sometimes critical) effects on people's physical well-being and personal relationships. We begin by looking at the connection between conflict management and abusive relationships, followed by research that links conflict to divorce and child adjustment problems.

You Hurt the Ones You Love

The Extent and Nature of Violence

Approximately 20% to 30% of marriages involve some form of physical, sexual, or verbal (psychological) abuse within the past year, with approximately 10% of marriages involving serious injury (Fincham, 2003; Marshall, 1994; Leonard & Roberts, 1998). As the following material shows, how people manage conflict plays a large role in whether or not they engage in abusive behaviors. This observation is clearly supported from studies that have compared physically abusive couples to other types (e.g., Babcock, Waltz, Jacobson, & Gottman, 1993; Gordis, Margolin, & Vickerman, 2005; Holtzworth-Munroe, Zmutzler, & Stuart, 1998). In our view, physical, sexual, and psychological abuse are behavioral strategies that partners (mostly men) adopt to get their way and these behavioral strategies intersect with conflict strategies in critically important ways.

Indeed, much of the research on spousal abuse is based on the premise that interventions into abusive relationships must take into account how couples manage conflict between them. As Burman, Margolin, and John (1993) stated:

We believe that that an important step in designing appropriate interventions is understanding the process whereby some couples are able to express disagreement and disapproval and yet move to conflict resolution, whereas others maintain a static cycle of anger and disapproval, and still others escalate into more severe forms of aggression. (p. 28)

This section discusses the research to date on this process.

Before continuing, it is important to acknowledge a difference between violence that occurs sporadically and violence that is ongoing. Johnson (1995, 2001) has identified two forms of violence in marriage—common couple violence and patriarchal terrorism. *Common couple violence* concerns sporadic forms of violence that are initiated by men and women alike. *Patriarchal terrorism* refers to violence that is used to control the partner in an ongoing manner, and it is largely male-initiated. In fact, Johnson (2001) found men and women equally engaged in common couple violence, but 97% of ongoing abuse was perpetrated by the male. The following paragraphs review the major findings concerning the link between conflict communication and spousal abuse.

Greater Negativity, Less Positivity

Partners in physically abusive relationships are much more likely than other partners to engage in a variety of negative conflict behaviors that do little to solve their problems. These include the following: signs of anger and contempt (Burman et al., 1993; Gordis et al., 2005; Holtzworth-Munroe et al., 1998); other demonstrations of hostility include exasperation, blaming, and critical assessments of the partner (Gordis et al., 2005; Holtzworth-Munroe et al., 1998); and the expression of critical feelings, interruptions, and dominance of the floor (Berns, Jacobson, & Gottman, 1999).

Conversely, physically abusive partners are less likely to rely on the following positive conflict management behaviors that promote resolution: showing affection/caring, positive energy, validation of the partner, backchannel responses, and humor (Berns et al., 1999; Burman et al., 1993; Gordis et al., 2005); negotiation and focus on the problem (Berns et al., 1999; Gordis et al., 2005); and flexibility (Gordis et al., 2005). In brief, the mere frequencies regarding these conflict strategies present a radically different profile of how couples in physically abusive marriages differ from those in non-physically abusive marriages. Both husbands and wives, ironically, engage in negative conflict strategies that reveal not only their dissatisfaction with their marriage but also their sheer contempt for their marital partner.

In addition, physically abusive partners are much more likely than others to engage in dysfunctional patterns of interaction over time. Burman et al. (1993) found that physically abusive couples "are characterized not only by more hostile affect overall but also by a number of contingent patterns involving anger" (p. 36). Two features of couple conflict patterns emerged: (1) physically abusive couples more likely initiate and perpetuate patterns of anger exchange; and (2) they have fewer alternative responses to anger (such as validation). The rigid patterns of negativity were likewise reported in Jacobson et al. (1994). In Jacobson et al., wives indicated that their husbands were likely to be violent when they (the wives) were violent, when they verbally defended themselves, and even when they attempted to withdraw from the conflict. Husbands indicated their violence continued only when the wife was violent or when she was emotionally abusive (p. 985).

A few studies have also found that physically abusive husbands engage in more frequent demand and withdrawal behavior. That is, physically abusive husbands demand change from the wife, which is counter to the norm in non-violent marriages where the wife is more likely to demand and the husband withdraws (e.g., Babcock et al., 1993; Berns et al., 1999; Holtzworth-Munroe et al., 1998). Berns et al. (1999) summarized their data accordingly (p. 672):

> Batterers put continued and exceedingly high levels of pressure on their wives for change. Yet they simultaneously avoided and withdrew from their wives' efforts to change them. In contrast, although their wives simultaneously demanded change, any tendencies they might have had to withdraw from their husbands' change demands were suppressed.

In other words, abusive husbands demand change but withdraw from conflict it their wives want change. But wives in abusive relationships do not appear to have the option to withdraw.

The Communication Skill Deficit Hypothesis

One of the more popular explanations of why some people turn to abuse concerns communicative skills. The *communication skill deficit* explanation holds that people turn to negative conflict tactics, including abuse, when their communication skills do not yield the outcomes they want (e.g., Marshall, 1994). It appears that competent communication differentiates physically abusive marriages from others. For example, Gordis et al. (2005) discovered that that "couples reporting recent aggression . . . had the poorest communication" (p. 187). Likewise, Babcock et al. (1993) examined the competence of spouses using the Behavioral Observation of Communication Skill (BOCS), a measure of communication clarity, organization, and other features. These authors found that communicatively incompetent husbands were more physically and psychologically abusive. Interestingly, wife BOCS was negatively correlated with husband psychological abuse. This means that if the wife was more competent, then their husbands tended to use less psychological warfare. These authors concluded their research in the following way:

> deficits in husband communication skill are particularly acute in the relationships of batterers. Perhaps these deficits are greatest when conflict issues are being discussed with the partner. If the wives of batterers are more adept

at verbal arguments and husbands are desperate to win those arguments, they may choose physical violence as their alternative. We can test such a hypothesis only by comparing couples' communication and arguing skills while they are engaged in direct interaction with one another. We plan to examine such interactions in future studies. (p. 48)

Aggression occurs as a predisposition as well as through actual interaction. As a predisposition, *argumentativeness* is the tendency to engage in argument when faced with a controversial topic (Infante & Rancer, 1982). Argumentativeness differs from *verbal aggression*, which is the tendency and behavior by using tactics that aim to hurt the other the other person's ego (for a review of approaches, see Beatty & Pence, 2010). Infante, Sabourin, Rudd, and Shannon (1990) identified ten types of verbally aggressive tactic: character attacks, competence attacks, background attacks (attacking the person's history), criticism of physical appearance, maledictions (e.g., telling someone to go to hell), teasing, ridicule, threats, swearing, and nonverbal emblems (e.g., raising an eyebrow to show disdain).

Research points to the functional utility of being predisposed to engage in argument behavior (i.e., to present a position and offer support). For instance, Infante, Chandler, and Rudd (1989) found that physically abusive marriages were characterized by lower self-reported argumentativeness and higher reports of spousal verbal aggressiveness. Likewise, Infante, Trebling, Shepard, and Seeds (1984) found that highly argumentative people were less likely than others to rely on aggression in roommate conflicts. Abuse appears to be a function of communicator incompetence and unwillingness to use communication to present and defend one's position.

Why Women Stay in Abusive Relationships

Many people wonder why women stay in abusive relationships. Naturally, people are complex and motivations for staying or leaving any relationship defy simple explanation. Also, people on the outside looking in likely underestimate the emotions that abused partners experience—their lives are in real danger.

We do know that abusive people learn various ways to gain control over their partners (Lloyd & Emery, 2000). For instance, abusive people might call their partners at all times of the day, listen on an extension to their telephone conversations with other people, not allow them to talk with certain friends or family members, refuse to discuss their relationships, follow them, monitor how they dress, limit their time away from home, and so forth. On this last example, Rusbult and Martz (1995) found that a primary predictor of remaining in an abusive relationship was the simple lack of transportation—women in abusive relationships tended not to own a car.

In short, women do not necessarily want to stay. They sometimes simply see no way out. Johnson (2001) framed the problem this way: "Women almost always do leave such relationships, as soon as they can put together the information and the financial resources they need to escape to a reasonably safe life for themselves and their children. Of course, that is what the women's shelter movement is all about" (p. 103).

In a summary of the research, Lloyd and Emery (2000) provided seven traits of ongoing intimate aggression. These traits each suggest ways that abuse might be revealed and discouraged. They are as follows:

(1) Most women do not believe that aggression will occur to them. Accordingly, most women are not on guard for the signs of an abusive partner.
(2) Aggression is not necessarily associated with relational dissatisfaction or instability. People sometimes interpret violent acts as signs of love.
(3) The discourse of aggression and intimate relationships entails cultural myths. In terms of *aggression*, people too often excuse the aggressor, blame the victim, confuse definitions of aggression, and render the nature of intimate violence as invisible. In terms of *intimate relationships*, the myths of equality between the sexes, idealized romance, and male need for sex all reinforce violence toward women.
(4) Interpersonal communication intersects with intimate violence, and these authors point to some of the research reviewed earlier in this chapter. Also, it is difficult for women to talk about being abused.
(5) Control is key to understanding intimate violence and aggression. Men control women in various ways, for instance, by cutting them off from friends and family (as mentioned above).
(6) Women feel betrayed and they blame themselves for what has happened to them. They feel betrayed by their partners and paradoxically feel responsible for their condition.
(7) Victims of physical and sexual violence are silenced in multiple ways. Both cultural factors (e.g., disagreement about what constitutes violence) and individual factors (e.g., shame) work against women discussing their experiences.

In brief, the research on abuse points to the process of conflict management as central to understanding how abuse occurs and continues. Reflecting on this issue and how communication can potentially work to discourage abuse, we could offer a number of principles. For instance, one take-away thought concerns how people who engage each other in clear and calm arguments manage to avoid abusive behaviors. Another is that women in particular need to protect themselves once such behaviors appear moot. Given the complexity and severity of the abuse issue, however, we would only plead with the reader to consider the following:

Conclusion 14.1: Ongoing abuse is different than common couple violence in that abuse involves attempts to control the partner through hurting the partner's self-esteem, emotional stability, and physical welfare.

Suggestion 14.1: For strategic conflict, rely on negotiation tactics, because abusive behaviors destroy the person and the relationship you want.

Conflict and Relationship Stability

Many studies have found that the manner in which couples manage conflict affects relational quality and stability. This section reviews that research, emphasizing the work of John Gottman. Gottman's work is emphasized because his is the most comprehensive in demonstrating how conflict tactics predict relational termination.

Gottman's Cascade Model of Divorce

Gottman's (1994) model delineates different processes that lead to satisfaction and stability, or dissatisfaction and instability. Gottman refers to his model as a "cascade model," where first one observes a "decline in marital satisfaction, which leads to consideration of separation or divorce, which leads to separation, which leads to divorce" (p. 88). Gottman's model is presented in Figure 14.1. As the

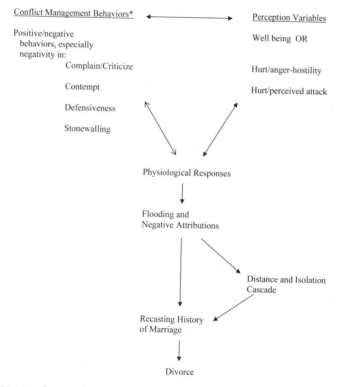

FIGURE 14.1 Gottman's Model of Dissolution

Note: From Gottman, 1994, p. 370. *Gottman also references these as "Flow" variables.

reader will see, this model focuses on how partners communicate with each other during conflict—and the way they communicate sets the stage for marital bliss or marital hell.

The initiating factor in Gottman's (1994) model concerns how married partners engage in positive or negative conflict strategies. The use of negative conflict tactics leads to initial reactions of feeling hurt and defensiveness or feeling hurt and angry. But the use of positive behaviors leads the partner to experience a sense of well-being, contentment, and safety.

According to Gottman, the ratio of positive/negative behaviors represents how the couple "balances" their relationship. Dissatisfied couples engage in a ratio of 1:1 positive-to-negative tactics. In laboratory studies, unstable and unhappy couples begin their problem-solving discussions using polite behavior, with 5:1 ratio of positive-to-negative tactics (the data actually show a 4.58 to 1 ratio; rather picky we know). After only a few minutes, however, partners in very unhappy relationships revert to fewer positive messages and greater negativity. Then their messages stabilize at one positive message for every negative message. In this manner, unhappy couples "balance" (as Gottman labels this phenomenon) a negative message with a positive message. Dissatisfied partners cannot act as positively as they did at the start because they cannot re-invent themselves to create different characters that communicate with strategic conflict. In other words, couples' conflict communication will largely remain the same across situations given the chance to argue.

On the other hand, highly stable and satisfied couples engage in a ratio of almost 5:1 positive-to-negative messages. Accordingly, highly satisfied partners largely approach incompatibilities by counter-balancing negative messages with a preponderance of positive ones. Satisfied couples begin their problem-solving conversations in a polite manner and they continue to be positive throughout the discussion. In that way, satisfied couples maintain their balance.

We should note, however, that the comparisons of highly stable and satisfied couples to very unstable and dissatisfied couples represent drastic contrasts. In a paper that compared highly satisfied to moderately satisfied couples (with no couple scoring below the mid-point on a standard satisfaction measure [Norton, 1983]), Canary, Mikesell, and Gustafson (2003) found that highly satisfied couples had an average of 4.5:1 positive to negative conflict tactics, and moderately satisfied couples had an average of 3:1 positive to negative tactics. The impact is that the 5:1 ratio that Gottman (1994) reports does not represent a critical threshold at which positive versus negative messages makes a difference. Instead, positive-to-negative conflict tactic ratios are incremental—so infusing more positivity can improve conflict tactic impacts on relational quality.

Four conflict behaviors appear to be especially corrosive to marital stability and quality. Gottman calls these the "Four Horsemen of the Apocalypse." As with the four horsemen of the Apocalypse who announce the end of the world (*Revelation*), four behaviors announce the end of the marriage. And these behaviors occur in order: *complaining/criticizing* the partner is followed by *contempt*, which is followed by *defensiveness*, which is followed by *stonewalling* (Gottman, 1994, p. 415). *Stonewalling*—or refusing to talk—is particularly corrosive as it signals one's complete disinterest in resolving a conflict or interacting with your partner.

However, Gottman, Coan, Carrere, and Swanson (1998) replicated some elements of Gottman's (1994) "Horsemen." Gottman et al. (1998) revised their "horsemen" to *defensiveness, contempt,* and *belligerence,* as well and milder forms of negativity, which among only wives predicted separation and divorce. Contrary to Gottman's and other research, reciprocity and complementarity were unrelated to relationship stability and satisfaction.

At this point, we wish to reflect the view (presented in Chapter 3) that the most recent literature on relationship quality often explores how conflict behaviors combine with some other form of positive interaction (e.g., sharing leisure time together). And we argued that *relational maintenance behaviors*—especially sharing time, positivity, and supportive messages—increase a nurturing relational environment that counteracts potential negative effects due to conflict. A nurturing relational environment must occur before the next stage of Gottman's model, as it represents the point of no return.

The Point of No Return

A relatively high proportion of negative behaviors lead to an extreme experience of flooding that Gottman (1994) calls *diffuse physiological arousal* (DPA). DPA is represented by increased blood pressure/heart rate, sweating, and other symptoms of the classic "fight versus flight" response (Gottman, 1990, 1994; Levenson & Gottman, 1983, 1985). At its best, DPA is confusing. When experiencing DPA, people are "surprised, overwhelmed, and disorganized by [one's] partner's expression of negative emotions" (Gottman, 1994, p. 21). Gottman terms this surprise aspect of DPA as *flooding,* to indicate one's inability to process information very well. Likewise, Zimmann (1993) has argued people's brains are short-circuited with DPA, at times so much so they have trouble interpreting the conflict issue, recognizing the partner's information, knowing how to respond to the partner, and so forth.

Moreover, negative messages are "absorbing," such that unhappy partners tend to focus on the negative features of a message, whereas happy partners tend to focus on the informational value in the message (Gottman, 1994; Levenson & Gottman, 1983, 1985; Levenson, Carstensen, & Gottman, 1994). As Gottman argued, negativity "as an absorbing state implies that all these social processes [e.g., functional use of metacommunication] have less of a chance of working, because what people attend to and respond to is the negativity" (p. 64). For instance, the observation, "You look like Santa Claus in that sweater" can be interpreted as a personal attack or as honest feedback about one's appearance. Whereas unsatisfied partners would probably be offended by the negative features of the message, satisfied partners would more likely tune in to the informational value of the message and perhaps do something about it (e.g., change clothes, join a gym).

Next, Gottman (1994) holds that people must somehow make sense of the negativity that they are faced with. Especially in unhappy and unstable marriages, people begin to see their relationships as the cause of their misery. More precisely, dissatisfied partners explain their marital problems as a function of who they married, not difficult events or any problems they bring to the relationship. That is, partners attribute their conflicts to the spouse's negative behaviors as global, stable, internal attributions versus specific, unstable, external, and praiseworthy causes (Fincham, Bradbury, & Scott, 1990). As we mentioned earlier, *globality* concerns how many different issues an explanation covers, *stability* concerns whether the explanation is consistent over time, and *internality* refers to whether the explanation offered focuses on features of a person or some external force. So global, stable, and internal causes of conflict are seen in explanations such as "he is lazy," "she is coldhearted," "he is dumb," "she is unfaithful," and so forth.

Accordingly, the reason why you might be unhappy and the reason why your partner uses negative and mean-spirited conflict messages is due to the kind of person your partner is. Why does this person criticize, condescend, and act rude? The answer is that this person is inherently selfish, inconsiderate, or worse. This person is an addict, a sociopath, or even the Devil himself. And when you finally wake up to the fact that you are sleeping with the Devil, it is near impossible to engage in effective strategic conflict strategies. You certainly do not want to disclose what you want out of the relationship or to trust what you partner says. According to Gottman, when partners begin interpreting their problems and conflicts using internal and negative attributions, then they have experienced "an abrupt flip in the perception of [their own] well-being . . . . This is the initial catastrophic change" (Gottman, 1994, p. 335). The change is catastrophic once you believe that your misery is due to some feature of your partner. Then the relationship proceeds to dissolution through the distance and isolation cascade and through rethinking the history of the marriage (see Figure 14.1). An alternative to dissolution is to change your beliefs about the marriage and attributions about your partner, which would likely require professional counseling for cognitive restructuring.

As indicated, the next phase of divorce involves two processes: increased isolation and distance, and rethinking the history of the marriage. We wish to note that the choice to remove yourself from your partner is your *strategic choice* as well as a psychological decision. It is strategic because one partner chooses avoidance as a path; she or he decides not to talk, not to listen, even not to be in the same room. But deciding not to discuss the relationship is a choice that works against the stability of the relationship. During this phase, people also rethink how they got into their relationships and they offer stories to friends and family members about the first signs of trouble, what a monster the spouse is, and so forth (Harvey, Orbuch, & Weber, 1991). Once these two events have simmered (avoidance and rethinking the history of the relationship), partners then separate and divorce.

Gottman's model of relational dissolution summarizes key events regarding relational stability and quality. Given the breadth and depth of Gottman's model of divorce and research on the topic:

> *Conclusions 14.2–14.11: (14.2) satisfied people engage in a higher ratio of positive to negative tactics; (14.3) people can perceive conflict tactics as comforting or threatening; (14.4) four fighting tactics appear to be especially damning—complaining/criticizing, showing contempt, acting defensively, and stonewalling; (14.5) in reaction to negative conflict tactics, people experience diffused physiological arousal (DPA); (14.6) people interpret the cause of conflicts containing negative conflict tactics using global, stable, and internal factors; (14.7) partners distance themselves when negativity becomes overbearing; (14.8) increases in isolation will occur; (14.9) partners will rethink the history of their relationship; (14.10) they will craft stories for friends that conveys this different history; and (14.11) separation/divorce will occur, beginning when partners make internal, stable, and global attributions about the other person.*

Being mindful of the above ten points, one suggestion is offered:

> *Suggestion 14.2: Strategically use negotiation and nonconfrontation tactics to create a more satisfying and stable relationship, especially when these tactics significantly outweigh strategic use of negative tactics.*

But What about the Kids?

Should partners in high-conflict relationships stay together for the sake of the children? We will address that question shortly. First, we need to establish whether conflict between partners has any effects on children. It is clear that the mismanagement of conflict has devastating effects on one's own intimate relationships. However, research also indicates that how parents manage conflict between them affects how well their children adjust. As one research team reported, "[destructive] conflict is the element in a disharmonious marriage which is most deleterious to children" (Jenkins & Smith, 1991, p. 805). Or as another research team put it, "marital conflict is more closely associated with children's problems than other individual aspects of distressed marriages" (Cummings, Goeke-Murphy, & Papp, 2001, p. 120).

Consistent with the research offered in previous sections of this chapter, the effects of parental conflict on child adjustment vary to the extent that parents are cooperative versus competitive with each other. For example, marital conflict has been linked to the quality of children's sleep. Good sleep is critical to the quality of one's life; lack of good sleep predicts poor performance at school, inattention, and emotionality (e.g., anger control; El-Sheikh, Buckhalt, Mize, & Acebo, 2006, p. 38).

El-Sheikh and colleagues conceptualized parental conflict as a cause of chronic stress for children that would disrupt their sleep. They examined the quality and quantity of sleep, based on mother reports, child self-reports, and an actigrah (a lightweight mechanism about the size of a wristwatch that measures tossing and turning). These researchers found that children in homes characterized by hostile conflict suffered in the extent to which they slept well, as opposed to children in homes where conflict was managed more constructively. Both mother and child reports of parental conflict were used. Interestingly, the assessment of marital conflict by the child (but not mother) predicted total sleep time, percentage of time sleeping when in bed, and activity (movement). Both mother and child reports of parental conflict predicted the child's self-reported level of sleepiness and activity. As one might anticipate, parental conflict affects more than sleep.

The instigation of conflict and displays of anger are especially upsetting to children. Cummings and colleagues (2001) summarized the effects of negative parental conflict on children. This summary is presented in Table 14.1. As Table 14.1 indicates, the effects of destructive conflict on children reflect in various the emotional, regulatory, and representational responses. Many of these effects are quite intuitive, whereas others are less obvious. For example, beginning at about five years of age, children sometimes attempt to intervene or mediate the conflicts between parents (Cummings et al., 2001). Or they might engage in behaviors that indirectly intervene in the parental conflicts in hopes of stopping them, such as pretending to be ill, getting in trouble in school, running away, or other deviations from the norm (Robin and Foster, 1989).

TABLE 14.1 Effects of Marital Conflict on Children

Emotional Reactivity
- Facial: Distress, anger
- Motor: Inhibition, freezing, play slows or stops
- Self-report: Anger, sadness, fear
- Physiological: Heart rate, blood pressure, skin conductance, vagal tone
- Interpersonal: Aggression, support of siblings or peers

Regulation of Marital Conflict
- Intervention, mediation, helping. Being good.
- Avoidance or withdrawal

Representations of Marital Relations
- Interpretation of the meaning or potential consequences for children's own well-being
- Interpretations of the meaning or potential consequences for others (e.g., the parents, siblings, family.

From Cummings et al. (2001).

In terms of children's adjustment, parental conflict affects the manner in which children cope internally. Several studies have found that children become more and more anxious, depressed, and withdrawn when parental conflict is competitive (for reviews, see Cummings & Davies, 2002; Emery, 1982). In addition, these effects are most prominent when children appraise the cause of the conflict as something that is threatening or when they blame themselves for causing of the conflict (Grych, Fincham, Jouriles, & McDonald, 2000). Grych et al. (2000) used both a community sample and a battered women's shelter to obtain data from children about the frequency and intensity of their parents' conflict. These authors found that when children felt threatened by parental conflict (e.g., they might get involved somehow) or when they blamed themselves for their parents' conflicts (e.g., they are the root cause of their parents' conflict), then destructive conflict leads to increases in anxiety, depression, and withdrawal. However, if the child did not feel threatened by parental conflict and did not self-blame, then the effects of destructive conflict on internationalization problems were greatly reduced.

Moreover, the effects of competitive conflict can be seen in externalizing adjustment problems. For instance, Grych et al. (2000) found that children's reports of their parents' destructive conflicts were positively associated with the children's aggression in both school and home (as reported by their teachers and mothers). And these effects held regardless of the appraisals made. Other studies have found that parental conflict predicts other forms of externalization problems, including problems related to developing friendships, getting bad grades, and poor scores on standardized tests (Cummings et al., 2001).

BOX 14.1   STUDENT STORY

Caught in the Middle
by
Richard Elliott

The conflict that I would like to elaborate upon is in regards to the manner in which my father views my relationship with my grandmother. My grandmother was the person mostly responsible for raising me, which has made her to be one of the most important parent figures that I have in my life. The relationship between my father and his mother has always been troublesome as he blames her for everything that has gone wrong in his life. My father, since my junior high years, has constantly been trying to pit me against her to ruin the relationship that I have with her. There has always been tension between my father and me when it came to her, and things have gradually gotten worse.

Several weeks ago, my family started to discuss the arrangements for attending my graduation this December. My father attending my graduation is very important to me. He was not at my high school graduation and has missed several other major events in my life, so him being there to watch me graduate college is very important. When I called him a few weeks back to ask him to come to my graduation, I expressed to him how important it is that he be there. His response to this was that he would of course be there and would not miss it for the world.

A few days passed and we spoke on the phone again. This time he immediately brought to my attention that he would *not* be there if my grandmother was there. I reminded him about the promise that he made to me before. But he said that he did not care, because he was not going to let my grandmother ruin my life as she did his. Things went back and forth between us for about five minutes and I eventually just hung up on him because I did not want to deal with the situation anymore. As it stood, he was not going to come and was trying to make me decide between him and my grandmother.

Throughout my life, I have always been reluctant to engage in an argument as being passive seemed to be the best way to feel safe and secure in my relationships. Many of my friends and romantic partners have said that I am very weak when it came to conflicts, and the fact that this one involved my own father made it even harder to deal with. I had a lot of limitations going into the conflict being that I knew the way that he felt about the situation and that I was counting on him wanting to attend the graduation. I am not sure if he knew this and used it to his advantage to hurt me necessarily, but the way the situation played out made it seem that way.

Many people, especially when it comes to their family, want to change things for the better. Sometimes you can, and sometimes making those changes is harder to do than just dealing with the problem. I am not sure if this experience with my father changed the way that I view conflict or the way in which I will handle it in the future. Looking at the situation, I think I have learned that no matter how I view my relationship with my father throughout my life, I cannot change the way he is. I may want him to be proud of me and want to be in my life, but if he chooses to not be there because a relationship that I have with my grandmother interferes with what he is comfortable with, he just may not be in it.

Discussion Questions

1. Have you ever been caught between two parents, as Richard is here?
2. What do you think of the tone of his account? Does it sound energized or subdued, perhaps even depressed?

3.   Do you think that the father's pressure to side with him affected the way Richard deals with conflict with others?

4.   What do you think of Richard's decision to side with his grandmother? What does that say about his attitude toward his father?

5.   What is your response when someone you care about forces you to choose between him/her or someone else you care about?

In addition, it appears that boys (more than girls) engage in externalizing problems (Robin & Foster, 1989). Emery (1982) suggested that girls usually engage in "overcontrolling" behaviors (e.g., withdrawal, overly positive and prosocial actions), whereas boys more frequently rely on "undercontrolling" behaviors (e.g., showing aggression, running away). In this manner, according to Emery, boys' signs of maladjustment are often more obvious than are girls' signs of maladjustment. So boys might receive more social support and accommodation, whereas girls are more often ignored.

For different reasons, including loyalty pressures by one or both parents, the child sometimes becomes involved in the parental conflict (or what researchers call "triangulation"). And research indicates that triangulation can have detrimental effects on children's experience of parental conflict as well as their emotional and behavioral adjustment (Grych, Raynor, & Fosco, 2004). For example, Grych et al. (2000) found that triangulation was positively associated with the extent to which adolescents perceived their parents' conflicts as threatening and as something for which they (the children) are to blame. In addition, these authors found that more conflicts between parents lead to increased feelings of triangulation, although adolescents who did take the side of one parent also felt triangulated in situations where conflicts were not very frequent. And when pressured to align, children tend to take the side of one parent and demonstrate hostility toward the other parent or they withdraw from both parents (Buchanan & Waizenhofer, 2001).

Finally, we address the question of whether unhappily married people should stay together for the sake of the children. Research by Amato and T. Afifi provide suggest the answer of a qualified "no." Amato and Keith (1991) published a meta-analysis related to this question. (A *meta-analysis* is the systematic and statistical summary of research on a particular topic to date.) According to Amato and Keith, unhappily married couples who engage in destructive conflict might in fact do more damage to their children's well-being than if they separated. Their summary indicates that children in high-conflict homes are significantly worse off (i.e., had more internalizing problems, poorer scores on homework and standardized tests, more aggression with peers) than children of divorce. Also, they reported that children of divorce whose parents did not enact destructive conflict behaviors were better adjusted than children of divorce whose parents displayed destructive conflict behaviors. As one might speculate, children in low conflict, intact homes enjoyed the highest internal and external adjustment of all groups. Finally, these authors found that having at least one supportive parent to provide a warm home environment also reduced the damaging effects of conflict and divorce.

Subsequent research has also shown that parents sometimes and sometimes unknowingly recruit their children to combat the partner (see Afifi, 2010). Two negative impacts of triangulation are (1) children are burdened with loyalty conflicts they should not have to deal with, and (2) children often will adopt the role of the absent parent—to be an adult who takes care of other members of the family. Accordingly,

> *Conclusion 14.12: Hostile interparental conflicts adversely affect children's social adjustment; triangulation is especially damaging.*
>
> *Suggestion 14.3: Provide your children examples of cooperative conflict management, if possible.*
>
> *Suggestion 14.4: If you engage in hostile conflict with your partner, do so outside the range of your children's field of vision and do not involve them in your conflicts.*
>
> *Suggestion 14.5: If separating, be sure that at least one of you consistently provides your children with uncritical thoughts about your ex-partner, signs of security, messages of comfort, and reassurance about their future well-being.*

Conclusion

This chapter has explored various ways that conflict messages have been linked to serious relational outcomes. These outcomes can be summarized by considering three questions. Ask yourself the following:

(1) How can I use conflict strategically to hurt my partner?
(2) How can I use conflict strategically to hurt my partnership?
(3) How can I use conflict strategically to hurt my children?

The point is that people often do not realize that their conflict strategies can have unintended and deleterious effects. And outcomes related to abuse, divorce, and child maladjustment are not the only problems that negative conflict strategies can cause! (See Chapter 12 regarding the health outcomes of conflict.) Nevertheless, given the possibility for you to experience any one or all of these disasters, you should be ready to become a smarter, more strategic communicator.

15

SEEKING RESOLUTION THROUGH FORGIVENESS

Anyone who has experienced conflict realizes the direct connection between conflict and forgiveness. Especially in ongoing relationships, sometimes one or both persons will engage in hurtful behaviors. The hurtful behaviors that accompany escalating and unregulated expression of conflict vary in degree of intensity and, therefore, in the pain they cause. The less serious may require only a mild reproach and a heartfelt concession to repair any damage to the relationship. However, serious breaches require a complete and heartfelt apology from the offender for there to be any chance of forgiveness and relationship repair. In some situations, no matter what offenders say or do, the people they have hurt can not or will not forgive, and even if they can forgive, they have no desire to continue in the relationship. The sense of hurt and betrayal is simply too deep for them to trust any more; the relationship has been irreparably harmed and must end.

The concept of forgiveness has been part of western civilization for at least 3500 years. People recognize forgiveness as an ideal, as a behavior prized in our society. Although forgiveness has long been discussed in both religion and philosophy, practical advice about how to achieve that ideal is limited; people observe and imitate what they see others do, or they may hear a sermon or homily about forgiving (McCullough, Sandage, & Worthington, 1997). Scientific research in the area of forgiveness is a recent development, still generally referred to as an "emerging field." But interest in the topic is widespread, so the research is interdisciplinary, including scientists, social scientists, and physicians (Heller, 1998, p. A18). The growth in research, which really began to develop after 1985, reflects a growing need for individuals, families, and even nations to understand and implement forgiveness to cope with events in their lives (Worthington, 1998). Careful research into this ancient concept should help people better understand the importance of forgiveness in our lives and provide some practical ways for people to forgive and thereby to receive the benefits, both emotional and physical, forgiving provides (McCullough, Pargament, & Thoresen, 2000).

The need for forgiveness exists after people cause deep personal hurt to others. The hurt can be psychological, physical, or moral, but the effects are roughly the same (Enright & Zell, 1989). People who have been hurt know that they have been harmed and believe the offenders intended the harm or at least were negligent enough to allow it to occur. Therefore, people believe that offenders have no right to expect sympathy for their behavior. Also, people know that their pain is legitimate and they own the right to feel negatively toward the people who hurt them (Fincham, Beach, & Davila, 2004). Enright refers to forgiveness as a moral choice that is also a paradox; people have a legitimate reason to be angry and hurt and to want to hold on to that hurt, yet they also know that letting go of those negative feelings is beneficial and the behavior our society expects and accepts (cited in Heller, 1998).

Although people who have been hurt desire apologies and requests for forgiveness, the decision to forgive is a personal one that is not dependent on the regret of the offender; people can decide to forgive in spite of the offender's lack of apology or repentance. People choose to forgive so that they can benefit by letting go of the anger and resentment that may be affecting their ability to trust in other relationships. Choosing to forgive gives people a renewed sense of control over events (Enright, Gassin, & Wu, 1992). The following material elaborates on the concept of forgiveness and how it might be achieved.

Defining Forgiveness

Definitions usually focus on explaining what something is, but Enright et al. (1992) believe that for people to understand forgiveness, they must clearly recognize what forgiveness is not. First, the familiar statement "I can forgive him, but I can't forget what happened" is valid. Forgiveness does not mean *forgetting*; even after forgiveness people remember what the offenders did to them. Nor is forgiveness *condoning* or *excusing*, both of which imply some type of excuse or justification for what happened. Both of these terms reduce the responsibility of the offender, and in fact can then negate the need for forgiveness. Forgiveness is not *pardoning*, which is a legal term that releases the perpetrator from any sanctioned punishment. And because people must make an effort to forgive, forgiveness is not *indifference*, which implies a lack of caring; people forgive because they care about themselves, the other person, and the relationship. Similarly, forgiveness does not deny the hurtful event, which implies that offended people don't even acknowledge that the event occurred (McCullough et al., 2000). Finally, forgiveness is not *reconciliation* or the reestablishment of the relationship. Although the two people might eventually reconcile, rebuilding the relationship is not required for forgiveness to occur (Enright & Zell, 1989).

Types of Forgiveness

Although many researchers agree about what forgiveness is not, similar agreement does not exist about a specific definition of forgiveness. Even so, all agree that people's responses to the offenders become more positive and less negative. Enright and his colleagues (1996) defined forgiveness as "a willingness to abandon one's right to resentment, condemnation, and subtle revenge toward an offender who acts unjustly, while fostering the undeserved qualities of compassion, generosity, and even love toward him or her" (p. 108). Rye and Pargament (2002) stated that forgiveness is the "letting go of negative affect, negative cognitions, and negative behavior in response to considerable injustice, and also may involve responding positively toward the offender [e.g., compassion]" (pp. 419–20). These definitions imply two basic types of forgiveness. First, *negative forgiveness* references the release of negative feelings (Gordon, Baucom, & Snyder, 2000). When experiencing *positive forgiveness*, the second type, people do not attempt to avoid the people who hurt them, and they work to understand the event differently by reconsidering and reinterpreting their feelings about what happened (Pargament, McCullough, & Thoresen, 2000). Negative forgiveness involves avoidance behavior whereas positive forgiveness requires approach behavior (Fincham & Beach, 2002; Fincham et al., 2004).

To forgive completely, people must experience both types of forgiveness because the absence of the negative feelings is a necessary but not a sufficient condition of forgiveness. In addition to letting go of the negative feelings, people must add positive emotions. Through the two types of forgiveness, elements are both removed and added. Negative emotions, including anger, resentment, and sadness, are relinquished, and people stop planning revenge. Simultaneously, more neutral emotions are added and can eventually lead to the existence of positive emotions and willingness to interact with the other person; in some cases relationships are even healed (Enright et al., 1992). Moreover, Fincham and Beach (2002) found that positive forgiveness and lack of retribution functioned in a way to mitigate the spouse's use of psychological warfare during conflict and promote the use of constructive conflict tactics.

Using somewhat different terminology, other researchers explain that as people try to cope with the hurtful behaviors of others, they can be either unforgiving or forgiving. *Unforgiveness* includes a variety of negative emotions including anger, bitterness, resentment, fear, and hostility (Worthington & Wade, 1999). Chronic unforgiveness also relates to negative physiological reactions such as increased blood pressure and heart rate (Witvliet, Ludwig, & Vander Laan, 2001). People maintain this level of negativity by repeatedly mulling over the event and the person. As a result, they can't move past this initial reaction. *Forgiveness*, in contrast, includes positive emotions such as empathy, compassion, sympathy, and affection (Worthington & Wade, 1999). Forgiveness shows self respect. The act also allows people to release their resentment, to change their negative thinking, and thus to move beyond the hurtful event (Enright & Group, 1996). Also, forgiving people experience less physiological stress (Witvliet et al., 2001).

Because the act of forgiveness is both cognitive and behavioral, it can also be viewed as both an intrapersonal and an interpersonal process. Forgiveness begins as an intrapersonal process involving changing negative emotions, thoughts, feelings, and motivations, including anger, resentment, and desire to seek revenge (Fincham et al., 2004). These changes in turn allow people to move on to the outward actions that are necessary for interpersonal forgiveness (North, 1987).

Using these two dimensions, Baumeister, Exline, and Sommer (1998) derived four possible types of forgiveness. The first type, *hollow forgiv*eness, means you have decided to forgive interpersonally but not intrapersonally. So even though you state your forgiveness to the other person, you hold on to resentment, anger, and hurt. This may occur because you have only begun to forgive internally, but you state the forgiveness to the other person in a way that implies that you have reached the final stage of forgiving. *Silent forgiveness* occurs when you have forgiven intrapersonally but not interpersonally. You have decided to forgive the other person, but you have not yet expressed that forgiveness. As a result, the person who hurt you continues to feel guilty, and you continue to appear to be the victim. By implication, one can use this type of forgiveness to manipulate the other person ("I really am over what happened, but I'm going to keep her guessing"). When you have not forgiven either intrapersonally or interpersonally, of course there is *no forgiveness*, the third type. Finally, when you forgive both intrapersonally and interpersonally, you have given *total forgiveness*. You have replaced the negative emotions, you no longer harbor feelings of resentment, and you have conveyed your forgiveness to the other person and allowed him/her to no longer feel guilt or shame.

From a somewhat different angle, Enright and colleagues identified two broad categories of forgiveness: exonerating and forgiving. *Exonerating* results when people learn more about the offenders' actions and situational influences and begin to see that the offenders were not responsible for what happened (Enright & Group, 1996). Hargrave (1994) added that the additional insight helps people identify the actual cause so they can better protect themselves in future situations. Once they understand more about why the offenders acted in such a hurtful way, they can deal with blame and allow themselves to release their anger. But exonerating doesn't necessitate reconciliation. People act this way to benefit themselves so that the destructive thinking caused by their initial understanding of the event won't continue and possibly harm other relationships.

When people *forgive*, the second category, they hold the offenders responsible for their behavior and provide opportunities for compensation. People generally move to forgiveness after they have carefully evaluated the importance or necessity of their relationships with the offenders and have decided they are ready to trust and love again. Forgiveness can occur only when both parties involved agree about the specifics of what happened during the hurtful event. Also, the offender must accept responsibility for what s/he did; s/he must also apologize to convey regret, understanding of what occurred, and assurance that s/he will not repeat the behavior that was so hurtful. The victim must then accept the apology and finally let go of any further desire for revenge (Hargrave, 1994).

Clearly, when all of these ideas about forgiveness are considered, the act of forgiveness is not necessary or appropriate for all situations; it seems most related to close relationships that people value highly (Hargrave, 1994). McCullough et al. (1997) explain that the empathy present in close relationships can help change the emotions and motivations that relate to forgiveness. Also, the high levels of caring in close relationships can help overshadow the offense so that people are more inclined to invest the effort necessary to forgive. If they can forgive, they can move away from self-protective behaviors that can be destructive for the relationship and move toward other types of behavior that will be more constructive. Their decision to forgive can be viewed as a turning point for the relationship (McCullough et al., 1997). Reaching the point of forgiveness does not occur quickly; it takes time during which the person begins to let go of the anger and hurt; even so, some anger may remain even when forgiveness is granted (Enright & Zell, 1989).

Motivations for Forgiveness

Because forgiveness is a choice, people need to be motivated to forgive; the act is neither automatic nor unconscious. In a study of motivations that people offered, Kelley (1998) identified four motivations for forgiveness. Restoring the relationship was mentioned most frequently. People said they forgave to continue the relationship, because of the nature of the relationship and because they perceived the value of the relationship to outweigh the transgression. The second most frequent reason was the strategy of the other person in recognizing the effects of their behavior. People mentioned the importance of apologies, remorse, and acceptance of responsibility. Third, people were motivated to forgive because of their own well-being, or in some situations the well-being of the other. They realized that forgiving would benefit them emotionally and/or physically. Finally, some people reported that they forgave because they loved the other person (a motivation the researcher saw as different from restoring the relationship because the two ideas were not always mentioned together).

Strategies of Forgiveness

In addition to these different motivations for forgiving, people employ a variety of strategies to forgive. Kelley (1998) identified three types. The most common strategy was for the victim to talk directly with the perpetrator about what had happened, including direct statements of forgiveness. Indirect strategies included humor; implying that the hurt was less than originally perceived; positive nonverbal displays of emotion such as hugging, touching, and establishing eye contact; and simply proceeding with the relationship as though nothing had happened. A third type was that the person forgave but with conditions attached. Using factor analysis, Waldron and Kelley (2005) expanded these types to five: *Nonverbal Display* (e.g., "I gave them a hug"), *conditional* (e.g., "I told then I would forgive them if the offense never happened again"), *minimizing* (e.g., "I told them it was no big deal"), *Discussion* (e.g., "I discussed the offense with them"), and *Explicit forgiveness* ("I told them I forgave them"). The use of Nonverbal Display, Discussion, and Explicit Forgiveness were positively related to the relationship being strengthened after a transgression. The use of Conditional was positively linked to the relationship becoming weaker. And Nonverbal was linked to the relationship being normalized.

Explicit forgiveness is difficult for many because it usually involves some degree of confrontation, what Kelley (1998) labels *reproach*. During the interaction, you as the person willing to forgive must make a direct reference to what happened and indicate your willingness to release the other from the "debt" incurred by the hurtful behavior. Of course, no confrontation is without risk; here the risk is that the other person might still not believe he or she did anything wrong and may become provoked by the description of the event or the idea that he or she is in your debt. In some situations, you can use implicit forgiveness by downplaying the seriousness of the hurt you suffered and simply resuming contact with the other person (Exline & Baumeister, 2000).

The Process of Forgiveness

Much as with the definition of forgiveness, researchers hold somewhat different understandings of how people forgive. Although they agree that forgiveness is a multi-step process, they identify the steps and stages somewhat differently. Enright and his colleagues (1992) discuss six styles of forgiveness in a cognitive–developmental model of forgiveness that are tied to six stages of the forgiveness process. Each style/stage is increasingly complex and requires higher levels of perspective taking. The first two stages are not viewed as true forgiveness because the motivation is punishment or reward; they confuse the concepts of justice and forgiveness. True forgiveness does not exact some form of payment. The next two stages involve social pressure; the forgiveness is not internally motivated. The fifth requires something to occur after the act of forgiveness: the restoration of social harmony. In all three of these stages, the forgiveness is incomplete because people still hold at least some remnants of their anger and hurt. Only the final type is viewed as true forgiveness.

1. *Revengeful forgiveness*—People in this stage view forgiveness as possible only if the offender is punished to a degree that is equal to the pain they have experienced. For example, your partner leaves you for another person, so you pray for the day that someone betrays your ex-partner.

2. *Restitutional forgiveness*—People in this stage offer forgiveness because the offender offers some form of restitution or because s/he feels guilty for holding a grudge against the offender. In this case, your partner pays for half the house plus a new car.

3. *Expectational forgiveness*—People forgive in response to social pressure; other people think they should forgive, so they do. Your friends at work think you should try to make amends and let the past be, so you do.

4. *Lawful expectational forgiveness*—People forgive in response to moral or religious pressure. Your minister stresses how forgiveness is essential to your spiritual walk.

5. *Forgiveness as social harmony*—People forgive to restore social harmony or to restore relationships. You realize that you would rather be friends with your ex than not to know him at all, so you approach him about being friends.

6. *Forgiveness as love*—This is true forgiveness because the forgiveness is offered unconditionally; people expect nothing in return. You realize that no-one is perfect, especially yourself, and that we all need grace, beginning at home.

Using a different model, Enright and Group (1996) offer a multi-step intervention process with four main phases: uncovering, decision to forgive, work of forgiveness, and outcome. During the first phase of *uncovering*, you become aware of what the other person has done and the hurt you have experienced. In this phase, you break down any resistance to acknowledging what has happened, you allow yourself to experience the negative emotions, and then you react to them. When you move into the second phase, *the decision to forgive*, you experience a change of heart and move toward the decision to let go of the negative emotions and even the desire for revenge. Next, you begin *the work to forgive*. You attempt to understand the hurtful actions of the other in ways you didn't previously know or accept. This effort leads to the ability to release the desire for revenge. Finally, you move into the final phase, *the outcome*. Here, you reinforce your decision to forgive and determine to continue to forgive the other. You also receive the benefit of improved psychological and even physical health, realizing personal positive outcomes from the act of forgiveness (Enright & Group, 1996). Table 15.1 provides the specific elements of each step offered by Enright and Group.

Worthington (1998) viewed the steps in the forgiveness process differently. His pyramid model, designed as a treatment model, includes five steps. During step 1, *recall the hurt*, you must acknowledge the pain the other person has caused and realize that unforgiveness is the default response. Only through these two actions can you overcome this almost conditioned response and move toward forgiveness. In Step 2, you *develop empathy* for the other person by attempting to identify that person's thoughts and feelings during the hurtful interaction. You try to create as many positive associations with the other person as you can recall. Developing this empathy is an important step in moving from unforgiveness toward forgiveness. Once you have decided to forgive, you move into step 3 by

TABLE 15.1 Processes of Forgiving Another

Uncovering Phase

1. Examination of your psychological defenses.
2. Confrontation of your anger to release the it.
3. Awareness of your shame and embarrassment.
4. Awareness of your cathexis (your emotional expenditure as you attempt to deal with the offense).
5. Awareness of your cognitive rehashing of the offense.
6. Understanding that you may be comparing yourself with offender.
7. Realizing that you may have been permanently changed by the offense.
8. Understanding that you may now see the justice or fairness of the world differently.

Decision Phase

9. Realizing that your old ways of dealing with the offense may not be working.
10. Realizing that you may be willing to forgive the offender.
11. Committing to forgive the offender.

Work Phase

12. Reframing your understanding and attribution of blame.
13. Developing empathy for the offender.
14. Recognizing your developing compassion for the offender.
15. Accepting and absorbing the pain from the offense.

Outcome Phase

16. Finding meaning for yourself and for others in the offense, the pain, and the forgiveness associated with the offense.
17. Recognizing that you have needed the forgiveness of others at points in your past.
18. Realizing that transgressing and needing forgiveness are universal events.
19. Realizing you may have developed a new purpose in your life as a result of your experience.

From Enright & Group (1996).

giving that altruistic gift to the other person. You approach this stage by recognizing and remembering guilt, humility, and the sense of receiving forgiveness you have experienced at other times in your life. This understanding allows you to grant the gift of forgiveness to the person who has hurt you. In step 4 you move from the internal granting of forgiveness to the external, *interpersonal act of granting forgiveness*. And finally, step 5, you *hold on to that decision to forgive* despite any other influences you might encounter.

Taking yet a different perspective, Kelley (1998) explained the process of forgiveness *as a parallel of the account process*. First, you must experience an interaction in which someone intentionally inflicts harm. Second, you must reproach the person who hurt you; you convey to the person your perception of what s/he did that hurt you. The offender must then provide some type of account for his/her behavior. Finally, based on the account provided and the personal characteristics of the person and the relationship, you respond with forgiveness when appropriate.

Offering a fourth perspective, Thoresen, Luskin, and Harris (1998) describe a six-step process using a cognitive-behavioral perspective. This approach begins with *recognizing the situation and the actions* that caused the hurt. Next, you *acknowledge your negative emotions and feelings*. Step 3 is *the act of forgiving*, making "a conscious decision to forgive before experiencing the emotional desire to do so" (p. 171). As this process continues, step 4 is accomplished, *healing the hurt*. Your negative emotions decrease until you finally no longer experience them when you recall the event. The last two steps of the process, while not required parts of forgiveness, may result from the previous decisions. They are *contact with the person who hurt you* (Step 5) and learning from the experience to *be less vulnerable* to hurt (Step 6) by developing more empathy, compassion, and love.

Although the existence of these different models may seem confusing and contradictory, the variety of approaches helps people to avoid prescriptive, one-size-fits-all approaches to forgiveness. They allow people to identify a path to forgiveness that will work best for that them in that particular situation. Additionally, the models share some basic characteristics. All are designed to help people understand the necessity of releasing the hurt if they want to heal, to develop empathy and compassion, and to reduce negative emotions. And all separate forgiveness from reconciliation (Thoresen, Luskin, & Harris, 1998).

Viewing forgiveness as a process emphasizes the time and effort required to reach true forgiveness. This process is difficult because it requires us to work against our immediate response to hurtful behavior—the desire for revenge. Forgiveness requires us to make a conscious effort to behave differently. The process cannot be rushed because internal changes must be real for external behavior to change and be lasting. All the models of the process of forgiveness indicate that we must face what happened to us, acknowledge our pain, and then work to move away from that pain and toward forgiveness and the benefits it provides.

Factors that Affect Forgiveness

Various factors influence what happens during the process of forgiveness. One strong factor is the *nature of the relationship*; the closer the relationship, the more likely people are to forgive after the offenders apologize. Commitment has been linked to people's motivation to forgive. More precisely, people's determination to remain in a relationship affected their motivation to forgive transgressions (Finkel, Rusbult, Kumashiro, & Hannon, 2002).

The *offender's behavior* after we have been hurt also affects our willingness to forgive. As stated earlier, people offer greater forgiveness when the offenders offer a sincere apology in which they express guilt, remorse, and sadness. Also, the offenders should ask for forgiveness rather than assume it will be granted and attempt to perform some positive behavior to try to compensate for the hurt that they caused. Contrastingly, if offenders offer insincere apologies, downplay or hide the offense, or blame the victim, people are much less likely to forgive (Exline & Baumeister, 2000). If the perpetrator refuses to acknowledge responsibility and accept blame, people may choose not to forgive as a way to substitute their blame for the other person's refusal to blame himself/herself. If no blame exists, the victim may fear that the person will repeat the behavior (Baumeister et al., 1998).

Another factor is the *type of account* provided. As discussed in Chapter 6, people make different attributions of responsibility based on the type of account provided. Excuses, concessions, and apologies allow people to make external attributions, thereby holding the person less responsible for the event. These external attributions lead people to be more motivated to forgive.

BOX 15.1   STUDENT STORY

Sister Sister
by
Jennifer Lopez

I was 17 and my sister was 22 when she had her daughter, Karin. I'd visit and spend time with the family because I enjoyed it and because I cared about them. My way of showing that love was through being available and making time for them. Since that time, they have had a son, Jackson. Now the children are seven and four.

Recently, my older sister seriously hurt me. After 2 1/2 months of avoiding me and not returning my calls, I phoned her. My niece answered and since it had been so long since I'd seen them, she had a lot to talk about. She mentioned her straight A's on her report card, so I told her we'd have to celebrate. I asked her what she wanted to do together and she said she wanted to go to Dairy Queen on Friday. Then she passed the phone to my sister. We caught up and spoke about her job, her husband's promotion, Karin's report card, Jackson starting school, the recent vacation they went on and whatever else was going on in their lives. It seemed like a positive and normal conversation.

On Friday, I contacted her to find out what their schedule was like for that evening to take Karin to Dairy Queen. She said she and her husband would be spending it together. The tone was suggesting that it wouldn't be convenient to have plans hat night. As I listened to her tone, I began to wonder if she was mad at me or if I offended her. I asked her, "Are you mad at me?"

The answer came back in the tone of surprise and annoyance, "Do you really want to get into this on the phone?" I was shocked and confused. I told her I didn't ever mean to offend her. In hopes to get her to open up, I told her that avoiding me and wouldn't get it resolved. It seemed to me that she didn't place much value on the relationship if she would feel angry this long and not take the time to discuss it with me.

As I racked my brain I recalled a phone conversation ten weeks before. The conversation was regarding my sister, her son, and me. Over the last 18 months, my sister had commented that Jackson, my nephew, was behaving badly. She often would say, "Why won't he obey me? I don't know what is wrong with him!" I felt a little helpless. I wasn't sure what to do with that situation so I didn't try to make suggestions.

However, recently I was talking to a friend whose daughter had some dramatic results with a homeopathic treatment for a behavioral disorder. I was interested in this finding and thought my sister might also be interested. I wanted to make the option available to her. She reacted in a defensive and offended manner. She yelled, "Nothing is wrong with my son! He's a normal little boy! You're accusing him of being A.D.D. or something. Mind your own business!" I apologized and backed down. Two or three days later I apologized for offending her, and I told her I was seeing a doctor myself for tiredness and anxiety, so that she would understand that my words were not meant the way they were taken. This seemed to make a difference and the conversation ended there.

Now it hit me that she must still be angry about that conflict so I asked her if this was true. Not only was it that situation specifically that had spurred this feeling toward me, but she explained that it was "ongoing problems" she has with me personally. She said that I should keep my "big nose" out of their business, all she wanted was an apology, and some other hateful comments.

I felt surprised and deeply hurt. It was no longer a confrontation, but a destruction of our rapport and trust we've taken years to establish by attacking my personality. At this point I didn't know what to say. I couldn't believe what I was hearing. I thought, "Why is she making such a big deal about this? Is this a reflection of how she feels about me?

She starting yelling things such as, "You love making people mad! You love causing arguments and conflicts! It makes you happy to do this, doesn't it?" I said that I didn't want to fight at all, but I wished she would've told me this before so we could've resolved it and clarified it earlier. Her words became more personal and hateful, so I interrupted, called her some names, and hung-up the phone. She called me back and said I could never see her kids again, and before I heard anything more, I hung-up again.

For two weeks we didn't talk or do anything to communicate. Every time I would think about how to resolve things, or what to say, I just went blank and became very emotional. I knew it wouldn't help to contact her while I was feeling this way, so I thought I would write her a letter. I still didn't know where to begin or how to express what I was feeling.

One night, while visiting my grandmother, she phoned and I answered the call. She asked for my grandma and I handed her the phone. In a moment, grandma passed the phone back to me. My sister asked if I wanted to talk and I said yes. We both started by expressing how badly we had felt over the past two weeks. We both knew that it was an emotionally charged argument and that it was blown out of proportion. We were each sorry for what we had done and said to hurt the other. We each agreed to communicate in a less competitive way next time, by listening more, asking questions more, and giving the benefit of the doubt concerning the other person's intentions.

Even though we have discussed everything and made amends, I still feel that this experience has done damage that was not necessary. We each have a bit less trust toward the other and a little more hesitancy toward the relationship. In some ways I think this is unfortunate. I know I will be more cautious and careful in relationships in the future and more aware of the other person's feelings before becoming defensive and hurt.

Discussion Questions

1. Family conflicts can be quite severe and painful. Have you experienced a situation like Jennifer's?
2. Has anyone in your family called you hurtful names? Have you ever forgotten them?
3. Do you think Jennifer and her sister have forgiven each other? Why or why not?
4. What steps, if any, would you advise Jennifer to take in order to heal her relationship with her sister?

Benefits of Forgiveness

A common misconception about forgiveness is that it benefits the forgiven more than the forgiver (Gassin, 1998). In contrast to this idea, often people choose to forgive because of the personal benefits they will receive through the act. These benefits include increased confidence, in addition to mental and physical health benefits (Exline & Baumesiter, 2000). McCullough et al. (1997) explain that the process of forgiving allows people to reestablish the sense that their actions make a difference in what happens to them, that they have some control over events. It also restores their sense of importance after the hurtful event told them they do not matter.

People who forgive may also want to avoid the negative mental health outcomes, which include social dysfunction, psychoticism, and depression (Maltby & Day, 2001).

Worthington and Scherer (2004) argue that unforgiveness has negative physical health effects because it is stressful. They base their claim on similarities in brain activity, hormonal patters, sympathetic nervous system activity, facial tension, and blood chemistry. The authors then proposed that forgiveness can positively affect physical health because it might reduce hostility, affect the immune system at both the cellular and neuro-endocrine levels, and affect central nervous system processes.

Refusing to Forgive

In spite of these benefits, some people have difficulty forgiving. Grudge theory helps explain why people would choose not to forgive. In some circumstances, people make a principled refusal to forgive; they believe that forgiveness in any form violates their moral standards. These people see a very blurry line between forgiveness and condoning (even though most research states directly that the two are different). This concern is especially strong in cases in which people find themselves repeatedly in situations in which they are hurt by the same person. They are concerned that the perpetrator will begin to assume that forgiveness will be granted and so will think less about the consequences of performing the hurtful behaviors. Other people limit principled refusal to extreme situations such as murder, abuse, or extreme cruelty (Baumeister et al., 1998).

A second reason is that people want rewards of some type from the person who hurt them. People might seek material rewards or damages, but forgiveness means they have to relinquish any demands. They may also want to maintain the moral superiority they feel to the perpetrator, and they think that forgiveness will cause them to lose this feeling (Baumeister et al., 1998).

A third reason is based on people's fear that the same offense will occur again; they don't want to make themselves vulnerable again. Victims sense that once something has happened to them, it very well may happen again. If they don't forgive, the person who hurt them may continue to experience guilt, which in turn may stop the person from repeating the hurtful behavior (Baumeister et al., 1998). This fear is most intense when the offense was severe, intentional, and repeated by a person who is not repentant. Repetition is more likely when a person has previously offered implicit forgiveness in which the feelings and specific details were not stated overtly and clearly. These behaviors may, to some people, convey condoning more than forgiveness; therefore, they believe it is acceptable for them to repeat the behavior (Exline & Baumeister, 2000).

Because they do not understand the true nature of forgiveness, some people fear that forgiving will make them appear weak. They are concerned that the offender may interpret their forgiveness as backing down or giving in. They perceive holding on to their anger and resentment as a way to establish or maintain their power over the other person (Exline & Baumeister, 2000). The hurtful actions of others usually wound our pride and attack our self esteem. We then think that forgiveness will imply an acceptance of this loss of face and somehow indicate that we should have acted in some way to defend ourselves and our rights (Baumeister et al., 1998). People also think that grudges and fantasies of revenge provide power, but in truth they lead to damage to mental and physical health as well as to the relationship. Thoughts of revenge also drain energy that could be put to more productive use (McCullough et al., 1997).

Others simply want to hold on to their status as victims and whatever benefits they perceive this status to convey (Exline & Baumeister, 2000). Being a victim allows one to explore the pain that must be endured, to dwell in it. Being a victim likewise suggests an opportunity for other people to offer their attention, sympathy, and support. Moreover, some people place blame on others routinely and view other people as responsible for all the problems that occur in their lives (McCullough et al., 1997). In that sense, being the victim is their *modus operandi*. In any case, being a victim does have its perks.

Also, some people do not forgive because of a cynical world view. The intentional and severe hurt caused by others can skew the way people view the world. Some people adopt a cynical world view as they try to cope with their hurt. They no longer see the world as fair, and they overlook all the fairness that surrounds and overshadows the hurtful behavior; they simply no longer believe that the world is just. In an effort to protect themselves, they become more suspicious and less trusting of everyone, not just of the person who hurt them (McCullough et al., 1997).

Finally, people may fear that forgiving may preclude justice. They fear that their forgiveness will be viewed as release. People who have a strong sense of retributive justice believe that the perpetrator must in some way be punished for the hurtful behavior. These people are more concerned about justice than about a relationship. From their perspective, without punishment, the perpetrator gets away with the hurtful actions; they pay no price and suffer no consequences (Exline & Baumesiter, 2000).

In spite of these very real concerns about granting forgiveness, holding grudges negatively affects people. In the absence of forgiveness, people continue to suffer and experience negative emotions; they also begin to weave the role of victim into their self concept. Each time they think of the event or encounter the perpetrator, their level of anger and resentment increases. They feel miserable again and again and again. Additionally, maintaining the role of a victim may interfere with people's ability to act decisively in areas beyond the relationship with the perpetrator. Holding a grudge may eventually destroy not just the relationship between the two; it may extend the negativity into other relationships connected to the original one (Baumeister et al., 1998). Failure to forgive also affects people psychologically. Maltby and Day (2004) found that both men and women who had not forgiven others scored higher on measures of depression. Additionally, men scored lower on social extraversion, and women's results indicated social dysfunction and psychotocism.

Seeking and Receiving Forgiveness

When people make the effort to apologize and seek forgiveness, they, too, will benefit. But people must recognize that forgiveness is a gift they receive from the person they have offended. And as with any gift, people give willingly—not when others demand that they do so (Enright & Group, 1996). People must wait for forgiveness, and they must even understand that sometimes it may not come despite their apologies and expressions of guilt and remorse (Gassin, 1998).

To seek forgiveness, people must be aware of their responsibility for the hurt the other person has suffered. Additionally, people must understand that seeking forgiveness involves a loss of face for them. They must be willing to, if necessary, offer repentance and restitution. Of course, these behaviors require humility. People usually seek forgiveness because of empathy for the person they hurt and their concern about the damage to the relationship (McCullough et al., 1997).

Being forgiven can allow people to feel that they have been released from their guilt and remorse. Positive results occur much more frequently than negative ones. A sense of relief and a sense of joy were the most commonly reported effects. The second most common was an obligation or desire not to hurt the person again. Forgiveness also produced changes in people's moral thoughts, feelings, commitment, and behavior. These positive outcomes occurred more when people had changed, or at least had tried to change, as a result of their guilt and remorse (Gassin, 1998).

People experience various motivations for seeking forgiveness. The most commonly mentioned motivation was well-being of self and/or other. People wanted to reduce or eliminate the negative feelings they or the other felt. Restoring the relationship was another common motivation. People wanted to reestablish the trust and maintain the relationship with the person they had hurt. People also attempted to receive forgiveness using a variety of strategies. Direct strategies included discussion to explain their actions, direct requests for forgiveness, and the use of third parties. Also viewed as direct strategies were apologizing, stating remorse, and accepting responsibility for the behavior. Indirect strategies were humor, having a third person request forgiveness, using ingratiation strategies, and using nonverbal displays of emotion. These strategies can be used alone or combined in ways to most effectively achieve the person's goal of receiving forgiveness (Kelley, 1998).

The Role of Forgiveness in Strategic Conflict

Forgiveness is central to managing future conflict. Without forgiveness, people build up resentment toward others who have hurt them, and that resentment may very well serve as fuel for the next conflict. Also, resentment and decreased good will toward a partner may cause people to believe that they are justified in using destructive behaviors during a future conflict (Fincham et al., 2004). Forgiveness, on the other hand, allows people to at minimum let go of the negative emotions and at best to reconcile. Forgiveness may break a recurring and reciprocal pattern of behavior and help people establish a new pattern of more productive conflict (Kim & Smith, 1993).

Worse, people who do not forgive may seek revenge, an attempt to harm the person who harmed them. They may set in motion a reciprocal pattern because after they hurt someone, that person may then want to hurt them again because this person now sees himself/herself as the victim. The two take turns as victim and perpetrator and have very different perceptions of the degree of harm they inflict on the other. Eventually, the degree of anger and the consequences of both people's behavior will be completely out of proportion to the original event (Kim & Smith, 1993).

To diminish the likelihood that desire for revenge may influence future conflict interaction and to ease the path to forgiveness, Kim and Smith (1993) suggested that during conflict people should try not to make comments that disparage the other's integrity. Comments should focus on content or instrumental goals and not on identity goals (Chapter 9). If the other person is offended, people should apologize immediately and appropriately (see Chapter 14). Finally, they also suggest that people be alert for the existence of the desire for revenge. Because revenge is no longer viewed as socially acceptable, people may hide their feelings and dwell on them until they explode during a future conflict.

BOX 15.2   CAN LEARNING ABOUT FORGIVENESS HELP?

Rye and Pargament (2002) compared Christian and secular female college students regarding the role of intervention in forgiveness. (A control group with no intervention was also included.) Female doctoral students were trained to conduct both religious and secular workshops. The sessions corresponded to Worthington's five stage process: recall the hurt, develop empathy toward the offender, altruistic gift, commitment to forgive, and hold on to the forgiveness. Participants in the religious workshops were actively encouraged to call on their religious beliefs, whereas religion and spirituality were not mentioned in the secular groups.

Results indicated that participants in *both* the secular and religious intervention situations improved significantly more than those who experienced no intervention in terms of their level of forgiveness for the specific offender and their knowledge of forgiveness. However, no significant difference was found for their likelihood to forgive across a variety of situations. Participants also indicated improvements in both existential well-being and their personal well-being, and these improvements increased between the pre-test and the six week post-test. But no treatment effects were found for hope, depression, religious well-being, and hostility. Contrary to expectations, no differences were found between the two types of intervention. Also, participants in both conditions viewed the intervention workshops favorably.

Reconciliation and Forgiveness

Reconciliation and forgiveness are different concepts. Although reconciliation can occur without forgiveness, possibly because people choose simply to move beyond the event or because outside factors necessitate the reconciliation, forgiveness usually precedes reconciliation. Several factors predict the likelihood of reconciliation; these include the length of the relationship, the level of trust and commitment in the relationship, what occurred after the offense (apology), and forgiveness. Because of the contribution of forgiveness to the model, it is evident that forgiveness facilitates reconciliation (Worthington, 1998).

Restoring the relationship is not a requirement of forgiveness, but it can be a result. Forgiveness can be granted by the victim alone, even in the absence of repentance by the perpetrator (Dorff, 1998), but reconciliation requires that both people want to restore the relationship (Hargrave, 1994). Reconciliation is based on the rebuilding of trust between the two people in the relationship. Forgiveness helps people move away from the hurtful event and move to more neutral ground. However, to move beyond this point, both people must enact specific and positive behaviors to rebuild trust and create the feelings that characterize close relationships (Worthington, 1998). Hargrave (1994) explains that, for people to move into reconciliation, they must agree on the specifics of what happened; the offender must acknowledge his/her responsibility for the pain s/he caused and must apologize. The apology serves as an overt statement that will ease the pain if at all possible and indicates that the person regrets his/her past actions and will attempt to be trustworthy in any future interactions between the two people. Finally, the victim must accept the apology.

In some circumstances, reconciliation is not the best outcome of forgiveness. Noll (2003) found that sexually abused girls who had let go of anger and a desire for revenge experienced higher self-esteem and less anxiety; girls who considered reconciliation, in contrast, had lower self-esteem and greater anxiety. Noll concluded that victims of abuse should be encouraged to forgive, but reconciliation shouldn't be encouraged because of the negative effects the thought of interacting with the perpetrator had on the girls.

Reconciliation does not always mean that the people return to a relationship that is identical to their previous one. Sometimes this ideal is reached, but in other circumstances the restored relationship is not the same. People may need to redefine their expectations and the relationship (Worthington, 1998). In other situations, the two can reach only a relationship in which they can function as acquaintances, interacting but without the closeness that characterized their previous relationship (Smedes, 1998). If both people value their relationship, the effort involved in forgiveness and reconciliation are worthwhile. They will generally experience more satisfaction in the future especially if their commitment to their relationship remains strong (Worthington, 1998).

Final Thoughts about Forgiveness and Conflict

Conflict, especially unrestrained conflict, too often results in damage to people and to their relationships. Once the comments have been made and the hurt has been inflicted, we cannot take back our words. We must find a way to deal with the consequences to have any chance to repair the damage. Providing accounts for our behavior is the first step because people rarely forgive without some adequate explanation for what happened. But once we have expressed our remorse and asked for forgiveness, we cannot control what then happens. The next step is controlled by the person who was hurt; s/he must decide if and when to forgive.

Holding on to the hurt can be damaging to you, both physically and psychologically, so many people ultimately decide to forgive. However, in some circumstances they do not decide to reconcile. They forgive to benefit themselves and the other person, but they are not able to reestablish the relationship. In some cases, though, the two people can reconstruct their relationship in some form, often in a way that differs from their original relationship.

Here are our last conclusions and suggestions:

> *Conclusion 15.1: Forgiveness functions to remediate relationships between you and another person.*
>
> *Conclusion 15.2: Forgiveness does not entail forgetting the harm done; it does alleviate the personal effects due to rumination, revenge planning, and other harmful thoughts.*
>
> *Suggestion 15.1: If you want to reconcile your relationship with the other person, forgive him or her.*
>
> *Suggestion 15.2: For your own sake, forgive.*

REFERENCES

Acitelli, L. K., & Antonucci, T. C. (1994). Gender differences in the link between marital support and satisfaction in older couples. *Journal of Personality and Social Psychology, 67,* 688–698.

Afifi, T. D., Aldeis, and Joseph, A. (2010). Family conflict. In W. R. Cupach, D. J. Canary, & B.H. Spitzberg (Eds.), *Competence in interpersonal conflict (2nd edition).* Prospect Heights, IL: Waveland Press.

Afifi, W., & Metts, S. (1998). Characteristics and consequences of expectation violations in close relationships. *Journal of Social and Personal Relationships, 15,* 365–392.

Ainsworth, M. D. S., Blehar, M. C., Waters, E., & Wall, S. (1978). *Patterns of attachment: A psychological study of the strange situation.* Hillsdale, NJ: Erlbaum.

Aivazyan, Tatyana A., Zaitsev, Vadim P., Khramelashvili, Viktor V., Golanov, Eugene V., Kichkin, Valeri I. (1988). Psychophysiological interrelations and reactivity characteristics in hypertensives. *Health Psychology, 7(Suppl),* 139–144.

Alberts, J. K. (1988). An analysis of couples' conversational complaints. *Communication Monographs, 55,* 184–197.

Allred, K. G. (2000). Anger and retaliation in conflict: The role of attribution. In M. Deutsch and P. T. Colerman (Eds.). *The handbook of conflict resolution, theory, and practice.* Boulder, CO: University of Colorado Press.

Amato, P. R., & Keith, B. (1991). Parental divorce and the well-being of children: A meta-analysis. *Psychological Bulletin, 110,* 26–46.

Andersen, P. A. (1986). Consciousness, cognition, and communication. *Western Journal of Speech Communication, 50,* 87–101.

Andersen, P. A., & Guerrero, L. K. (1998). *The handbook of communication and emotion.* San Diego CA: Academic Press.

Antonioni, D. (1998). Relationship between the Big Five personality factors and conflict management styles. *International Journal of Conflict Management, 9,* 336–355.

Applegate, J. L., & Leichty, G. B. (1984). Managing interpersonal relationships: Social, cognitive and strategic determinants of competence. In R. N. Bostrom (Ed.), *Competence in communication: A multidisciplinary approach* (pp. 33–54). Beverly Hills, CA: Sage.

Apt, C., Hurlbert, D. F., Pierce, A. P., & White, L. C. (1996). Relationship satisfaction, sexual characteristics, and the psychosocial well being of women. *The Canadian Journal of Human Sexuality, 5*, 195–210.

Argyle, M, & Furnham, A. (1983). Sources of satisfaction and conflict in long-term relationships. *Journal of Marriage and the Family, 45*, 481–493.

Argyle, M., & Henderson, M. (1984). The rules of friendship. *Journal of Social and Personal Relationships, 1*, 211–237.

Argyle, M., & Martin, M. (1991). The psychological causes of happiness. In F. Strack, M. Argyle, & N. Schwarz (Eds.), *Subjective well-being: An interdisciplinary perspective* (pp. 77–100). New York: Pergamon Press.

Aron, A., Norman, C. C., & Aron, E. N. (2001). Shared self-expanding activities as a means of maintaining and enhancing close romantic relationships. In J. H. Harvey & A. Wenzel (Eds.), *Close romantic relationships: Maintenance and enhancement* (pp. 47–66). Mahwah, NJ: Routledge.

Aron, A., Norman, C. C., Aron, E. N., & Lewandowski, G. Jr. (2002). Shared participation in self-expanding activities: Positive effects on experienced marital quality. In P. Noller & J. Feeney (Eds.), *Understanding marriage: Developments in the study of couple interaction* (pp. 177–194). New York: Cambridge University Press.

Aron, A., Norman, C. C., Aron, E. N., McKenna, C., & Heyman, R. E. (2000). Couples' shared participation in novel and arousing activities and experienced relationship quality. *Journal of Personality and Social Psychology, 78*, 273–284.

Austin, J. T., & Vancouver, J. B. (1996). Goal constructs in psychology: Structure, process, and content. *Psychological Bulletin, 120*, 338–375.

Averill, J. R. (1993). Illusions of anger. In R. B. Felso & J. T. Tedshi (Eds.), *Aggression and violence: Social interactionist perspectives* (pp. 171–193). Washington DC: APA.

Avtgis, T. A., & Rancer, A. S. (Eds.) (2010). *Arguments, aggression, and conflct: New directions in theory and research.* New York: Routledge.

Babcock, J. C., Waltz, J., Jacobson, N. S., & Gottman, J. M. (1993). Power and violence: The relation between communication patterns, power discrepancies, and domestic violence. *Journal of Consulting and Clinical Psychology, 61*, 40–50.

Bachman, G. F., & Guerrero, L. K. (2006). Relational quality and communicative responses following hurtful events in dating relationships: An expectancy violations analysis. *Journal of Social and Personal Relationships, 23*, 943–963.

Bakeman, R., & Gottman, J. M. (1997). *Observing interaction: An introduction to sequential analysis.* Cambridge, UK: Cambridge University Press.

Bandura, A. (1989). Self-regulation of motivation and action through internal standards and goal systems. In L. A. Pervin (Ed.), *Goal concepts in personality and social psychology* (pp. 19–85). Hillsdale, NJ: Lawrence Erlbaum.

Barbuto, J.E. & Moss, J.A. (2006). Dispositional effects in intra-organizational influence tactics: A meta-analytic review. *Journal of Leadership and Organizational Studies, 12*, 3, 30–52.

Baucom, D. H., & Epstein, N. (1990). *Cognitive-behavioral marital therapy.* New York: Brunner/Mazel.

Baucom, D. H., Sayers, S. L., & Duhe, A. (1989). Attributional style and attributional patterns among married couples. *Journal of Personality and Social Psychology, 56*, 596–607.

Baumeister, R. F., Exline, J. J., & Sommer, K. L. (1998). The victim role, grudge theory, and two dimensions of forgiveness. In E. L. Worthington (Ed.), *Dimensions of forgiveness: Psychological research and theological perspectives* (pp. 79–104). Radnor, PA: Templeton Foundation.

Baumeister, R. R., Stillwell, A., & Wortman, S. R. (1990). Victim and perpetrator accounts of interpersonal conflict: Autobiographical narratives about anger. *Journal of Personality and Social Psychology 59*, 994–1005.

Baxter, L. A. (1986). Gender differences in the heterosexual relationship rules embedded in break-up accounts. *Journal of Social and Personal Relationships, 3*, 289–306.

Baxter, L. A., & Dindia, K. (1990). Marital partners' perceptions of marital maintenance strategies. *Journal of Social and Personal Relationship, 7*, 187–208.

Beach, S. R. H., Martin, J. K., Blum, T. C., & Roman, P. M. (1993). Effects of marital and co-worker relationships on negative affect: Testing the central role of marriage. *American Journal of Family Therapy, 21*, 312–322.

Beatty, M. J., & Pence, M.E. (2010). Verbal aggressiveness as an expression of selected biological influences. In T. A. Avtgis & A. S. Rancer (Eds). In T. A. Avtgis & A. S. Rancer. *Arguments, aggression, and conflict: New directions in theory and research* (pp. 3–25). New York: Routledge.

Beck, U., & Beck-Gernsheim, E. (2001). *Individualization*. London: Sage.

Bell, R. A. (1985). Conversational involvement and loneliness. *Communication Monographs, 52*, 218–235.

Belsky, J., Spanier, G. B., & Rovine, M. (1983). Stability and change in marriage across the transition to parenthood. *Journal of Marriage and the Family, 45*, 567–577.

Bennett, J. M., & Bennett, M. J. (2004). Developing intercultural sensitivity: An integrative approach to global and domestic diversity. In D. Landis, J. Bennett, & M. Bennett (Eds.), *Handbook of intercultural training* (3rd ed., pp. 147–165). Thousand Oaks, CA: Sage.

Benoit, P. J., & Benoit, W. L. (1990). To argue or not to argue: How real people get into and out of interpersonal arguments. In R. Trapp & J. Schuetz (Eds.), *Perspectives on Argument: Essays in Honor of Wayne Brockriede* (pp. 55–72). Prospect Heights: Waveland Press.

Benoit, W. L., & Benoit, P. J. (1987). Everyday argument practices of naïve social actors. In J. W. Wentzel (Ed.), *Argument and critical practices: Proceedings of the Fifth SCA/AFA Conference on Argumentation* (pp. 465–473). Annandale, VA: Speech Communication Association.

Berg, C. A., Johnson, M. M., Meegan, S. P., & Strough, J. (2003). Collaborative problem-solving interactions in young and old married couples. *Journal of Psychology, 35*, 33–58.

Berger, C. R. (1993). Goals, plans, and mutual understanding in relationships. In S. Duck (Ed.), *Individuals in relationships* (pp. 30–59). Newbury Park, CA: Sage.

Berger, C. R. (1997). *Planning strategic interaction*. Mahwah, NJ: Lawrence Erlbaum.

Berger, C. R., & DiBattista, P. (1993). Communication failure and plan adaptation: If at first you don't succeed, say it louder and slower. *Communication Monographs, 60*, 220–238.

Berger, C. R., & Kellermann, K. (1994). Acquiring social information. In J. A. Daly & J. M. Wiemann (Eds.), *Strategic interpersonal communication* (pp. 1–27). Hillsdale, NJ: Lawrence Erlbaum.

Berger, C. R., Knowlton, S. W., & Abrahams, M. F. (1996). The hierarchy principle in strategic communication. *Communication Theory, 6*, 111–142.

Bergmann, T. J., & Volkema, R. J. (1994). Issues, behavioral responses, and consequences in interpersonal conflicts. *Journal of Organizational Behavior, 15*, 467–471.

Berkowitz, L. (1993). Towards a general theory of anger and emotional aggression. Implications of the cognitive-neoassociationistic perspective for the analysis of anger and other emotions. In R.S. Wyer, Jr., & T.K. Srull (Eds.), *Perspectives on anger and emotion: Vol. VI. Advances in social cognition* (pp. 1–46). Hillsdale, NJ: Erlbaum.

Berns, S. B., Jacobson, N. S., & Gottman, J. M. (1999). Demand-withdraw interaction in couples with a violent husband. *Journal of Consulting and Clinical Psychology, 67,* 666–674.

Berry, J. W., & Worthington, E. L. (2001). Forgiveness, relationship quality, stress while imagining relationship events, and physical and mental health. *Journal of Counseling Psychology, 48,* 447–455.

Berscheid, E. (1983). Emotion. In H. H. Kelley et al. (Eds.), *Close relationships* (pp. 110–168). New York: W. H. Freeman.

Berscheid, E., & Regan, P. (2005). *The psychology of interpersonal relationships.* Upper Saddle River, NJ: Pearson/Prentice Hall.

Berstene, T. (2004). The inexorable link between conflict and change. *The Journal for Quality and Participation, 27 (2),* 4–10.

Betancourt, H., & Blair, I. (1992). A cognition (attribution)-emotion model of violence in conflict situations. *Personality and Social Psychology, 18,* 343–350.

Bevan, J. L., Hale, J. L., & Williams, S. L. (2004). Identifying and characterizing goals of dating partners engaging in serial argumentation. *Argumentation and Advocacy, 41,* 28–40.

Billings, A. (1979). Conflict resolution in distressed and nondistressed married couples. *Journal of Consulting and Clinical Psychology, 47,* 368–376.

Bingham, S. G., & Burleson, B. R. (1989). Multiple effects of messages with multiple goals: Some perceived outcomes of responses to sexual harassment. *Human Communication Research, 16,* 184–216.

Bippus, A. M., & Rollin, E. (2003). Attachment style differences in relational maintenance and conflict behaviors: Friends' perceptions. *Communication Reports, 16,* 113–123.

Bird, G. W., Stith, S. M., & Schladale, J. (1991). Psychological resources, coping strategies, and negotiation styles as discriminators of violence in dating relationships. *Family Relations, 40,* 45–50.

Bisanz, G. L., & Rule, B. G. (1989). Gender and the persuasion schema: A search for cognitive invariants. *Personality and Social Psychology Bulletin, 15,* 4–18.

Bisanz, G. L., & Rule, B. G. (1990). Children's and adult's comprehension of narratives about persuasion. In M. J. Cody & M. L. McLaughlin (Eds.), *The psychology of tactical communication* (pp. 48–69). Clevedon, England: Multilingual Matters, Ltd.

Bjorkqvist, K., Osterman, K., & K. M. J. Lagerspetz. (1994). Sex differences in covert aggression among adults. *Aggressive Behavior, 20,* 27–33.

Bleil, M. E., McCaffery, J., M., Muldoon, M. F., Sutton-Tyrrell, K., & Manuck, S. B. (2004). Anger-related personality traits and carotid artery atherosclerosis in untreated hypertensive men. *Psychosomatic Medicine, 66,* 633–639.

Bochner, A. P., & Kelly, C. W. (1974). Interpersonal competence: Rationale, philosophy, and implementation of a conceptual framework. *The Speech Teacher, 23,* 279–301.

Bolger, N., & Zuckerman, A. (1995) A framework for studying personality in the stress process. *Journal of Personality and Social Psychology, 69,* 890–902.

Bolger, N., Delongis, A., Kessler, R. C. & Schilling, E. A. (1989). Effects of daily stress on negative mood. *Journal of Personality and Social Psychology, 57,* 808–818.

Bono, G., McCullough, M. E., & Root, L. M. (2008). Forgiveness, feeling connected to others, and well-being: Two longitudinal studies. *Personality and Social Psychology Bulletin, 34,* 182–194.

Booth, A, Crouter, A. C., & Clements, M. (2001). *Couples in conflict.* Mahwah, NJ: Earlbaum.

Booth-Butterfield, M., Anderson, R. H., & Booth-Butterfield, S. (2000). Adolescents' use of tobacco, health locus of control, and self-monitoring. *Health Communication, 12,* 137–148.

Bowlby, J. (1969). *Attachment and loss: Vol 1. Attachment.* New York: Basic Books.

Boyle, S. H., Williams, R. D., Mark, D. B., Brummett, B. H., Siegler, I. C., Helms, M. J., & Barefoot, J. C. (2004). Hostility as a predictor of survival in patients with coronary heart disease. *Psychosomatic Medicine, 66,* 629–632.

Bradbury, T. N., & Fincham, F. D. (1990). Attributions in marriage: Review and critique. *Psychological Bulletin, 107,* 3–33.

Braiker, H. B., & Kelley, H. H. (1979). Conflict in the development of close relationships. In R. L. Burgess & T. L. Huston (Eds.), *Social exchange in developing relationships* (pp. 135–168). New York: Academic Press.

Bristow, W. (2004). *100 tips to be happy together.* Hauppauge, NY: Barrons Educational Series.

Brown, J. G. (2004). The role of apology in negotiation. *Marquette Law Review, 87,* 665–673.

Brown, J., & Langer, E. (1990). Mindfulness and intelligence: A comparison. *Educational Psychologist, 25,* 305–335.

Brown, P., & Levinson, S. (1987). *Politeness: Some universals in language usage.* New York: Cambridge University Press.

Brown, S. L. (2000). Union transitions among cohabitors: The significance of relationship assessments and expectations. *Journal of Marriage and the Family, 62,* 833–846.

Buchanan, C. M., & Waizenhofer, R. (2001). The impact of interparental conflict on adolescent children: Considerations of family systems and family structure. In A. Booth, A. C. Crouter, & M. Clements (Eds.), *Couples in conflict* (pp. 149–159). Mahwah, NJ: Lawrence Erlbaum Associates.

Burggraf, C. S., & Sillars, A. L. (1987). A critical examination of sex differences in marital communication. *Communication Monographs, 54,* 276–294.

Burgoon, J. K., Johnson, M., & Koch, P. T. (1998). The nature and measurement of interpersonal dominance. *Communication Monographs, 65,* 308–335.

Burleson, B. R. (2002). Personal communication to Daniel Canary.

Burleson, B. R. (2003). Social support. In J. Greene & B. Burleson (Eds.), *Handbook of communication and social interaction skills.* Mahwah, NJ: Lawrence Erlbaum and Associates.

Burleson, B. R., & Denton, W. H. (1997). The relationship between communication skills and marital satisfaction. *Journal of Marriage and the Family, 59,* 884–902.

Burleson, B. R., & Goldsmith, D. (1998). How the comforting process works: Alleviating emotional distress through conversationally induced reappraisals. In P. A. Andersen & L. K. Guerrero (Eds.), *The handbook of communication and emotion: Research, theory, applications, and contexts* (pp. 245–280). San Diego: Academic Press.

Burleson, B. R., & Samter, W. (1985). Consistencies in theoretical and naive evaluations of comforting messages. *Communication Monographs, 52,* 103–123.

Burman, B., Margolin, G., & John, R. S. (1993). America's angriest home videos: Behavioral contingencies observed in home reenactments of marital conflict. *Journal of Consulting and Clinical Psychology, 61,* 28–39.

Burnette, J. L., Davis, D. E., Green, J. D., Worhington, E. L. Jr., & Bradfield, E. (2009). Insecure attachment and depressive symptoms: The mediating role of rumination, empathy, and forgiveness. *Personality and Individual Differences, 46,* 275–280.

Burpee, L. S. & Langer, E. L. (2005). Mindfulness and marital satisfaction. *Journal of Adult Development, 12,* 43–51.

Bushman, B., J., & Baumeister, R. F. (1998). Threatened egotism, narcissism, self-esteem, and direct and displaced aggression: Does self-love or self-hate lead to violence? *Journal of Personality and Social Psychology, 75,* 219–229.

Bushman, B. J., & Cooper, H. M. (1990). Effects of alcohol on human aggression: An intergrative research review. *Psychological Bulletin, 107,* 341–354.

Buunk, B. P., Schaap, C., & Prevoo, N. (1990). Conflict resolution styles attributed to self and partner in premarital relationships. *Journal of Social Psychology, 130,* 821–823.

Cahn, D. D. (1990). *Intimates in conflict: A communication perspective.* Hillsdale, NJ: Erlbaum.

Cahn, D. D. (1992). *Conflict in intimate relationships.* New York: Guilford.

Cahn, D. D. (1994). *Conflict in personal relationships.* Hillsdale, NJ: Erlbaum.

Cahn, D. D., & Lloyd, S. A. (1996). *Family violence from a communication perspective.* Hillsdale, NJ: Erlbaum.

Cai, D. A., & Fink, E. L. (2002). Conflict style differences between individualists and collectivists. *Communication Monographs, 69,* 67–87.

Cameron, J. J., Ross, M., & Holmes, J. G. (2002). Loving the one you hurt: Positive effects of recounting a transgression against an intimate partner. *Journal of Experimental Social Psychology, 38,* 307–314.

Campbell, W. K., & Foster, C. A. (2002). Narcissism and commitment in close relationships: An investment model analysis. *Personality and Social Psychology Bulletin, 28,* 484–495.

Campbell, W. K., Foster, C. A., & Finkel, E. J. (2002). Soes self-love lead to love for others? A story of narcissistic game playing. *Journal of Personality and Social Psychology, 83,* 340–354.

Canary, D. J., Brossmann, J. E., Brossmann, B. G., & Weger, H. (1995). Toward a theory of minimally rational argument: Analyses of episode-specific effects of argument structures. *Communication Monographs, 62,* 183–212.

Canary, D. J., Cody, M. J., & Marston, P. J. (1986). Goal types, compliance-gaining, and locus of control. *Journal of Language and Social Psychology, 5,* 249–303.

Canary, D. J., Cunningham, E. M., & Cody, M. J. (1988). Goal types, gender, and locus of control in managing interpersonal conflict. *Communication Research, 15,* 426–446.

Canary, D. J., & Cupach, W. R. (1988). Relational and episodic characteristics associated with conflict tactics. *Journal of Social and Personal Relationships, 5,* 305–325.

Canary, D. J., Cupach, W. R., & Messman, S. J. (1995). *Relationship conflict: Conflict in parent-child, friendship, and romantic relationships.* Thousand Oaks, CA: Sage.

Canary, D. J., Cupach, W. R., and Serpe, R. T. (2001) A competence-based approach to examining interpersonal conflict. *Communication Research 28,* 79–104.

Canary, D. J., & Dainton, M. (Eds.) (2003). *Maintaining relationships through communication: Relational, contextual and cultural variations.* Mahwah, NJ: Routledge.

Canary, D. J., Erickson, E. L., Tayfoya, M. A. & Bachman, G. (2002 November). *Attachment styles, conflict management behaviors, and relational characteristics.* Paper presented at the annual National Communication Convention, New Orleans, LA.

Canary, D. J., & Lakey, S. G. (2006). Managing conflict in a competent manner: A mindful look at events that matter. In J. G. Oetzel, & S. Ting-Toomey (Eds.), *The Sage handbook of conflict communication: Integrating theory, research, and practice* (pp. 185–210). Thousand Oaks, CA: Sage.

Canary, D. J., Pfleiger, J., & Cupach, W. R. (2008). *Actor-Partner effects on competence assessments of conflict strategies*. Paper presented at the International Association of Relationship Researcher conference.

Canary, D. J., & Spitzberg, B. H. (1987). Appropriateness and effectiveness perceptions of conflict strategies. *Human Communication Research, 14*, 93–118.

Canary, D. J., & Spitzberg, B. H. (1990). Attribution biases and associations between conflict strategies and competence outcomes. *Communication Monographs, 57*, 139–151.

Canary, D. J., Spitzberg, B. H., & Semic, B. A. (1998). The experience and expression of anger in interpersonal settings. In P. A. Andersen & L. K. Guerrero (Eds.), *Handbook of communication and emotion: Research, theory, and contexts* (pp. 191–213). New York: Academic Press.

Canary, D. J., & Stafford, L. (2001). Equity in the preservation of personal relationships. In J. H. Harvey & A. Wenzel (Eds.), *Close romantic relationships: Maintenance and enhancement* (pp. 133–152). Mahwah, NJ: Routledge.

Canary, D. J., Stafford, L., Hause, K. S., & Wallace, L. A. (1993). An inductive analysis of relational maintenance strategies: Comparisons among lovers, relatives, friends, and others. *Communication Research Reports, 10*, 5–14.

Canary, D. J., Stafford, L., & Semic, B. A. (2002). A panel study of the associations between maintenance strategies and relational characteristics. *Journal of Marriage and Family, 64*, 395–406.

Canary, D. J., & Wahba, J. (2006). Do women work harder than men at maintaining relationships? In K. Dindia & D. J. Canary (Eds.), *Sex differences and similarities in communication* (pp. 359–389). New York: Lawrence Erlbaum Associates.

Cano, A., O'Leary, K. D., & Heinz, W. (2004). Short-term consequences of severe marital stressors. *Journal of Social and Personal Relationships, 21*, 419–431.

Carl, D., Gupta, V., & Javidan, M. (2004). Power distance. In R. House, P. Hanges, M. Javidan, P. Dorfman, & V. Gupta (Eds.), *Culture, leadership, and organizations: The GLOBE study of 62 societies* (pp. 513–563). Thousand Oaks, CA: Sage.

Catanzaro, S. J., & Laurent, J. (2004). Perceived family support, negative mood regulation expectancies, coping, and adolescent alcohol use: Evidence of mediation and moderation effects. *Addictive Behaviors, 29*, 1779–1797.

Catanzaro, S. J., & Mearns, J. (1990). Measuring generalized expectancies for negative mood regulation: Initial scale development and implications. *Journal of Personality Assessment, 54*, 546–563.

Caughlin, J. P., & Golish, T. D. (2002). An analysis of the association between topic avoidance and dissatisfaction: Comparing perceptual and interpersonal explanations. *Communication Monographs, 69*, 275–295.

Caughlin, J. P., & Huston, T. L. (2002). A contextual analysis of the association between demand/withdraw and marital satisfaction. *Personal Relationships, 9*, 95–119.

Caughlin, J. P., & Huston, T. L. (2006). The affective structure of marriage. In A. L. Vangelisti & D. Perlman (Eds.), *The Cambridge handbook of personal relationships* (pp. 131–156). New York: Cambridge University Press.

Caughlin, J. P., & Vangelisti, A. L. (1999). Desire for change in one's partner as a predictor of the demand/withdraw pattern of martial communication. *Communication Monographs, 66*, 66–89.

Caughlin, J. P., & Vangelisti, A. L (2000). An individual difference explanation of why married couples engage in demand/withdraw pattern of conflict. *Journal of Social and Personal Relationships, 17*, 523–551.

Caughlin, J. P., & Vangelisti, A. (2006). Conflict in dating and marital relationships. In J.

G. Oetzel, & S. Ting-Toomey (Eds.), *The Sage handbook of conflict communication: Integrating theory, research, and practice* (pp. 129–158). Thousand Oaks, CA: Sage.

Cegala, D. J., & Waldron, V. R. (1992). A study of the relationship between communicative performance and conversation participants' thoughts. *Communication Studies, 43,* 107–123.

Chapman, G. (1992). *The five love languages: How to express heartfelt commitment to your mate.* Chicago: Northfield.

Christensen, A., & Heavey, C. L. (1990). Gender and social structure in the demand/withdraw pattern of marital conflict. *Journal of Personality and Social Psychology, 59,* 73–81.

Christopher, F. S., & Sprecher, S. (2000). Sexuality in marriage, dating, and other relationships: A decade review. *Journal of Marriage and the Family, 62,* 999–1017.

Cialdini, R. B. (1993). *Influence: Science and practice* (3rd ed.). New York: HarperCollins.

Clark, R. A., & Delia, J. G. (1979). Topoi and rhetorical competence. *Quarterly Journal of Speech, 65,* 187–206.

Claxton, A., & Perry-Jenkins, M. (2008). No fun anymore: Leisure and marital quality across the transition to parenthood. *Journal of Marriage and Family, 70,* 28–43.

Clements, M. L., Cordova, A. D., Markman, H. J., & Lawrenceau, J. (1997). The erosion of marital satisfaction over time and how to prevent it. In R. J. Sternberg & M. Hojjat (Eds.), *Satisfaction in close relationships* (pp. 335–355). New York: Guilford Press.

Clore, G. L., & Ortony, A. (1991). What more is there to emotion concepts than prototypes? *Journal of Personality and Social Psychology, 60,* 48–50.

Clore, G. L., Ortony, A., Dienes, B., & Fujita, F. (1993) Where does anger dwell? In R. W. Wyer & T. K. Srull (Eds.), *Perspectives on anger and emotions* (vol. 6). Hillsdale, NJ: Erlbaum.

Cloven, D. H., & Roloff, M. E. (1991). Sense-making activities and interpersonal conflict: Communicative cures for the mulling blues. *Western Journal of Speech Communication, 55,* 134–158.

Cloven, D. H., & Roloff, M. E. (1993a). Sense-making activities and interpersonal conflict. Part 2. The effects of communicative intentions of internal dialogue. *Western Journal of Speech Communication, 57,* 309–329.

Cloven, D. H., & Roloff, M. E. (1993b). The chilling effect of aggressive potential on the expression of complaints in intimate relationships. *Communication Monographs, 60,* 199–219.

Cloven, D. H., & Roloff, M. E. (1995). Cognitive tuning effects on anticipating communication of thought about an interpersonal conflict. *Communication Reports, 8,* 1–9.

Cody, M. J., Canary, D. J., & Smith, S. W. (1994). Compliance-gaining goals: An inductive analysis of actors' goal types, strategies, and successes. In J. Daly & J. Wiemann (Eds.), *Communicating strategically: Strategies in interpersonal communication* (pp. 33–90). Hillsdale, NJ: Lawrence Erlbaum.

Cohen, S., Frank E., Doyle, W. J., Skinner, D. P., Rabin, B. S., Gwaltney, J. M. (1998). Types of stressors that increase susceptibility to the common cold in healthy adults. *Health Psychology, 17,* 214–223.

Coleman, P. T. (2000a). Power and conflict. In M. Deutsch & P. T. Coleman (Eds.) *The Handbook of conflict resolution: Theory and practice* (pp. 108–130). New York: Jossey-Bass.

Coleman, P. T. (2000b). Intractable conflict. In M. Deutsch & P. T. Coleman (Eds.), *The handbook of conflict resolution: Theory and practice* (pp. 428–450). San Francisco: Jossey-Bass.

Coleman, P. T. (2003). Characteristics of protracted, intractable conflict: Towards the development of a metaframework – I. *Peace and Conflict: Journal of Peace Psychology, 9*(1), 1–37.

Collins, N. L., & Read, S. J. (1990). Adult attachment: Implications for explanation, emotion and behavior. *Journal of Personality and Social Psychology, 58*, 644–663.

Conrad, C. (1991). Communication in conflict: Style-strategy relationships. *Communication Monographs, 58*, 135–155.

Covey, S. R. (1989). *The seven habits of highly effective people.* New York: Fireside.

Cowan, C. P., & Cowan, P. A. (1988). Who does what when partners become parents: Implications for men, women, and marriage. *Marriage and Family Review, 12*, 105–131.

Crawford, D. W., Houts, R. M., Huston, T. L., & George, L. J. (2002). Compatibility, leisure, and satisfaction in marital relationships. *Journal of Marriage and Family, 64*, 433–449.

Creasey, G. (2002). Associations between working models of attachment and conflict management behavior in romantic couples. *Journal of Counseling Psychology, 49*, 365–375.

Creasey, G., & Ladd, A. (2004). Negative mood regulation expectancies and conflict behaviors in late adolescent college student romantic relationships: The moderating role of generalized attachment representations. *Journal of Research on Adolescence, 14*, 235–255.

Crews, T., & Boettiger, A. (2009). Impulsivity, frontal lobes, and risk for addiction. *Pharmacology Biochemistry and Behavior, 93*, 237–247.

Cromwell, R. E., & Olson, D (Eds.). (1975). *Power in Families.* New York: Wiley and Sons.

Cummings, E. M., Goeke-Morey, M. C., & Papp, L. M. (2001). Couple conflict, children, and families: It's not just you and me, babe. In A. Booth, A. C. Crouter, & M. Clements (Eds.), *Couples in conflict* (pp. 117–147). Mahwah, NJ: Lawrence Erlbaum Associates.

Cunradi, C. B., Caetano, R., & Schafer, John. (2002). Alcohol-related problems, drug use, and male intimate partner violence severity among US couples. *Alcoholism: Clinical and Experimental Research, 26*, 493–500.

Cupach, W. R., & Canary, D. J. (2000). *Competence in interpersonal conflict.* Prospect Heights, IL: Waveland Press.

Cupach, W. R., Canary, D. J., & Spitzberg, B. S. (2010). *Competence in interpersonal communication, 2nd edition.* Prospect Heights, IL: Waveland Press.

Cupach, W. R., & Metts, S. (1994*). Facework.* Thousand Oaks, CA: Sage.

Cutrona, C. E. (1996). Social support as a determinant of marital quality: The interplay of negatice and supportive behaviors. In G. R. Pierce, B. R., Sarason, & I. G., Sarason (Eds.), *Handbook of social support and the family* (pp. 173–194). New York: Birhauser.

Cutrona C. E., & Suhr J. A. (1993). Social support communication in the context of marriage: An analysis of couples' supportive interactions. In B. Burleson, T. Albrecht, & I. Sarason (Eds.), *The communication of social support: Messages, interactions, relationships, and community,* (pp. 113–135) Newbury Park, CA: Sage.

D'Augelli, A., & D'Augelli, J. F. (1985). The enhancement of sexual skills and competence: Promoting lifelong sexual unfolding. In L. L'Abate, & M. A. Milan (Eds.), *Handbook of social skills training and research* (pp. 170–191). New York: Wiley.

DeDreu, C. K. W., Natua, A., & van de Vliert, E. (1995). Self-serving evaluations of conflict behavior and escalation of the dispute. *Journal of Applied Social Psychology, 25*, 2049–2066.

DeLongis, A., Folkman, S., & Lazarus, R. S. (1988). The impact of daily stress on health and mood: Psychological and social resources as mediators. *Journal of Personality and Social Psychology, 54,* 486–495.

DeTurck, M. A. (1987). When communication fails: Physical aggression as a compliance-gaining strategy. *Communication Monographs, 54,* 106–112.

Deutsch, M. (1973). *The resolution of conflict: Constructive and destructive processes.* New Haven, CT: Yale University Press.

Diener, E., & Seligman, M. E. P. (2000). Very happy people. *Psychological Science, 13,* 81–84.

Dillard, J. P. (1989). Types of influence goals in personal relationships. *Journal of Social and Personal Relationships, 6,* 293–308.

Dillard, J. P. (1990a). A goal-driven model of interpersonal influence. In J. P. Dillard (Ed.), *Seeking compliance: The production of interpersonal influence messages* (pp. 41–56). Scottsdale, AZ: Gorsuch-Scarisbrick.

Dillard, J. P. (1990b). The nature and substance of goals in tactical communication. In M. J. Cody & M. L. McLaughlin (Eds.), *The psychology of tactical communication* (pp. 70–89). Philadelphia: Multilingual Matters LTD.

Dillard, J. O. (1997). Explicating the goal construct: Tools for theorists. In J. O. Greene (Ed.), *Message production: Advances in communication theory* (pp. 47–69). Mahwah, NJ: Lawrence Erlbaum.

Dillard, J. P., & Wilson, B. J. (1993). Communication and affect: Thoughts, feelings, and issues for the future. *Communication Research, 20,* 637–646.

Dillard, J. P., Palmer, M. T., & Kinney, T. A. (1995). Relational judgments in an influence context. *Human Communication Research, 21,* 331–353.

Dillard, J. P., Segrin, C., & Harden, J. M. (1989). Primary and secondary goals in the production of interpersonal influence messages. *Communication Monographs, 56,* 19–37.

Dindia, K. (2000). Relational maintenance. In C. Hendrick & S. S. Hendrick (Eds.), *Close relationships: A sourcebook* (pp. 287–300). Thousand Oaks, CA: Sage.

Dindia, K., & Baxter, L. A. (1987). Strategies for maintaining and repairing marital relationships. *Journal of Social and Personal Relationships, 4,* 143–158.

Dindia, K., & Canary, D.. J. (Eds.) (2006). *Sex differences and similarities in communication, 2nd edition.* Mahwah, NJ: Lawrence Erlbaum Associates.

Dobson, M., & Markham, R. (1992). Individual differences in anxiety level and eyewitness memory. *Journal of General Psychology, 119,* 343–350.

Doherty. (1981). Cognitive processes in intimate conflict I: Extending attribution theory. *American Journal of Family Therapy, 9,* 3–13.

Donnely, D. A. (1993). Sexually inactive marriages. *The Journal of Sex Research, 30,* 171–179.

Donohue, W. A., & Kolt, R. (1992). *Managing interpersonal conflict.* Newbury Park, CA: Sage.

Dorff, E. N. (1998). Dimensions of forgiveness: Psychological research and theoretical perspectives. In E. L. Worthington (Ed.). *Dimensions of forgiveness: Psychological research and theological perspectives* (pp. 29–55). Philadelphia, PA: Templeton.

Driver, J. & Gottman, J. (2004). Daily marital interactions and positive affect during marital conflict among newlywed couples. *Family Processes, 43,* 301–315.

Duggan, A. P. (2007). Sex differences in communicative attempts to curtail depression: An inconsistent nurturing as control perspective. *Western Journal of Communication, 71,* 114–135.

Duggan, A. P., & Le Poire, B. A. (2006). One down, two involved: An application and extension of inconsistent nurturing as control theory to couples including one depressed individual. *Communication Monographs, 73,* 379–405.

Dumlao, RT., & Botta, R. A. (2000). Family communication patterns and the conflict styles young adults use with their fathers. *Communication Quarterly, 48,* 174–189.

Dunbar, N. E. (2004). Dyadic power theory: Constructing a communication-based theory of relational power. *The Journal of Family Communication, 4,* 235–248.

Dunbar, N. E. & Abra, G. (2010). Observations of dyadic power in interpersonal interaction. *Communication Monographs, 77,* 657–684.

Dunbar, N. E., & Burgoon, J. K. (2005). Perceptions of power and interactional dominance in interpersonal relationships. *Journal of Social and Personal Relationships, 22,* 207–233.

Dunbar, N. E., Bippus, A. M., & Young, S. L. (2008). Interpersonal dominance in relational conflict: A view from dyadic power theory. *Interpersona, 1,* 1–33.

Du Rocher Schudlich, T. D., Papp, L. M., & Cummings, E. M. (2004). Relations of husbands' and wives' dysphoria to marital conflict resolution strategies. *Journal of Family Psychology, 18,* 171–183.

Eagly, A. H., & Chaiken, S. (1993). *The psychology of attitudes.* Orlando, FL: Harcourt, Brace, Jovanovich.

Easterbrook, J. A. (1959). The effect of emotion on cue utilization and the organization of behavior. *Psychological Review, 66,* 183–201.

Eberhart, N. K., & Hammen, C. L. (2009). Interpersonal predictors of stress generation. *Personality and Social Psychology Bulletin, 35,* 544–556.

Eldridge, K. A., & Christensen, A. (2002). Demand-withdraw communication during couple conflict: A review and analysis. In P. Noller & J. A. Feeney (Eds.), *Understanding marriage: Developments in the study of couple interaction* (pp. 289–322). Cambridge, UK: Cambridge University Press.

Ellis, B. J., & Malamuth, N. M. (2000). Love and anger in romantic relationships: A discrete systems model. *Journal of Personality, 68,* 525–556.

El-Sheikh, M., & Cheskes, J. (1995). Background verbal and physical anger: A comparison of children's responses to adult-adult and adult-child arguments. *Child Development, 66,* 446–458.

El-Sheikh, M., Buckhalt, J. A., Mize, J., & Acebo, C. (2006) Marital conflict and disruption of children's sleep. *Child Development, 77,* 31–43.

Emery, R. E. (1982). Interparental conflict and the children of discord and divorce. *Psychological Bulletin, 92,* 310–330.

Emmers, T. M., & Canary, D. J. (1996). The effect of uncertainty reducing strategies on young couples' relational repair and intimacy. *Communication Quarterly, 44,* 166–182.

Emmers-Sommer, T. M. (2003). When partners falter: Repair after a transgression. In D. J. Canary & M. Dainton (Eds.), *Maintaining relationships through communication: Relational, contextual, and cultural variations* (pp. 185–208). Mawah, NJ: Erlbaum.

Emmers-Sommer, T. M. (2004). The effect of communication quality and quantity indicators on intimacy and relational satisfaction. *Journal of Social and Personal Relationships, 21,* 399–411.

Enright, R. D., & Group (1996). Counseling within the forgiveness triad: On forgiving, receiving forgiveness, and self-forgiveness. *Counseling and Values, 40,* 107–127.

Enright, R. D., & Zell, R. L. (1989). Problems encountered when we forgive one another. *Journal of Psychology and Christianity, 8,* 52–54.

Enright, R., Gassin, E., & Wu, C. (1992). Forgiveness: A developmental view. *Journal of Moral Education, 21,* 101.

Erbert, L. (2000). Conflict and dialectics: Perceptions of dialectical contradictions in marital conflict. *Journal of Social and Personal Relationships, 17*, 638–659.

Exline, J. J., & Baumeister, R. F. (2000). Expressing forgiveness and repentance: Benefits and barriers. In McCullough, M. E., Pargament, K. I., & Toresen, C. E. (Eds.). *Forgiveness: Theory, research and practice* (pp. 133–155). London: Guilford Press.

Exline, J. J., Deshea, L, & Holeman, V. T. (2007). Is apology worth the risk? Predictors, outcomes, and ways to avoid regret. *Journal of Social and Clinical Psychology, 26*, 479–504.

Falbo, T. (1977). A multidimensional scaling of power strategies. *Journal of Personality and Social Psychology, 35*, 537–547.

Feeney, J. A. (2005). Hurt feelings in couple relationships: Exploring the role of attachment and perceptions of personal injury. *Personal Relationships, 12*, 253–271.

Feeney, J. A., & Noller, P. (1990). Attachment style as a predictor of adult romantic relationships. *Journal of Personality and Social Psychology, 58*, 281–291.

Fehr, R., & Gelfand, M. J. (2010). When apologies work: How matching apology components to victims' self-construals facilitates forgiveness. *Organizational Behavior and Human Decision Processes, 113*, 37–50.

Felmlee, D. H. (2001). No couple is an island: A social network perspective on dyadic stability. *Social Forces, 79*, 1259–1287.

Feltman, R., Robinson, M. D., & Ode, S. (2009). Mindfulness as a moderator of neuroticism-outcome relations: A self-regulation perspective. *Journal of Research in Personality, 43*, 953–961.

Feshbach, S. (1986). Reconceptualizations of anger: Some research perspectives. *Journal of Social and Clinical Psychology, 4*, 123–132.

Fields, N. S. (1983). Satisfaction in long-term marriages. *Social Work, 28*, 37–41.

Fincham, F. D. (2003) Marital conflict: Correlates, structure, and context. *Current Directions in Psychological Science, 12*, 23–27.

Fincham, F. D., & Beach, S. R. H. (1999). Conflict in marriage: Implications for working couples. *Annual Review of Psychology, 50*, 47–77.

Fincham, F. D., & Beach, S. R. H. (2002). Forgiveness and marriage: Implications for psychological aggression and constructive communication. *Personal Relationships, 9*, 239–251.

Fincham, F. D., & Bradbury, T. N. (1987). Cognitive processes and conflict in close relationships: An attribution-efficacy model. *Journal of Personality and Social Psychology, 53*, 1106–1118.

Fincham, F. D., & Bradbury, T. N. (1987). The impact of attributions in marriage: A longitudinal analysis. *Journal of Personality and Social Psychology, 53*, 510–517.

Fincham, F. D., & Bradbury, T. N. (1992). Assessing attributions in marriage: The relationship attribution measure. *Journal of Personality and Social Psychology, 62*, 457–468.

Fincham, F. D., & Linfield, K. J. (1997). A new look at marital quality: Can spouses feel positive and negative about their marriage? *Journal of Family Psychology, 11*, 489–502.

Fincham, F. D., Beach, S. R. H., & Davila, J. (2004). Forgiveness and conflict resolution in marriage. *Journal of Family Psychology, 18*, 72–82.

Fincham, F. D., Beach, S. R. H., & Nelson, G. (1987). Attribution processes in distressed and nondistressed couples: 3, Causal and responsibility attributions for spouse behavior. *Cognitive Therapy and Research, 11*, 71–86.

Fincham, F. D., Bradbury, T. N., & Grych, J. H. (1990). Conflict in close relationships:

The role of intrapersonal phenomena. In S. Graham & V. S. Folkes (Eds.), *Attribution theory: Applications to achievement, health, and interpersonal conflict* (pp. 161–184). Hillsdale, NJ: Erlbaum.

Fincham, F. D., Bradbury, T. N., & Scott, C. K. (1990). Cognition in marriage. In F. D. Fincham (Ed.), *The psychology of marriage, basic issues and applications* (pp. 118–149). New York: Guilford.

Finkel, E. J., Rusbult, C. E., Kumashiro, M., & Hannon, P. A. (2002). Dealing with betrayal in close relationships: Does commitment promote forgiveness? *Journal of Personality and Social Psychology, 82*, 956–974.

Fisher, R., & Davis, W. H. (1987). Six basic interpersonal skills for a negotiatior's repertoire. *Negotiation Journal, 3*, 117–125.

Fiske, S. T., & Taylor, S. E. (1984). *Social cognition*. New York: Random House.

Fitness, J. (2001). Betrayal, rejection, revenge, and forgiveness: An interpersonal script approach. In M. Leary (Ed.), *Interpersonal rejection* (pp. 73–103). New York: Oxford University Press.

Fitness, J., & Fletcher, G. J. O. (1993). Love, hate, anger, and jealousy in close relationships: A prototype and cognitive appraisal analysis. *Journal of Personality and Social Psychology, 65*, 942–958.

Fitzgibbons, R. P. (1986). The cognitive and emotional uses of forgiveness in the treatment of anger. *Psychotherapy, 23*, 629–633.

Flannery, D. J., Montemayor, R., Eberly, M., & Torquati, J. (1993). Unraveling the ties that bind: Affective expression and perceived conflict in parent-adolescent interactions. *Journal of Social and Personal Relationships, 10*, 495–509.

Foa, E. B., Cascardi, M., Zoellner, L. A., Feeny, N. C. (2000). Psychological and environmental factors associated with partner violence. *Trauma, Violence, and Abuse, 1*, 67–91.

Forgas, J. (1999). Feeling and speaking: Mood effects on verbal communication strategy. *Personality and Social Psychology Bulletin, 25*, 850–863.

Forgas, J. P. (1983). *Language, goals, and situations. Journal of Language and Social Psychology, 2*, 267–293.

Forgas, J. P. (1994). Sad or guilty: Affective influences on the explanation of conflict episodes. *Journal of Personality and Social Psychology, 66*, 56–68.

Forgas, J. P. (1995). Mood and judgment: The affect infusion model (AIM). *Psychological Bulletin, 116*, 39–66.

Forgas, J. P. (1995). Strange couples: Mood effects on judgments and memory about prototypical and atypical targets. *Personality and Social Psychology Bulletin, 21*, 747–765.

Forgas, J. P. (1998a). Asking nicely? The effects of mood on responding to more or less polite requests. *Personality and Social Psychology Bulletin, 24*, 173–185.

Forgas, J. P. (1998b). Feeling good and getting your way: Mood effects on negotiating strategies and outcomes. *Journal of Personality and Social Psychology, 74*, 565–577.

Forgas, J. P. (1998c). Happy and mistaken? Mood effects on the fundamental attribution error. *Journal of Personality and Social Psychology, 75*, 318–331.

Forgas, J. P. (1999). On feeling good and being rude: Affective influences on language use. *Journal of Personality and Social Psychology, 76*, 928–939.

Forgas, J. P. (2001). Affective influences on communication and attribution in relationships. In V. Manusov & J. H. Harvey (Eds.), *Attribution, communication, behavior, and close relationships: Advances in personal relations* (pp. 3–20). New York: Cambridge University Press.

Forgas, J. P., & East, R. (2008). How real is that smile? Mood effects on accepting or rejecting the veracity of emotional facial expressions. *Journal of Nonverbal Behavior, 32,* 157–170.

Forgas, J. P., Bower, G. H., & Moylan, S. J. (1990). Praise or blame? Mood effects on attributions for success and failure. *Journal of Personality and Social Psychology, 59,* 809–819.

Forgas, J. P., Levinger, G., & Moylan, S. (1994). Feeling good and feeling close: Mood effects on the perceptions of intimate relationships. *Personal Relationships, 2,* 165–184.

Fortado, B. (2001). The metamorphosis of workplace conflict. *Human Relations, 54,* 1189–1221.

Foster, J. D., Shira, I., Campbell, W. K. (2006). Theoretical models of narcissism, sexuality, and relationship commitment. *Journal of Social and Personal Relationships, 23,* 367–386.

French, J. R., & Raven, B. (1959). The bases of social power. In D. Cartwright (Ed.), *Studies in social power* (150–167). Ann Arbor MI: Institute for Social Research.

Frijda, N. H. (1986). *The emotions.* Cambridge, UK: Cambridge University Press.

Frijda, N. H., Kuipers, P, & ter Shure, E. (1989). The relationship between emotion, appraisal, and emotional action readiness. *Journal of Personality and Social Psychology, 57,* 212–228.

Fruzetti, A. E., & Jacobson, N. S. (1990). Toward a behavioral conceptualization of adult intimacy: Implications for marital therapy. In E. A. Blechman (Ed.), *Emotions and the family: For better or for worse* (pp. 117–136). Hillsdale, NJ: Lawrence Erlbaum Associates.

Fukushima, O., & Ohbuchi, K. (1996). Antecedents and effects of multiple goals in conflict resolution. *International Journal of Conflict Management, 7,* 191–208.

Gabrielidis, C., Stephan, W. G., Ybarra, O., Pearson, V. M., & Villareal, L. (1997). Preferred styles of conflict resolution: Mexico and the United States. *Journal of Cross Cultural Psychology, 28,* 661–677.

Gaelick, L., Bodenhausen, G. V., & Wyer, R. (1985). Emotional communication in close relationships. *Journal of Personality and Social Psychology, 49 (5),* 1246–1265.

Gager, C. T., & Sanchez, L. (2003). Two as one?: Couples' perceptions of time spent together, marital quality, and the risk of divorce. *Journal of Family Issues, 24,* 21–50.

Galinsky, A. D., Gruenfeld, D. H., & Magee, J. C. (2003). From power to action. *Journal of Personality and Social Psychology, 85,* 453–466.

Gallo, L. C. & Smith, T. W. (2001). Attachment style in marriage: Adjustment and responses to interaction. *Journal of Social and Personal Relationships, 18,* 263–289.

Gassin, E. (1998). Receiving forgiveness as moral education: A theoretical analysis and initial empirical investigation. *Journal of Moral Education, 27,* 71–88.

Gelles, R. J. (1972). *The violent home: A study of physical aggression between husbands and wives,* Sage, Thousand Oaks, CA.

Goldberg, L. (1992). The development of markers of the Big Five factor structure. *Psychology Assessment, 4,* 26–42.

Goldberger & S. Breznitz (Eds.), *Handbook of stress: Theoretical and clinical aspects* (pp. 342–367). New York: The Free Press.

Goldberger, L. (1993). Sensory deprivation and overload. In L. Goldberger & S. Breznitz (Eds.), *The handbook of stress* (2nd ed., pp. 333–341). New York: Free Press.

Goldner, V. (2004), Attachment and Eros: Opposed or synergistic? *Psychoanalytic Dialogues, 14,* 381–396.

Goldsmith, D. J. (2004). *Communicating social support.* New York: Cambridge University Press.

Goodstadt, B. E., & Hjelle, L. A. (1973). Power to the powerless: Locus of control and the use of power. *Journal of Personality and Social Psychology, 27,* 190–196.

Goodyear-Smith, F., & Buetow, S. (2001). Power issues in the doctor–patient relationship. *Health Care Analysis, 9,* 449–462.

Gordis, E. B., Margolin, G., & Vickerman, K. (2005). Communication and frightening behavior among couples with past and recent histories of physical marital aggression. *American Journal of Community Psychology, 36,* 177–191.

Gordon, K.C., Baucom, D. H., & Snyder, D. K. (2000). The use of forgiveness in marital theapy. In M. F. McCullough, K. I, Pargament, & C. F. Thoresen (Eds.), *Forgiveness: Theory, research and practice* (pp. 203–227). London: Guilford Press.

Gottman, J. M. (1979). *Marital interaction: Experimental investigations.* New York: Academic Press.

Gottman, J. M. (1994). *What predicts divorce? The relationship between marital processes and marital outcomes.* Hillsdale, NJ: Lawrence Erlbaum Associates.

Gottman, J. M. (1999). *The marriage clinic: A scientifically-based marital therapy.* New York: W. W. Norton.

Gottman, J. M., Coan, J., Carrere, S., & Swanson, C. (1998). Predicting marital happiness and stability from newlywed interactions. *Journal of Marriage and the Family, 60,* 5–22.

Gottman, J. M., & Krokoff, L. J. (1989). Marital interaction and marital satisfaction: A longitudinal view. *Journal of Consulting and Clinical Psychology, 57,* 47–52.

Gottman, J. M., & Levenson, R. W. (1988). The social psychophysiology of marriage. In P. Noller & M. A. Fitzpatrick (Eds.), *Perspectives on marital interaction* (pp. 182–200). Philadelphia: Multilingual Matters.

Gottman, J. M., & Levenson, R. W. (1992). Marital processes predictive of later dissolution: behavior, physiology, and health. *Journal of Personality and Social Psychology, 63,* 221–233.

Gottman, J. M., & Levenson, R. W. (2000). The timing of divorce: Predicting when a couple will divorce over a 14-year period. *Journal of Marriage and the Family, 62,* 737–745.

Gottman, J. M., & Levenson, R. W. (2002). A two-factor model for predicting when a couple will divorce: Explanatory analyses using a 14-year longitudinal data. *Family Process, 41,* 83–96.

Graham, S., & Folkes, V. S. (1990). *Attributrion theory: Appliction to achievement, mental health, and interpersonal conflict.* Hillsdale, NJ: Lawrence Erlbaum.

Graig, E. (1993). Stress as a consequence of the urban physical environment. In L. Goldberger & S. Breznitz (Eds.), *The handbook of stress* (2nd ed., pp. 316–332). New York: Free Press.

Graziano, W. G., Jensen-Campbell, L. A., & Hair, E. C. (1996). Perceiving interpersonal conflict and reacting to it: The case for agreeableness. *Journal of Personality and Social Psychology, 70,* 820–835.

Greefe, A. P., & DeBruyne, T. (2000). Conflict management style and marital satisfaction. *Journal of Sex and Marital Therapy, 26,* 321–334.

Greene, J., & Burleson, B. (2003). *Handbook of communication and social interaction skills.* Mahwah NJ: Erlbaum.

Greene, J. O., & Lindsey, A. E. (1989). Encoding processes in the production of multiple-goal messages. *Human Communication Research, 16,* 130–140.

Grenyer, G. F. S., & Luborsky, L. (1996). Dynamic change in psychotherapy: Mastery of interpersonal conflicts. *Journal of Consulting and Clinical Psychology, 64,* 411–416.

Grimshaw, A. D. (1990). *Research on conflict talk.* Cambridge, UK: Cambridge University Press.

Gudykunst, W. B., & Ting-Toomey, S. (1996). Communication in personal relationships across cultures: An introduction. In W. B. Gudykunst, S. Ting-Toomey, & T. Nishida (Eds.), *Communication in personal relationships across cultures* (pp. 3–16). Thousand Oaks, CA: Sage.

Gudykunst, W. B., Matsumoto, Y., Ting-Toomey, S., Nishida, T., Kim, K., & Heyman, S. (1996). The influence of cultural individualism-collectivism, self construals, and individual values on communication styles across cultures. *Human Communication Research, 22,* 510–543.

Guerrero, L. K. (1994). "I'm so mad I could scream": The effects of anger expression on relational satisfaction and communication competence. *Southern Communication Journal, 59,* 125–141.

Guerrero, L. K. (1996). Attachment-style differences in intimacy and involvement: A test of the four-category model. *Communication Monographs, 63,* 269–292.

Guerrero, L. K., & Andersen, P. A. (1998). Jealousy experience and expression in romantic relationships. In P. A. Andersen & L. K. Guerrero (Eds.), *Handbook of communication and emotion: Research, theory, applications, and contexts* (pp. 155–188). San Diego, CA: Academic Press.

Guerrero, L. K., & Bachman, G. F. (2010). Forgiveness and forgiving communication in dating relationships: An expectancy-investment explanation. *Journal of Social and Personal Relationships, 27,* 801–824.

Guerrero, L. K., & La Valley, A. G. (2006). Conflict, emotion, and communication. In J. G. Oetzel, & S. Ting-Toomey (Eds.), *The Sage handbook of conflict communication: Integrating theory, research, and practice* (pp. 69–96). Thousand Oaks, CA: Sage.

Guerrero, L. K., Farinelli, L., and McEwan, B. (2008) Attachment and relational satisfaction: The mediating effect of emotional communication. *Communication Monographs. 76,* 487–514.

Gunderson, P. R., & Ferrari. J. R. (2008). Forgiveness of sexual cheating in romantic relationships: Effects of discovery method, frequency of offense, and presence of apology. *North American Journal of Psychology, 10,* 1–14.

Grych, J. H., Raynor, S. R., & Fosco, G. M. (2004). Family processes that shape the impact of interparental conflict on adolescents. *Development and Psychopathology, 16,* 649–665.

Grych, J. H., Fincham, F. D., Jouriles, E. N., & McDonald, R. (2000). Interparental conflict and child adjustment: Testing the mediational role of appraisals in the cognitive-contextual framework. *Child Development, 71,* 1648–1661.

Haferkamp, C. J. (1992). Oreintations to conflict: Gender, attributions, resolution strategies, and self-monitoring. *Current Psychology, 10,* 227–241.

Hall, B. J. (1991). An elaboration of the structural possibilities for engaging in alignment episodes. *Communication Monographs, 68,* 79–100.

Hall, E. T. (1976). *Beyond culture.* New York: Doubleday.

Hample, D., & Cionea, I. A. (2010). Taking conflict personally and its connections with aggressiveness. In T. A. Avtgis & A. S. Rancer (Eds.), *Arguments, aggression, and conflict: New directions in theory and research* (pp. 372–387). New York: Routledge.

Hample, D., & Dallinger, J. (1992). The use of multiple goals in cognitive editing of arguments. *Argumentation and Advocacy, 28,* 109–122.

Hargrave, T. D. (1994). *Families and forgiveness.* New York: Brunner/Mazel.

Harris, P. R., & Lightsey, O. R. (2005). Constructive thinking as a mediator of the relationship between extraversion, neuroticism and subjective well-being. *European Journal of Personality, 19*, 409–426.

Harvey, J. H., Orbuch, T. L., & Weber, A. L. (Eds.). (1991). *Attributions, accounts, and close relationships*. New York: Springer-Verlag.

Hayashi, G. M., & Strickland, B. R. (1998), Long-term effects of parental divorce on love relationships: Divorce as attachment disruption. *Journal of Social and Personal Relationships 15*, 23–38.

Hazan, C., & Shaver, P. R. (1987). Romantic love conceptualized as an attachment process. *Journal of Personality and Social Psychology, 52*, 511–524.

Heller, S. (1998, July 17). Emerging field of forgiveness studies explores how we let go of grudges. *Chronicle of Higher Education*, A-19.

Henderson-King, D. H., & Veroff, J. (1994). Sexual satisfaction and marital well being in the first years of marriage. *Journal of Social and Personal Relationships, 11*, 509–534.

Henne, E., Buysse, A., & Van Oost, P. (2007). An interpersonal perspective on depression: the role of marital adjustment, conflict communication, attributions and attachment within a clinical sample. *Family Process, 46*, 499–515

Hindin, T. R., & Schriesheim, C. A. (1989). Development and application of new scales to measure the French and Raven bases of social power. *Journal of Applied Psychology, 7*, 561–576.

Hill, M. S. (1988). Marital stability and spouses' shared time: A multidisciplinary hypothesis. *Journal of Family Issues, 9*, 427–451.

Hinchliffe, M. K., Hooper, D., & Roberts, J. (1978). *The melancholy marriage: Depression in marriage and psychosocial approaches to therapy*. New York: Wiley.

Hindin, T. R., & Schriesheim, C. A. (1989). Development and application of new scales to measure the French and Raven bases of social power. *Journal of Applied Psychology, 7*, 561–576.

Hinton, P. R. (1993). *Psychology of interpersonal perception*. London: Routledge.

Hofstede, G. (2001). *Culture's consequences: Comparing values, behaviors, institutions, and organizations across cultures* (2nd ed.). Thousand Oaks, CA: Sage.

Holahan, C. J., & Moos, R. H. (1990). Life stressors, resistance factors, and improved psychological functioning: An extension of the stress resistance paradigm. *Journal of Personality and Social Psychology, 58*, 909–1017.

Holt, R. R. (1993). Occupational stress. In L. Goldberger & S. Breznitz (Eds.), *The handbook of stress* (2nd ed., pp. 342–367). New York: Free Press.

Holtzworth-Munroe, A., & Jacobson, N. S. (1985). Causal attributions of marital couples: When do they search for causes? What do they conclude when they do? *Journal of Personality and Social Psychology, 48*, 1398–1412.

Holtzworth-Munroe, A., Smutzler, N., & Stuart, G. L. (1998). Demand and withdraw communication among couples experiencing husband violence. *Journal of Consulting and Clinical Psychology, 66*, 731–743.

Honeycutt, J. M., Cantrill, J. G., Kelly, P., & Lambkin, D. (1998). How do I love thee? Let me consider my options: Cognition, verbal strategies, and the escalation of intimacy. *Human Communication Research, 25*, 39–63.

Honeycutt, J. M., & Eidenmuller, M. E. (2000). Communication and attribution: An exploration of the effects of music and mood on intimate couples' verbal and nonverbal conflict resolution behaviors. In V. Manusov & J. H. Harvey (Eds.). *Attribution, communication behavior, and close relationships* (pp. 21–37). Cambridge, UK: Cambridge University Press.

Hope, D. (1987). The healing paradox of forgiveness. *Psychotherapy, 24,* 240–244.

Howat, GT., & London, M. (1980). Attributions of conflict management strategies ini supervisor-subordinate dyads. *Journal of Applied Psychology, 65,* 172–175.

Hoyt, W.T., Fincham, F. D., McCullough, M. E., Maio, G, & Davila, J. (2005). Responses to interpersonal transgressions in families: Forgivingness, forgivability, and relationship-specific effects. *Journal of Personality and Social Psychology, 89,* 375–394.

Hubbard, A. S. E. (2001). Conflict between relationally uncertain romantic partners: The influence of relational responsiveness and empathy. *Communication Monographs, 68,* 400–414.

Huber, V. L., & Neale, M. A. (1987). Effects of self- and competitor goals on performance in an interdependent bargaining task. *Journal of Applied Psychology, 72,* 197–203.

Hull, J. G., & Bond, C. F. Social and behavioral consequences of alcohol consumption and expectancy: A meta-analysis. *Psychological Bulletin, 99,* 347–360.

Huston, T. (1983). Power. In H. H. Keeley, E. Berscheid, A. Christesen, J. Harvey, T. Huston, G. Levinger, E. McClintock, A. Peplau, & D. Peterson (Eds.), *Close relationships* (pp. 169–219). New York: W. H. Freeman.

Huston, T. L., & Vangelisti, A. L. (1995). How parenthood affects marriage. In M. A. Fitzpatrick & A. L. Vangelisti (Eds.), *Explaining family interactions* (pp. 147–176). Thousand Oaks, CA: Sage.

Huston, T. L., Caughlin, J. P., Houts, R. M., Smith, S. E., & George, L. J. (2001). The connubial crucible: Newlywed years as predictors of marital delight, distress, and divorce. *Journal of Personality and Social Psychology, 80, 237–252.*

Huston, T., Robins, E., Atkinson, J., & McHale, S. (1987). Surveying the landscape of marital behavior: A behavioral self-report approach to studying marriage. In S. Oskamp (Ed.), *Family processes and problems: Social psychological aspects* (pp. 45–71). Beverly Hills, CA: Sage.

Infante, D. A., & Rancer, A. S. (1982). A conceptualization and measure of argumentativeness. *Journal of Personality Assessment, 46,* 72–80.

Infante, D. A., & Wigley, C. J. (1986). Verbal aggressiveness: An interpersonal model and measure. *Communication Monographs, 53,* 61–69.

Infante, D. A., Chandler, T. A., & Rudd, J. E. (1989). Test of an argumentative skill deficiency model of interspousal violence. *Communication Monographs, 56,* 163–177.

Infante, D. A., Sabourin, T. C., Rudd, J. E., & Shannon, E. A. (1990). Verbal aggression in violent and nonviolent marital disputes. *Communication Quarterly, 38,* 361–371.

Infante, D. A., Hartley, D. C., Martin, M. M., Higgins, M. A., Bruning, S. D., & Hur, G. (1992). Initiating and reciprocating verbal aggression: Effects on credibility and credited valid arguments. *Communication Studies, 43,* 182–190.

Infante, D. A., Trebling, J. D., Shepard, P. E., & Seeds, D. E. (1984). The relation of argumentativeness to verbal aggression. *Southern Speech Communication Journal, 50,* 67–77.

Jacobs, S., & Jackson, S. (1983). Speech act structure in conversation: Rational aspects of pragmatic coherence. In R. T. Craig & K. Tracy (Eds.), *Conversational coherence: Form, structure, and strategy* (pp. 47–67). Beverly Hills, CA: Sage.

Jacobson, N. S., Gottman, J. M., Waltz, J., Rushe, R., Babcock, J., & Holtzworth-Munroe, A. (1994). Affect, verbal content, and psychophysiology in the arguments of couples with a violent husband. *Journal of Consulting and Clinical Psychology, 62,* 982–988.

Jenkins, J. M., & Smith, M. A. (1991). Marital disharmony and children's behavior problems: Aspects of a poor marriage that affect children adversely. *Journal of Child Psychology and Psychiatry, 32,* 793–810.

Jensen-Campbell, L.. A., & Graziano, W. G. (2000). Beyond the schoolyard: Relationships as moderators of interpersonal conflict. *Personality and Social Psychology Bulletin, 26*, 925–935.

Jensen-Campbell, L.A., & Graziano, W. G. (2001). Agreeableness as a moderator of interpersonal conflict. *Journal of Personality, 69*, 323–362.

Jensen-Campbell, L. A., Gleason, K. A., Adams, R., & Malcolm, K. T. (2003). Interpersonal conflict, agreeableness, and personality development. *Journal of Personality, 71*, 1059–1085.

Johnson, P. E., & Evans, J.P. (1997). Power, communicator styles, and conflict management styles: A web of interpersonal constructs for the school principal. *International Journal of Educational Reform, 6*, 40–53.

Johnson, K. L., & Roloff, M. E. (1998). Serial arguing and relational quality: Determinants and consequences of perceived resolvability. *Communication Research, 25*, 327–343.

Johnson, K. L., & Roloff, M. E. (2000a). Correlates of the perceived resolvability and relational consequences of serial arguing in dating relationships: Argumentative features and the use of coping strategies. *Journal of Social and Personal Relationships, 17*, 676–686.

Johnson, K. L., & Roloff, M. E. (2000b). The influence of argumentative role (Initiator vs. Resistor) on perceptions of serial argument resolvability and relational harm. *Argumentation, 14*, 1–15.

Johnson, M. P. (1995). Patriarchal terrorism and common couple violence: Two forms of violence against women. *Journal of Marriage and the Family, 57*, 283–294.

Johnson, M. P. (2001). Conflict and control: Symmetry and asymmetry in domestic violence. In A. Booth, A. C. Crouter, & M. Clements (Eds.), *Couples in conflict* (pp. 95–104). Mahwah, NJ: Lawrence Erlbaum Associates.

Johnson, P. E., & Evans, J.P. (1997). Power, communicator styles, and conflict management styles: A web of interpersonal constructs for the school principal. *International Journal of Educational Reform, 6*, 40–53.

Jones, E. E., & Davis, K. (1965). From acts to dispositions: The attribution process in person perception. In L. Berkowitz (Ed.), *Advances in experimental social psychology* (Vol. 2, pp. 219–267). New York: Academic Press.

Jones, T. S., & Brinkert, R. (2008). *Conflict coaching: Conflict management strategies and skills for the individual.* Thousand Oaks, CA: Sage.

Jones, W., & Gallois, C. (1989). Spouses impressions of rules for communication in public and private marital conflicts. *Journal of Marriage and the Family, 51*, 957–967

Jones, W. H., Moore, D. S., Schratter, A., & Negel, L. A. (2001). Interpersonal transgressions and betrayals. Behaving badly: Aversive behaviors in interpersonal relationships. In R. M. Kowalski (Ed.), *Behaving badly: Aversive behaviors in interpersonal relationships,* (pp. 233–256): Washington, DC: American Psychological Association.

Jourdain, K. (2004). Communication styles and conflict. *The Journal for Quality and Parication, 27* (2), 23–25

Julien, D., & Markman, H. J. (1991). Social support and social networks as determinants of individual and marital outcomes. *Journal of Social and Personal Relationships, 8*, 549–568.

Julien, D., Chartrand, E., Simard, M,. Bouthillier, B., & Begin, J. (2003). Conflict, social support, and relationship quality: An observational study of heterosexual, gay male, and lesbian couples' communication. *Journal of Family Psychology, 17*, 419–428.

Keeley-Dyreson, M., Burgoon, J., & Bailey, W. (1991). The effects of stress and gender on non verbal decoding accuracy in kinesic and vocalic channels. *Human Communication Research, 17*, 584–605.

Kellermann, K. (1984). The negativity effect and its implications for initial interaction. *Communication Monographs, 51*, 37–55.

Kellerman, K. (1992). Communication: Inherently strategic and primarily automatic. *Communication Monographs, 59*, 288–300.

Kellermann, K. (2004). A goal-directed approach to gaining compliance relating to differences among goals to differences in behaviors. *Communication Research, 31*, 397–445.

Kelley, H. H. (1973). The processes of causal attribution. *American Psychologist, 28*, 107–128.

Kelly, D. (1998). The communication of forgiveness. *Communication Studies, 49*, 255–271.

Kelley, D. L., & Waldron, V. R. (2005). An investigation of forgiveness-seeking communication and relational outcomes. *Communication Quarterly, 53*, 339–358.

Kelman, H. C. (1961). Processes of opinion change. *Public Opinion Quarterly, 25*, 57–78.

Keltner, D., Gruenfeld, D. H., & Anderson, C. (2003). Power, approach, and inhibition. *Psychological Review, 110*, 265–284.

Keltner, P., Ellsworth, P. C., & Edwards, K. (1993). Beyond simple pessimism: Effects of sadness and anger on social perception. *Journal of Personality and Social Psychology, 64*, 740–752.

Kennedy, K. A., & Pronin, E. (2008). When disagreement gets ugly: Perceptions of bias and the escalation of conflict. *Personality and Social Psychology Bulletin, 34*, 833–848.

Kessing, R. (1974). Theories of culture. *Annual Review of Anthropology, 3*, 73–97.

Kiecolt-Glaser, J. K., & Newton, T. L. (2001). Marriage and health: His and hers. *Psychological Bulletin, 127*, 472–503.

Kiecolt-Glaser, J. K., Gouin, J., & Hantsoo, L. (2010). Close relationships, inflammation, and health. *Neuroscience & Biobehavioral Reviews, 35*, 33–38.

Kiecolt-Glaser, J. K., Malarkey, W. B., Chee, M. A., Newton, T., Cacioppo, J. T., Mao, H. Y., & Glaser, R. (1993). Negative behavior during marital conflict is associated with immunological down-regulation. *Psychosomatic Medicine, 55*, 395–409.

Kiecolt-Glaser, J. K., McGuire, L., Robles, T. F., Glaser, R. (2003). Psychoneuroimmunology: Psychological influences on immune function and health. *Journal of Consulting and Clinical Psychology, 70*, 537–547.

Kiecolt-Glaser, J. K., Newton, T., Cacioppo, J. T., MacCallum, R. C., Glaser, R., & Malarkey, W. B. (1996). Marital conflict and endocrine function: Are men really more physiologically affected than women? *Journal of Counseling and Clinical Psychology, 64*, 324–332.

Killmann, R. H., & Thomas, K. W. (1977). Developing a forced-choice measure of conflict-handling behavior: The MODE instrument. *Educational and Psychological Measurement, 37*, 309–325.

Kim, M-S., & Leung, T. (2000). A multicultural view of conflict management styles: Review and critical synthesis. In M. E. Roloff (Ed.), *Communication Yearbook 23* (pp. 227–269). Thousand Oaks, CA: Sage.

Kim, S. H., & Smith, R. H. (1993). Revenge and conflict escalation. *Negotiation Journal, 9 (1)*, 37–43.

Kingston, P. W., & Nock, S. L. (1987). Time together among dual-earner couples. *American Sociological Review, 52*, 391–400.

Kitzmann, K. M., & Cohen, R. (2003). Parents' versus children's perceptions of interparental conflict as predictors of children's friendship quality. *Journal of Social and Personal Relationships, 20*, 689–700.

Klausner, W. J. (1968). An experiment in leisure. *Science Journal, 4*, 81–85.

Kluwer, E. S., deDreu, C. K. W., & Buunk, B. P. (1998). Conflict in intimate vs. nonintimate relationships: When gender role stereotyping overrides biased self-other judgment. *Journal of Social and Personal Relationships, 15*, 637–650.

Kluwer, E. S., Heesink, J. A. M., & van de Vliert, E. (1997). The marital dynamics of conflict over the division of labor. *Journal of Marriage and the Family, 59*, 635–653.

Knapp, M. L., Stafford, L, & Daly, J. A. (1987). Regrettable messages: Things people wish they hadn't said. *Journal of Communication, 36*, 40–59.

Koerner, F. A., & Fitzpatrick, M. A. (2002). You never leave your family in a fight: The impact of family of origin on conflict behavior in romantic relationships. *Communication Studies, 53*, 2334–251.

Koesten, J., & Anderson, K. (2004). Exploring the influence of family communication patterns, cognitive complexity, and interpersonal competence on adolescent risk behaviors. *The Journal of Family Communication, 4*, 99–121.

Komter, A. (1989). Hidden power in marriage. *Gender and Society, 3*, 187–216.

Kowalski, R. M. (2000). "I was only kidding": Victim and perpetrators perceptions of teasing. *Personality and Social Psychology Bulletin, 26*, 231–241.

Kowalski, R., Walker, S., Wilkenson, R., Queen, A., & Sharpe, B. (2003). Lying, cheating, complaining, and other aversive interpersonal behaviors: A narrative examination of the darker side of relationships. *Journal of Social and Personal Relationships, 20*, 471–490.

Kumar, P. (1986). Psychological study of factors in marital happiness. *Indian Journal of Current Psychological Research, 1*, 73–76.

Kuppens, P., & Tuerlinckx, F. (2007). Personality traits predicting anger in self-, ambiguous-,and other caused unpleasant situations. *Personality and Individual Differences 42*, 1105–1115.

Kurdek, L. A. (1993). Nature and prediction of changes in marital quality for first-time parent and nonparent husbands and wives. *Journal of Family Psychology, 6*, 255–265.

Kurdek, L. A. (1994). Conflict resolution styles in gay, lesbian, heterosexual nonparent, and heterosexual parent couples. *Journal of Marriage and the Family, 56*, 705–722.

Lakey, S. G., & Canary, D. J. (2002). Actor goal achievement and sensitivity to partner as critical factors in understanding interpersonal communication competence and conflict strategies. *Communication Monographs, 69*, 217–235.

Lam, J. A., Rifkin, J., & Townley, A. (1989). Reframing conflict: Implications for fairness in parent-adolescent mediation. *Mediation Quarterly, 7 (1)*, 15–31.

Langer, E. J. (1989a). *Mindfulness.* Reading, MA: Addison-Wesley.

Langer, E. J. (1989b). Minding matters: The consequences of mindlessness-mindfulness. *Advances in Experimental Social Psychology, 22*, 137–173.

Lanthier, R. P. (2007). Personality traits and sibling relationships in emerging adults. *Psychologial Reports, 100*, 672–674.

Laursen, B., Finkelstein, B. D., & Betts, N. T. (2001). A developmental meta-analysis of peer conflict resolution. *Developmental Review, 21*, 421–449.

Lazarus, R. S. (1993). Why we should think of stress as a subset of emotion. In L. Golderberger & S, Breznitz (Eds.) *Handbook of stress.* New York: Free Press.

Lazarus, R. S., & Folkman, S. (1984) *Stress, appraisal, and coping.* New York: Springer.

Le, T. N. (2005). Narcissism and immature love as mediators of vertical individualism and ludic love style. *Journal of Social and Personal Relationships, 22*, 543–560.

Leary, M. (2001). *Interpersonal rejection.* New York: Oxford University Press.

LeBaron, M. (2003). *Bridging cultural conflicts: A new approach for a changing world*. San Francisco: Jossey Bass/John Wiley.

Lefcourt, H. M. (1982). *Locus of control: Current trends in theory and research (2nd ed.)*. Hillsdale, NJ: Erlbaum.

Lefcourt, H. M., Martin, R. A., Fick, C. M., & Saleh, W. E. (1985). Locus of control for affiliation and behavior in social interactions. *Journal of Personality and Social Psychology, 48*, 755–769.

Lefcourt, H. M., Von Bayer, C. L., Ware, E. E., & Cox, D. J. (1979). The Multidimensional-Multiattributional Scale: The development of a goal-specific locus of control scale. *Canadian Journal of Behavioral Science, 11*, 286–304.

Leith, K. P., & Baumeister, R. F. (1998). Empathy, shame, guilt, and narratives of interpersonal conflicts: Guilt-prone people are better at perspective taking. *Journal of Personality, 66*, 1.

Leonard, K. E., & Roberts, L. J. (1998). The effects of alcohol on the marital interactions of aggressive and nonaggressive husbands and their wives. *Journal of Abnormal Psychology, 107*, 602–615.

Levenson, R. W., & Gottman, J. M. (1983). Marital interaction: Physiological linkage and affective predictors of change in relationship satisfaction. *Journal of Personality and Social Psychology, 45*, 587–597.

Levenson, R. W., & Gottman, J. M. (1985). Physiological and affective predictors of change in relationship satisfaction. *Journal of Personality and Social Psychology, 49*, 85–94.

Levenson, R. W., Carstensen, L. L., & Gottman, J. M. (1994). The influence of age and gender on affect, physiology, and their interrelations: A study of long-term marriages. *Journal of Personality and Social Psychology, 45*, 587–597.

Levine, T. R., & Boster, F. J. (1996). The impact of self and others' argumentativeness on talk about controversial issues. *Communication Quarterly, 44*, 345–358.

Levine, T. R., & Kotowski, M. R. (2010). Measuring argumtativeness and verbal aggression: psychometric concerns and advances. In Avtgis, T. A., & Rancer, A. S. (Eds.) (2010). *Arguments, aggression, and conflct: New directions in theory and research* (pp. 67–82). New York: Routledge.

Lipkus, I., & Rusbult, C. (1993). Reactions to individuals who are consistently positive or negative: The impact of differing interaction goals. *Human Relations, 46*, 481–499.

Littlejohn, S. W., & Jabusch, D. M. (1982). Communication competence: Model and application. *Journal of Applied Communication Research, 10*, 29–36.

Lloyd, S. A. (1987). Conflict in premarital relationships: Differential perceptions of males and females. *Family Relations, 36*, 290–294.

Lloyd, S. A., & Emery, B. C. (2000) The context and dynamics of intimate aggression against women. *Journal of Social and Personal Relationships, 17*, 503–522.

Locke, E. A., & Latham, G. P. (1990) *A theory of goal setting and task performance*. Englewood Cliffs, NJ: Prentice Hall.

Locke, H. J. (1951). *Predicting adjustment in marriage*. New York: Holt.

Lubit, R., & Russett, B. (1984). The effects of drugs on decision-making. *Journal of Conflict Resolution, 28*, 85–102.

Macdonald, G., Zanna, M. P, & Holmes, J. G. (2000). An experimental test of the role of alcohol in relationship conflict. *Journal of Experimental Social Psychology, 36*, 182–193.

MacGeorge, E., & Burleson, B. R. (2003). Comforting messages. In M. L. Knapp, J. A. Daly, & G. R. Miller (Eds.), *Handbook of interpersonal communication, 3rd edition*. Thousand Oaks, CA: Sage.

Makepeace, J. M. (1983). Life events, stress, and courtship violence. *Family Relations, 30,* 97–102.

Malarkey, W. B., Kiecolt-Glaser, J. K., Perl, D., & Glaser, R. Hostile behavior during marital conflict alters pituitary and adrenal hormones. *Psychosomatic Medicine, 56,* 41–51.

Malis, R. S. (2006). Serial arguing in relationships: Implications for individuals' well-being. Dissertation completed at Northwestern University.

Malis, R. S., & Roloff, M. E. (2006a). Demand/withdraw patterns in serial arguments: Implications for well-being. *Human Communication Research, 32,* 198–216.

Malis, R. S., & Roloff, M. E. (2006b). Features of serial arguing and coping strategies: Links with stress and well-being. In B. A. Le Poire, & R. M. Dailey (Eds.) *Applied research in interpersonal communication: Family communication, health communication, and communicating across social boundaries.* New York: Peter Lang Publishers.

Maltby, J., & Day, L. (2004). Forgiveness and defense style. *The Journal of Genetic Psychology, 165,* 99–109.

Maltby, J., Macaskill, A., & Day, L. (2001). Failure to forgive self and others: A replication and extension of the relationship between forgiveness, personality, social desirability and general health. *Personality and Individual Differences, 30,* 881–885.

Mandler, G. (1993) Thought, memory, and learning: Effects of emotional stress. In L. Goldberger & S. Breznitz (Eds.), *The handbook of stress* (2nd ed., pp. 40–55). New York: Free Press.

Manusov, V. & Harvey, J. H. (2001) (Eds.). *Attribution, communication behavior, and close relationships.* Cambridge, UK: Cambridge University Press.

Margolin, G., & Wampold, B. E. (1982). Sequential analysis of conflict and accord in distressed and nondistressed marital partners. *Journal of Consulting and Clinical Psychology, 49,* 554–567.

Margolin, G., John, R. S., & Gleberman, L. (1988). Affective responses to conflictual discussions in violent and nonviolent couples. *Journal of Consulting and Clinical Psychology, 56,* 24–33.

Markman, H. J., Renick, M. J., Floyd, F. J., Stanley, S. M., & Clements, M. (1993). Preventing marital distress through communication and conflict management training: A 4-and 5-year follow up. *Journal of Consulting and Clinical Psychology, 61,* 70–77.

Marks, S. R., Huston, T. L., Johnson, E. M., & MacDermid, S. M. (2001). Role balance among White married couples. *Journal of Marriage and Family, 63,* 1083–1098.

Markus, H. R., & Kitayama, S. (1991). Culture and the self: Implications for cognition, emotion, and motivation. *Psychological Review, 2,* 224–253.

Markus, H. R., & Kitayama, S. (1998). The cultural psychology of personality. *Journal of Cross-Cultural Psychology 29,* 63–87.

Marshall, L. L. (1994). Physical and psychological abuse. In W. R. Cupach & B. H. Spitzberg (Eds.), *The dark side of interpersonal communication* (pp. 281–311). Hillsdale, NJ: Erlbaum.

Marshall, L. L., & Rose, P. (1987). Gender, stress, and violence in the adult relationships of a sample of college students. *Journal of Social and Personal Relationships, 4,* 299–316.

Martin, L. L., Achee, J. W., Ward, D. W., & Harlow, T. F. (1993). The role of cognition and effort in the use of emotions to guide behavior. In R. E. Wyer, T. K. Srull, & L. Berkowitz (Eds.). *Perspectives on anger and emotions* (vol. 6, pp. 147–157). Hillsdale, NJ: Erlbaum.

Martin, M. M., Anderson, C. M., & Horvath, G. L. (1996). Feelings about verbal aggression: Justifications for sending and hurt from receiving verbally aggressive messages. *Communication Research Reports, 13,* 19–26.

Marwell, G., & Schmitt, D. R. (1967). Dimensions of compliance-gaining behaviors: An empirical analysis. *Sociometry, 30,* 350–364.

McCarthy, B. W. (1997). Strategies and techniques for revitalizing a nonsexual marriage. *Journal of Sex & Marital Therapy, 23,* 231–240.

McCarthy, B. W. (2001). Integrating sex therapy strategies and techniques into marital therapy. *Journal of Family Psychotherapy, 12,* 45–53.

McCarthy, B. W. (2003). Marital sex as it ought to be. *Journal of Family Psychotherapy, 14,* 1–12.

McCarthy, B., & McCarthy, E. (2009). *Discovering your couple sexual style: The key to sexual satisfaction.* Boca Raton, FL: CRC Press.

McCullough, M. E., & Rachal, K. C. (1997). Interpersonal forgiving in close relationships. *Journal of Personality and Social Psychology, 73,* 321–336.

McCullough, M. E., Pargament, K. I., & Toresen, C. E. (2000). The psychology of forgiveness: History, conceptual issues, and overview. In M. E. McCullough, K. I., Pargament, & C. E. Toresen (Eds.), *Forgiveness: Theory, research and practice* (pp. 1–14). London: Guilford Press.

McCullough, M. E., Pargament, K. I., & Toresen, C. E. (Eds.). (2000). *Forgiveness: Theory, research and practice.* London: Guilford Press.

McCullough, M. E., Sandage, S. J., & Worthington, L. L. (1997). *To forgive is human.* Downers Grove IL: Intervarsity Press.

McDonald, G. W. (1980). Family power: The assessment of a decade of theory and research. 1970–1979. *Journal of Marriage and the Family, 42,* 841–854.

McEwen, B. S. (1998). Protective and damaging effects of stress mediators. *New England Journal of Medicine, 388,* 171–179.

McGraw, K. M. (1987). Guilt following transgression: An attribution of responsibility approach. *Journal of Personality and Social Psychology, 53,* 247–256.

McLaughlin, M. L., Cody, M. J., & French, K. (1990). Account-giving and the attribution of responsibility: Impressions of traffic offenders. In M. J. Cody & M. L. McLaughlin (Eds.), *The psychology of tactical communication.* Clevedor, Avon, England: Multilingual Matters. LTD.

Messman, S. J., & Canary, D. J. (1998). Conflict patterns. In W. R. Cupach & B. H. Spitzberg (Eds.), *The darkside of interpersonal relationships.* Mahwah, NJ: Lawrence Erlbaum Associates.

Metz, M. E., & Epstein, N. (2002). Assessing the role of relationship conflict and in sexual dysfunction. *Journal of Sex and Marital Therapy, 28,* 139–164.

Miller, J. D., & Campbell, W. K. (2010). The case for using research on trait narcissism as a building block for understanding narcissistic personality disorder. *Personality Disorders: Theory, Research, and Treatment, 1(3),* 180–191.

Miller, C. W., & Roloff, M. E. (2006). The perceived characteristics of irresolvable, resolvable and resolved intimate conflicts: Is there evidence of intractability? *International Journal of Conflict Management, 17,* 291–315.

Mischel, W. (2004). Toward an integrative model for CBT: Encompassing behavior, cognition, affect, and process. *Behavior Therapy, 35,* 185–203.

Molden, D. C., & Finkel, E. J. (2010). Motivations for promotion and prevention and the role of trust and commitment in interpersonal forgiveness. *Journal of Experimental Social Psychology, 46,* 255–268.

Mongeau, P. A., & Hale, J. L. (1990). *Attributions of responsibility for relational transgressions.* Paper presented at the Annual meeting of the Western Speech Communication Association. Sacramento CA.

Mongrain, M., & Vettese, L. C. (2003). Conflict over emotional expression: Implications for interpersonal communication. *Personality and Social Psychology Bulletin, 29,* 545–555.

Morf, C. C., & Rhodewalt, F. (2001). Unraveling the paradoxes of narcissism: A dynamic self-regulatory processing model. *Psychologial Inquiry, 12, 177–196.*

Morokoff, P. J., & Gillilland, R. (1993). Stress, sexual functioning, and marital satisfaction. *The Journal of Sex Research, 30,* 43–53.

Morrill, C., & Thomas, C. K. (1992). Organizational conflict management as a disputing process: The problem of social escalation. *Human Communication Research, 18,* 400–429.

Newell, S. E., & Stutman, R. K. (1991). The episodic nature of social confrontation. In A. Andersen (Ed.), *Communication Yearbook 14.* Beverly Hills, CA: Sage.

Newton, D. A., & Burgoon, J. K. (1990a). Nonverbal conflict behaviors: Functions, strategies, and tactics. In D. D. Cahn (Ed.) *Intimates in conflict: A communication perspective* (pp. 77–104). Hillsdale, NJ: Erlbaum.

Newton, D. A., & Burgoon, J. K. (1990b). The use and consequences of verbal influence strategies during interpersonal disagreements. *Human Communication Research, 16,* 477–518.

Nicotera, A. M., & Dorsey, L. K. (2006). Individual and interactive process in organizational conflict. In J. G. Oetzel, & S. Ting-Toomey (Eds.), *The Sage handbook of conflict communication: Integrating theory, research, and practice* (pp. 293–326). Thousand Oaks, CA: Sage.

Nicotera, A. M., & Robinson, N. M. (2010). Culture and aggressive communication. In Avtgis, T. A., & Rancer, A. S. (Eds.) (2010). *Arguments, aggression, and conflict: New directions in theory and research.* (pp. 100–123). New York: Routledge.

Nisbett, R. E., & Ross, L. (1980). *Human inference: Strategies and shortcomings of social judgment.* Englewood Cliffs, NJ: Prentice-Hall.

Noll, J. (2003). The process of forgiving childhood sexual abuse: A prospective study. Paper presented at the Conference of Forgiveness in Atlanta.

Noller, P., Feeney, J. A., Bonnell, D., & Callen, V. (1994). A longitudinal study of conflict in early marriage. *Journal of Social and Personal Relationships, 11,* 233–252.

Novaco, R., Stokols, D., & Milanesi, L. (1990). Objective and subjective dimensions of travel impedance as determinants of commuting stress. *American Journal of Community Psychology, 18,* 231–257.

North, J. (1987). Wrongdoing and forgiveness. *Philosophy, 62,* 499–508.

O'Keefe, B. J. (1988). The logic of message design: Individual differences in reasoning about communication. *Communication Monographs, 55,* 80–103.

O'Keefe, B. J. (1991). Message design logic and the management of multiple goals. In K. Tracy (Ed.), *Understanding face-to-face interaction: Issues linking goals and discourse* (pp. 131–166). Hillsdale, NJ: Lawrence Erlbaum.

O'Keefe, B. J., & McCornack, S. A. (1987). Message design logic and message goal structure: Effects on perceptions of message quality in regulative communication situations. *Human Communication Research, 14,* 68–92.

O'Keefe, B. J., & Shepherd, G. J. (1987). The pursuit of multiple objectives in face-to-face persuasive interactions: Effects of construct differentiation on message selection. *Communication Monographs, 54,* 396–419.

O'Sullivan, P. B. (2000). What you don't know won't hurt me: Impression management functions of communication channels in relationships. *Human Communication Research, 26,* 403–431.

Oetzel, J. G., & Ting-Toomey, S. (2003). Face concerns in interpersonal conflict: A cross-cultural empirical test of the face negotiation theory. *Communication Research, 30,* 599–624.

Oetzel, J. G., & Ting-Toomey, S. (2006) (Eds.), *The Sage handbook of conflict communication: Integrating theory, research, and practice.* Thousand Oaks, CA: Sage.

Oetzel, J. G., Ting-Toomey, S., & Yokochi, Y. (2000). A typology of facework behaviors in conflicts with best friends and relative strangers. *Communication Quarterly, 48,* 397–419.

Oetzel, J. G., Ting-Toomey, S., Yokochi, Y., Masumoto, T., & Takai, J. (2000). A typology of facework behaviors in conflicts with best friends and relative strangers. *Communication Quarterly, 48,* 397–419.

Oetzel, J. G., Arcos, B., Mabizela, P., Weinman, A. M., Zhang, Q. (2006). Historical, political, and spritual factors of conflict: Understanding conflict perspectives and communication in the Muslim World, China, Colombia, and South Africa. In J. G. Oetzel, & S. Ting-Toomey (Eds.), *The Sage handbook of conflict communication: Integrating theory, research, and practice* (pp. 549–576). Thousand Oaks, CA: Sage.

Oetzel, J., Ting-Toomey, S., Chew-Sanchez, M. I., Harris, R., Wilcox, R., & Stumpf, S. (2003). Face and facework in conflicts with parents and siblings: A cross-cultural comparison of Germans, Japanese, Mexicans, and U.S. Americans. *Journal of Family Communication, 3,* 67–93.

Oetzel, J. G., Ting-Toomey, S., Masumoto, T., Yokochi, Y., Pan, X, Takai, J., & Wilcox, R. (2001). Face behaviors in interpersonal conflicts: A cross-cultural comparison of Germany, Japan, China, and the United States. *Communication Monographs 68,* 235–258.

Ognibene, T. C., & Collins, N. L. (1998). Adult attachment styles: Perceived social support and coping strategies. *Journal of Social and Personal Relationships, 15,* 323–345.

Ohbuchi, K. I., Chiba, S., & Fukushima, O. (1996). Mitigation of interpersonal conflicts: Politeness and time pressure. *Personality and Social Psychology Bulletin, 22,* 1035–1042.

Ohbuchi, K. I., Kameda, M, & Agarie, N. (1989). Apology as aggression control: Its role in mediating appraisal of and response to harm. *Journal of Personality and Social Psychology, 56,* 219–227.

Ohbuchi, K. I., & Tedeschi, J. T. (1997). Multiple goals and tactical behaviors in social conflicts. *Journal of Applied Social Psychology, 27,* 2177–2199.

Olson, L., & Braithwaite, D. (2004). "If you hit me again, I'll hit you back." Conflict management strategies of individuals experiencing aggression during conflicts. *Communication Studies, 55,* 271–285.

Orden, S. R., & Bradburn, N. M. (1968). Dimensions of marriage happiness. *The American Journal of Sociology, 73,* 715–731.

Orthner, D. K. (1975). Leisure activity patterns and marital satisfaction over the marital career. *Journal of Marriage and Family, 37,* 91–102.

Orthner, D. K., & Mancini, J. A. (1990). Leisure impacts on family interaction and cohesion. *Journal of Leisure Research 22,* 125–137.

Orthner, D. K., & Mancini, J. A. (1991). Benefits of leisure for family bonding. In B. L. Driver, P. J. Brown, & G. L. Peterson, (Eds.), *Benefits of leisure,* (pp. 215–247). State College, PA: Venture Publishing.

Oyserman, D., Coon, H. M., & Kemmelmeir, M. (2002). Rethinking individualism and collectivism: Evaluation of theoretical assumptions and meta-analysis. *Psychological Bulletin, 128,* 3–72.

Paolucci, E. O., & Violato, C. (2004). A meta-analysis of the published research on the affective, cognitive, and behavioral effects of corporal punishment. *Journal of Psychology, 138,* 197–221.

Papp, L. M., Kouros, C. D., & Cummings, E. M. (2009) Demand-withdraw patterns in marital conflict in the home. *Personal Relationships, 16,* 285–300.

Pargament, K. I., McCullough, M. E., & Thoresen,, C. F. (2000). The frontier of forgiveness: Seven directions for psychological study and practice. In M. F. McCullough, K. I., Pargament, & C. F. Thoresen (Eds.), *Forgiveness: Theory, research and practice* (pp. 299–319). London: Guilford Press.

Pasch, L. A., & Bradbury, T. N. (1998). Social support, conflict, and the development of marital dysfunction. *Journal of Consulting and Clinical Psychology, 66,* 219–230.

Pasch, L. A., Bradbury, T. N., Davila, J., & Sullivan, K. T. (1999). Social support and the development of marital dysfunctions: Extension of previous findings. In K. W. Harris (Chair), *Beyond marital conflict: Social support and the search for unexplained variance.* Symposium conducted at the 33rd annual meeting of the Association for the Advancement of Behavior Therapy, Toronto.

Pauhus, D, L. (1998). Interpersonal and intrapsychic adaptiveness of trait enhancement: A mixed blessing? *Journal of Personality and Social Psychology, 74,* 1197–1208.

Pearce, W. B., & Cronin, V. F. (1980). *Communication, action, and meaning: The creation of social reality.* New York: Praeger.

Pearson, J. C., & Daniels, T. D. (1988). On, what tangled webs we weave: Concerns about current conceptualizations of communication competence. *Communication Reports, 1,* 95–100.

Pervin, L. A. (1989a). Goal concepts in personality and social psychology: A historical introduction. In L. A. Pervin (Ed.), *Goal concepts in personality and social psychology* (pp. 1–13). Hillsdale, NJ: Lawrence Erlbaum.

Pervin, L. A. (1989b). Goals concepts: Themes, issues, and questions. In L. A. Pervin (Ed.), *Goal concepts in personality and social psychology* (pp. 473–479). Hillsdale, NJ: Lawrence Erlbaum.

Peterson, C. C., & Peterson, J. L. (1990). Fight or flight: Factors influencing children's and sults; decisions to avoid of confront conflict. *Journal of Genetic Psychology, 151,* 461–471.

Peterson, D. R. (1989). Interpersonal goal conflict. In L. A. Pervin (Ed.), *Goal concepts in personality and social psychology* (pp. 327–361). Hillsdale, NJ: Lawrence Erlbaum.

Pierce, G. R., Sarason, B. R., & Sarason, I. G. (1992). General and specific support expectations and stress as predictors of perceived supportiveness: An experimental study. *Journal of Personality and Social Psychology, 63,* 297–307.

Pines, A.M. (1993) Burnout. In L. Goldberger & S. Breznitz (Eds.) *Handbook of Stress* (2nd Ed. pp. 386–402). New York: Free Press.

Pistole, M. C. (1989). Attachment in adult romantic relationships: Style of conflict resolution and relationship satisfaction. *Journal of Social and Personal Relationships, 6,* 505–510.

Planap. S. (1999). *Communicating emotions: Social, moral, and cultural process.* Cambridge, UK: Cambridge University Press.

Popper, M. (2002). Narcissism and attachment patterns of personalized and socialized charismatic leaders. *Journal of Social and Personal Relationships, 19,* 797–809.

Portello, J. Y., & Long, B. C. (2002). Appraisals and coping with workplace interpersonal stress: A model for women managers. *Journal of Counseling Psychology, 48*, 144–156.

Powers, R. S., & Reiser, C. (2006). Gender and self-perceptions of social power. *Social Behavior and Personality, 33*, 553–568.

Powers, S. I., Pietromonaco, P. R., Gunlicks, M., & Sayer, A. (2006). Dating couples' attachment styles and patterns of cortisol reactivity and recovery in response to a relationship conflict. *Journal of Personality and Social Psychology, 90*, 613–628

Powers, R. S., & Reiser, C. (2006). Gender and self-perceptions of social power. *Social Behavior and Personality, 33*, 553–568.

Pronin, E. (2007). Perception and misperception of bias in human judgment. *Trends in Cognitive Sciences, 11*, 37–43.

Proulx, C. M., Buehler, C., & Helms, H. (2009). Moderators of the link between marital hostility and change in spouses' depressive symptoms. *Journal of Family Psychology, 23*, 540–550.

Putnam, L. L. (2006). Definitions and approaches to conflict and communication. In J. G. Oetzel, & S. Ting-Toomey (Eds.), *The Sage handbook of conflict communication: Integrating theory, research, and practice* (pp. 1–12). Thousand Oaks, CA: Sage.

Putnam, L. L., & Folger, J. P. (1988). Communication, conflict, and dispute resolution: the study of interaction and the development of conflict theory. *Communication Research, 15*, 349–359.

Putnam, L. L., & Jones, T. S. (1992). The role of communication in bargaining. *Human Communication Research, 8*, 262–280.

Putnam, L. L., & Poole, M. S. (1987). Conflict and negotiation. In F. M. Jablin, L. L. Putnam, K. H. Roberts, & L. W. Porter (Eds.), *Handbook of organizational communication* (pp. 549–599). Beverly Hills, CA: Sage.

Putnam, L. L., & Wilson, C. E. (1982). Communicative strategies in organizational conflicts: Reliability and validity of a measurement scale. In M. Burgoon (Ed.), *Communication yearbook 6* (pp. 131–144). New York: Praeger.

Rahim, M. A. (1983). A measure of styles of handling interpersonal conflict. *Academy of Management Journal, 26*, 368–376.

Rahim, M. A. (1990). *Theory and research in conflict management.* New York: Praeger.

Raush, H. L., Barry, W.A., Hertel, R. J., & Swain, M.A. (1974). *Communication, conflict, and marriage.* San Francisco, CA: Jossey-Bass.

Raven, B. H., & Kruglanski, A. W. (1970). *The Structure of conflict.* New York: Academic Press.

Read, S. J., & Miller, L. C. (1989). Inter-personalism: Toward a goal-based theory of persons in relationships. In L. A. Pervin (Ed.), *Goal concepts in personality and social psychology* (pp. 413–471). Hillsdale, NJ: Lawrence Erlbaum.

Repenning, N. P., & Sterman, J. (2002). Capability traps and self-confirming attribution errors in the dynamics of process improvement. *Administrative Science Quarterly, 47*, 265–295.

Repetti, R. L. (1993). The effects of workload and the social environment at work on health. In L. Goldberger & S. Breznitz (Eds.), *The handbook of stress* (2nd ed., pp. 368–385). New York: Free Press.

Repetti, R. L. (1994). Short-term and long-term processes linking job stressors to father-child interaction. *Social Development, 3*, 1–15.

Repetti, R. L., & Wood, J. (1997). Effects of daily stress at work on mothers' interaction with preschoolers. *Journal of Family Psychology, 11*, 90–108.

Retzinger, S. M. (1991b). Shame, anger, and conflict: case-study of emotional violence. *Journal of Family Violence, 6*(1), 37–59.

Richardson, D. R., Green, L. R., & Lago, T. (1998). The relationship between perspective taking and nonaggressive responding in the face of an attack. *Journal of Personality, 66*, 235–256.

Risen, J.L., & Gilovich, T. (2007). Target and observer differences in the acceptance of questionable apologies. *Journal of Personality and Social Psychology, 92*, 418–433.

Rivers, S. E., Brackett, M.A., Katulak, N. A., & Salovey, P. (2007). Regulating anger and sadness: An exploration of discrete emotions in emotion regulation. *Journal of Happiness Studies, 8*, 393–427.

Robey, E. B., Canary, D. J., & Burggraf, C. S. (1998). Conversational maintenance behaviors of husbands and wives: An observational analyses. In D. J. Canary & K. Dindia (Eds.), *Sex differences and similarities in communication: Critical essays and empirical investigations of sex and gender in interaction* (pp. 373–392). Hillsdale, NJ: Lawrence Erlbaum Associates.

Robin, A. L., & Foster, S. L. (1989). *Negotiating parent–adolescent conflict: A behavioral systems approach*. New York: Guilford.

Robinson, M. D., & Johnson, J. T. (1997). Is it emotion or is it stress? Gender stereotypes and the perception of subjective experience. *Sex Roles, 36*, 235–248.

Robles, T. F., & Kiecolt-Glaser, J. K. (2003). The physiology of marriage: Pathways to health. *Physiology and Behavior, 79*, 409–416.

Rogan, R. G., & LaFrance, B. H. (2003). An examination of the relationship between verbal aggressiveness, conflict management strategies, and conflict interaction goals. *Communication Quarterly, 51*, 458–469.

Rogers, B. (2004). Intelligent conflict: Growth through awareness and change. *The Journal for Quality and Participation, 27 (2)*, 14–16.

Rogge, R. D., & Bradbury, T. N. (1999). Till violence does us part: The differing roles of communication and aggression in predicting adverse marital outcomes. *Journal of Consulting and Clinical Psychology, 67*, 340–351.

Rohsenow, D., & Bachorowski, J. (1984). Effects of alcohol and expectancies on verbal aggression in men and women. *Journal of Abnormal Psychology, 93*, 418–432.

Roloff, M. E. (1987). Communication and conflict. In C. R. Berger & S. H. Chaffee (Eds.), *Handbook of communication science* (pp. 484–534). Thousand Oaks, CA: Sage.

Roloff, M. E. (2009). Links between conflict management research and practice. *Journal of Applied Communication Research, 37*, 339–348.

Roloff, M. C., & Cloven, D. H. (1990). The chilling effect in interpersonal relationships: The reluctance to speak one's mind. D. D. Cahn et al. (Eds.), *Intimates in conflict: A communication perspective* (pp. 49–76). Hillsdale, NJ: Erlbaum.

Roloff, M. E., & Cloven, D. H. (1994). When partners transgress: Maintaining violated relationships. In D. J. Canary & L. Stafford (Eds.), *Communication and relational maintenance* (pp. 23–43). San Diego: Academic Press, Inc.

Roloff, M. E., & Ifert D. (1998). Antecedents and consequences of explicit agreements to declare a topic taboo in dating relationships. *Personal Relationships, 5*, 191–205.

Roloff, M. E., & Janiszewski, C. A. (1989). Overcoming obstacles to interpersonal compliance: A principle of message construction. *Human Communication Research, 16*, 33–61.

Roloff, M. E., & Johnson, K. L. (2002). Serial arguing over the relational life course: Antecedents and consequences. In A. L. Vangelisti, H. T. Reis, & M. A. Fitzpatrick (Eds.), *Stability and change in relationships. Advances in personal relationships* (pp. 107–128). New York: Cambridge University Press.

Roloff, M. E., & Reznik, R. M. (2008). Communication during serial arguments: Connections with individuals' mental and physical well-being. In M. T. Motley (Ed.), *Studies in Applied Communication* (pp. 97–119). Thousand Oaks, CA: Sage.

Rose, A. J., & Asher, S. R. (1999). Children's goals and strategies in response to conflicts within a friendship. *Developmental Psychology, 35,* 69–79.

Rotter, J. B. (1966). Generalized expectancies for internal vs. external locus of control of reinforcement. *Psychological Monographs, 80* (Whole No. 609).

Ruesch, J. & Bateson, G. (1951). *Communication, the social matrix of psychiatry.* New York: WW Norton & Co.

Rule, B. G., Bisanz, G. L., & Kohn, M. (1985). Anatomy of a persuasion schema: Targets, goals, and strategies. *Journal of Personality and Social Psychology, 48,* 1127–1140.

Rusbult, C. E., & Martz, J. M. (1995). Remaining in an abusive relationship: An investment model analysis of nonvoluntary dependence. Personality *and Social Psychology Bulletin, 21,* 558–571.

Rye, M. S., & Pargament, K. I. (2002). Forgiveness and romantic relationships in college: Can it heal a wounded heart? *Journal of Clinical Psychology, 58,* 419–441.

Sabourin, T. C., Infante, D. C., & Rudd, J. E. (1993). Verbal aggression in marriages: A comparison of violent, distressed, and nondistressed couples. *Human Communication Research, 20,* 245–267.

Saeki, M. & O'Keefe, B. J. (1994). Refusals and rejections: Designing messages to serve multiple goals. *Human Communication Research, 21,* 67–102.

Sahl, J. C., Cohen, L. H., & Dasch, K. B. (2009). Hostility, interpersonal competence, and daily dependent stress: A daily model of stress generation. *Cognitive Theory Research, 33,* 199–210.

Samp, J. A., & Solomon, D. H. (1999). Communicative responses to problematic events in close relationships II. *Communication Research, 26,* 193–239.

Sanders, R. E. (1991). The two-way relationship between talk in social interactions and actors' goals and plans. In K. Tracy (Ed.), *Understanding face-to-face interaction: Issues linking goals and discourse* (pp. 167–188). Hillsdale, NJ: Lawrence Erlbaum.

Sanderson, S. A., & Karetsky, K. H. (2002). Intimacy goals and strategies of conflict resolution in dating relationships: A mediational analysis. *Journal of Social and Personal Relationships, 19,* 317–337.

Scaife, J. C., & Duka, T. (2009). Behavioural measures of frontal lobe function in a population of young social drinkers with binge drinking pattern. *Pharmacology, Biochemistry, and Behavior, 93,* 354–362.

Schafer, R., B., Wickrama, K. A. S., & Keith, P. M. (1998). Stress in marital interaction and change in depression. *Journal of Family Issues, 19,* 578–594.

Schaller, M., Conway, L. G. (1999). Influence of impression-management goals on the emerging contents of group stereotypes: Support for a social-evolutionary process. *Personality and Social Psychology Bulletin, 25,* 819–833.

Schieman, S. (2000). Education and the activation, course, and management of anger. *Journal of Health and Social Behavior, 41,* 20–39.

Schlenker, B. R., & Barby, B. W. (1981). The use of apologies in social predicaments. *Social Psychology Quarterly, 44,* 271–278.

Schlenker, B. R., & Weigold, M. F. (1989). Goals and the self-identification process: Constructing desired identities. In L. A. Pervin (Ed.), *Goal concepts in personality and social psychology* (pp. 243–283). Hillsdale, NJ: Lawrence Erlbaum.

Schönbach, P. (1990). *Account episodes: The management or escalation of conflict.* New York: Cambridge University Press.

Schönbach, P, & Kleibaumhuter, P. (1990). Severity of reproach and devensiveness of accounts. In M. J. Cody & M. L. McLaughlin (Eds.), *The psychology of tactical communication.* Clevedon, Avon, England: Multilingual Matters.

Schriber, J., Larwook, L, & Peterson, J. (2001). Bias in the attribution of marital conflict. *Journal of Marriage and Family, 47,* 717–722.

Schumann, K., & Ross, M. (2010). Why women apologize more than men: Gender differences in thresholds for perceiving offensive behavior. *Psychological Science Online First,* 1–7.

Sedikides, C. (1990). Effects of fortuitously activated constructs versus activated communication goals on person impressions. *Journal of Personality and Social Psychology, 58,* 397–408.

Segrin, C. (1990). A meta-analytic review of social skill deficits in depression. *Communication Monographs, 57,* 292–308.

Seibold, D. R., Cantrill, J. G., & Meyers, R. A. (1994). Communication and interpersonal influence. In M. L. Knapp & G. R. Miller (Eds.), *Handbook of interpersonal communication, 2nd edition* (pp. 542–588). Thousand Oaks, CA: Sage.

Selman, R. L. (1980). *The growth of interpersonal understanding: Developmental and clinical analyses.* New York: Academic Press.

Sereno, K. K., Welch, M., & Braaten, D. (1987). Interpersonal conflict: Effects of variations in manner of expressing anger and justification for anger upon perceptions of appropriateness, competence, and satisfaction. *Journal of Applied Communication Research, 15,* 128–143.

Sessa, B. I. (1996). Using perspective taking to manage conflict and affect in teams. *The Journal of Applied Behavioral Science, 32,* 101–115.

Shiner, D. (1998). Aggressive driving: the contribution of the drivers and the situation. *Transportation Research Part F: Traffic Psychology and Behavior, 1,* 137–160.

Siegert, J. R., & Stamp, G. H. (1994). "Our first big fight" as a milestone in the development of close relationships. *Communication Monographs, 61,* 345–360.

Siegman, A. W., & Snow, S. C. (1997). The outward expression of anger, the inward experience of anger and CVR: The role of vocal expression. *Journal of Behavioral Medicine, 20,* 29–45.

Sillars, A. L. (1980). The sequential and distributional structure of conflict interactions as a function of attributions concerning the locus of responsibility and stability of conflicts. In D. Nimmo (Ed.), *Communication Yearbook 4* (pp. 217–235). New Brunswick, NJ: Transaction.

Sillars, A. L. (1985). Interpersonal perception in relationships. In W. J. Ickes (Ed.), *Compatible and incompatible relationships* (pp. 277–305). New York: Springer-Verlag.

Sillars, A. L. (1998). (Mis)Understanding. In B. H. Spitzberg & W. R. Cupach (Eds.). *The dark side of personal relationships* (pp. 73–102). Mahwah, NJ: Lawrence Earlaum Associates.

Sillars, A. L., & Canary, D. J. (in press). Conflict and relational quality in families. In A. L. Vangelisti (Ed.), *Handbook of family communication* (2nd ed.). New York: Routledge.

Sillars, A. L., Canary, D. J., & Tafoya, M. (2004). Communication, conflict, and the quality of family relationships. In A. L. Vangelisti (Ed.), *Handbook of family interaction* (pp. 413–446). Mahwah, NJ: Lawrence Erlbaum Associates.

Sillars, A. L., Coletti, S. F., Parry, D., & Rogers, M. A. (1982). Coding verbal conflicts: Non-verbal and perceptual correlates of the "avoidance-distributive-integrative" distinction. *Human Communication Research, 9,* 83–95.

Sillars, A. L., & Parry, D. (1982). Stress, cognition, and communication in interpersonal conflicts. *Communication Research, 9,* 201–226.

Sillars, A. L., Pike, G. R., Jones, T. S., and Murphy, M. A. (1984) Communication and understanding in marriage. *Human Communication Research. 10,* 317–350.

Sillars, A. L., Roberts, L. J., Dun, T., & Leonard, K. (2001). Affective influences on communication and attribution in relationships. In V. Manusov & J. H. Harvey (Eds.), *Attribution, communication, behavior, and close relationships: Advances in personal relations* (pp. 193–210). New York: Cambridge University Press.

Sillars, A. L., Roberts, L. J., Leonard, K. E., & Dun, T. (2000), Cognition during marital conflict: The relationship of thought and talk. *Journal of Social and Personal Relationships, 1,* 479–502.

Sillars, A. L., Smith, T., & Koerner, A. (2010) Misattributions contributing to empathic (in)accuracy during parent–adolescent conflict discussions. *Journal of Social and Personal Relationships, 27,* 727–748.

Sillars, A. L., & Weisberg, J. (1987). Conflict as a social skill. In M. E. Roloff & G. R. Miller (Eds.), *Interpersonal processes: New directions in communication research* (pp. 140–171). Newbury Park, CA: Sage.

Sillars, A. L., Weisberg, J., Burggraf, C. S., & Zietlow, P. H. (1990). Communication and understanding revisited: Married couples' understanding and recall of conversations. *Communication Research, 17,* 500–522.

Sillars, A. L., & Wilmot, W. W. (1994). Communication strategies in conflict and mediation. In J. A. Daly & J. M. Wiemann (Eds.), *Strategic interpersonal communication* (pp. 163–190). Hillsdale, NJ: Erlbaum.

Simpson, J. A., Collins, W. A., Tran, S. S., & Haydon, K. C. (2007). Attachment and the experience and expression of emotion in romantic relationships: A developmental perspective. *Journal of Personality and Social Psychology, 92,* 355–367.

Simpson, J. A., Rholes, W. S., & Phillips, D. (1996). Conflict in close relationships: An attachment perspective. *Journal of Personality and Social Psychology, 71,* 899–914.

Smedes, L. B. (1998). Stations on the journey from forgiveness to hope. In E. L. Worthington (Ed.). *Dimensions of forgiveness: Psychological research and theological perspectives* (pp. 341–354). Philadelphia, PA: Templeton.

Smith, K. J., Snyder, T. J., & Monsma, B. R. (1988). Predicting relationship satisfaction from couple's use of leisure time. *American Journal of Family Therapy, 16,* 3–13.

Smith, P. B., Dugan, S., Peterson, A. F., & Leung, W. (1998). Individualism: Collectivism and the handling of disagreement. A 23 country study. *International Journal of Intercultural Relations, 22,* 351–367.

Solomon, D., Knobloch, L., & Fitzpatrick, M. (2004). Relational power, marital schema, and decisions to withhold complaints: An investigation of the chilling effect on confrontation in marriage. *Communication Studies, 55,* 146–169.

Soto, C. J., John, O. P., Gosling, S. D.,& Potter, J. (2008). The developmental psychometrics of big five self-reports: Acquiescence, factor structure, coherence, and differentiation from ages 10 to 20. *Journal of Personality and Social Psychology, 94,* 718–737.

Spitzberg, B. H. (2010). Intimate violence. In W. R. Cupach, D. J. Canary, & B. H. Spitzberg (Eds.), *Competence in interpersonal conflict* (pp. 211–251).

Spitzberg, B. H., Canary, D. J., & Cupach, W. R. (1994). A competence-based approach to the study of interpersonal conflict. In D. D. Cahn (Ed.), *Conflict in personal relationships* (pp. 183–202). Hillsdale, NJ: Lawrence Erlbaum.

Spitzberg, B. H., & Cupach, W. R. (1984). *Interpersonal communication competence.* Beverly Hills, CA: Sage.

Spitzberg, B. H., & Cupach, W. R. (1989). *Handbook of interpersonal competence research.* New York: Springer-Verlag.

Stafford, L., & Canary, D. J. (1991). Maintenance strategies and romantic relationship type, gender, and relational characteristics. *Journal of Social and Personal Relationships, 8,* 217–242.

Stafford, L., & Canary, D. J. (2006). Equity and interdependence as predictors of relational maintenance strategies. *Journal of Family Communication, 6,* 227–254.

Stern, S. B. (1999). Anger management in parent-adolescent conflict. *The American Journal of Family Therapy, 27,* 181–193.

Storti, C. (2001). *Old world/new world.* Yarmouth, ME: Intercultural Press.

Stoyva, J. M., & Carlson, J. G. (1993) In L. Goldberger & S. Breznitz (Eds.), *The handbook of stress* (2nd ed., pp. 724–756). New York: Free Press.

Strong, G., & Aron, A. (2006). The effect of shared participation in novel and challenging activities on experienced relationship quality. In K. D. Vohs & E. J. Finkel (Eds.), *Self and relationships: Connecting intrapersonal and interpersonal processes* (pp. 342–359). New York: The Guilford Press.

Suarez, E. C. (2004) C-Reactive Protein is associated with psychological risk factors of cardiovascular disease in apparently healthy adults. *Psychosomatic Medicine, 66,* 684–691.

Suarez, E. C., Harlan, E., Peoples, M. C., & Williams, R. B., Jr. (1993). Cardiovascular and emotional responses in women: The role of hostility and harassment. *Health Psychology, 12,* 459–468.

Suarez, E. C., Kuhn, C. M., Schanberg, S. M., Williams, R. B., Jr., Zimmermann, E. A. (1998). Neuroendocrine, cardiovascular, and emotional responses of hostile men: The role of interpersonal challenge, *Psychosomatic Medicine, 60,* 78–88.

Sullivan, K. T., Pasch, L. A., Johnson, M. D., & Bradbury, T. N. (2010). Social support, problem solving, and the longitudinal course of marriage. *Journal of Personality and Social Psychology, 98,* 631–644.

Sypher, B. D., & Sypher, H. E. (1984). Seeing ourselves as others see us: Convergence and divergence in assessments of communication behavior. *Communication Research, 11,* 97–115.

Takaku, S. (2001). Attribution and perspective taking on interpersonal forgiveness: A dissonance-attribution model of interpersonal conflict. *The Journal of Social Psychology, 141,* 494–508.

Tavris, C. (1989). *Anger, the misunderstood emotion.* New York: Simon and Schuster.

Tedeschi, J. T. (2001). Social power, influence, and aggression. In J. P. Forgas & K. D. Williams (Eds.), *Social influence: Direct and indirect processes* (pp. 109–128). New York: Psychology Press.

The good heart (2005). *Newsweek,* October 3, 2005.

Thompson, M.P., Saltzman, L. E., & Johnson, H. (2003). A comparison of risk factors for intimate partner violence-related injury across two national surveys on violence against women. *Violence Against Women, 9,* 438–457.

Thoresen, C. E., Luskin, F., & Harris, A. H. S. (1998). Science and forgiveness interventions: Reflection and recommendation. In E. L. Worthington (Ed.), *Dimensions of forgiveness: Psychological research and theological perspectives* (pp. 163–191). Philadelphia, PA: Templeton.

Ting-Toomey, S. (1983). An analysis of verbal communication patterns in high and low marital adjustment groups. *Human Communication Research, 9,* 306–319.

Ting-Toomey, S. (1985). Toward a theory of conflict and culture. In W. Gudykunst, L.

Steward, & S. Ting-Toomey (Eds.), *Communication, culture, and organizational processes* (pp. 71–86). Beverly Hills, CA: Sage.

Ting-Toomey, S. (1994). Managing intercultural conflicts effectively. In L. Samovar & R. Porter (Eds.), *Intercultural communication* (7th ed.) (pp. 360–373). Belmont, CA: Wadsworth.

Ting-Toomey, S. (1999). *Communicating across cultures.* New York: Guilford.

Ting-Toomey, S. (2004). Translating conflict face-negotiation theory into practice. In D. Landis, J. Bennett, & M. Bennett (Eds.), *Handbook of intercultural training* (3rd ed., pp. 217–248). Thousand Oaks, CA: Sage Publications.

Ting-Toomey, S. (2005). The matrix of face: An updated Face-Negotiation Theory. In W. B. Gudykunst (Ed.), *Theorizing about intercultural communication* (pp. 71–92). Thousand Oaks, CA: Sage.

Ting-Toomey, S. (2010). Intercultural conflict interaction competence: From theory to practice. In M. Guilherme, E. Glaser, & M. C. Mendez-Garcia (Eds.), *The intercultural dynamics of multicultural working* (pp. 21–40). Clevedon, Avon, UK: Mullilingual Matters.

Ting-Toomey, S., & Oetzel, J. G. (2001). *Managing intercultural conflict effectively.* Thousand Oaks, CA: Sage.

Ting-Toomey, S., Oetzel, J. G., & Yee-Jung, K. (2001). Self-construal types and conflict management styles. *Communication Reports, 14,* 87–104.

Ting-Toomey, S. & Takai, J. (2006). Explaining intercultural conflict: Promising approaches and future directions. In J. G. Oetzel & Ting-Toomey (Eds.). *The Sage handbook of conflict communication: Integrating theory, research, and practice* (pp. 691–724). Thousand Oaks, CA: Sage.

Thomsen, D. G., & Gilbert, D. G. (1998). Factors characterizing marital conflict states and traits: Physiological, affective, behavioral, and neurotic variable contributions to marital conflict and satisfaction. *Personality and Individual Differences, 25,* 833–855.

Tomaka, J., Blascovich, J., Kelsey, R. M., & Leitten, C. L. (1993). Subjective, physiological, and behavioral effects of threat and challenge appraisal. *Journal of Personality and Social Psychology, 65,* 248–260.

Tracy, K. (1984). The effect of multiple goals on conversational relevance and topic shift. *Communication Monographs, 51,* 274–288.

Tracy, K., & Coupland, N. (1990). Multiple goals in discourse: An overview of issues. *Journal of Language and Social Psychology, 9,* 1–13.

Trapp, R., & Hoff, N. (1985). A model of serial argument in interpersonal relationships. *Journal of the American Forensic Association, 22,* 1–11.

Trentham, S., & Larwood, L. (2001). Power and gender influences on responsibility attributions: The case of disagreements in relationships. *Journal of Social Psychology, 141,* 730–751.

Triandis, H. (1995). *Individualism and collectivism.* Boulder, CO: Westview.

Trubisky, P., Ting-Toomey, S., & Lin, S. (1991). The influence of individualism-collectivism and self-monitoring on conflict styles. *International Journal of Intercultural Relations, 16,* 65–84.

Trudel, G. (2002). Sexuality and marital life: Results of a survey. *Journal of Sex & Marital Therapy, 28,* 229–249.

Trumpeter, N., Watson, P. J., & O'Leary, B.J. (2006). Factors within multidimensional perfectionism scales: Complexity of relationships with self-esteem, narcissism, self-control, and self-criticism. *Personality and Individual Differences, 41,* 849–860.

Tsang, J., McCullough, M. E., & Fincham, F. (2006). The longitudinal association between forgiveness and relationship closeness and commitment. *Journal of Social and Clinical Psychology, 25*, 448–472.

Tucker, J. S., & Anders, S. L. (1999). Attachment style, interpersonal perception accuracy and relationship satisfaction in dating couples. *Personality and Social Psychology Bulletin, 25*(4), 403–412.

Turk, D. R., & Monahan, J. L. (1999). "Here I go again": An examination of repetitive behaviors during interpersonal conflicts. *Southern Communication Journal, 64*, 232–244.

Tutzauer, F., & Roloff, M. E. (1988). Communication processes leading to integrative agreements: Three paths to joint benefits. *Communication Research, 15*, 360–375.

Twenge, J. M., Konrath, S., Foster, Joshua D., Campbell, W. K., & Bushman, B. J. (2008). Further evidence of an increase in narcissism among college students. *Journal of Personality, 76*, 919–928.

Tyler, J. M. & Feldman, R. S. (2007). The double-edged sword of excuses: When do they help, when do they hurt. *Journal of Social and Clinical Psychology, 26*, 659–688.

Van de Vliert, E., & Euwema, M. C. (1994). Agreeableness and activeness as components of conflict behaviors. *Journal of Personality and Social Psychology, 66*, 674–687.

Van Kleef, G. A. (2010). Don't worry, be angry? Effects of anger on feelings, thoughts and actions in conflict and negotiation. In M. Potegal, G. Stemmler, & C. Spielberger (Eds). *International handbook of anger: Constituent and concomitant biological, psychological, and social processes.* pp. 5445–5559.

Van Kleef, G. A., DeDreu, C. K. W., & Manstead, A. S. R. (2010). An interpersonal approach to emotion in social decision making: The emotions as Social Information Model. *Advances in Experimental Social Psychology, 42*, 45–96.

Vangelisti, A. (2001). Making sense of hurtful interactions in close relationships: When hurt feelings create distance. Affective influences on communication and attribution in relationships. In V. Manusov & J. H. Harvey (Eds.), *Attribution, communication, behavior, and close relationships: Advances in personal relations* (pp. 38–58). New York: Cambridge University Press.

Vangelisti, A., & Young, S. L. (2000). When words hurt: The effects of perceived intentionality on interpersonal relationships. *Journal of Social and Personal Relationships, 17*, 395–424.

Varga, K. (1972). Marital cohesion as reflected in time budgets. In A. Szalai (Ed.), *The use of time* (pp. 82–104). The Hague, The Netherlands: Morton.

Voorpostel, M., Gershuny, J., & van der Lippe, T. (2007). Spending time together—changes in joint activities of couples over four decades. Retrieved from http://www.atususers.umd.edu/wip2/papers_i2007/Voorpostel.pdf.

Vuchinich, S. (1987). Starting and stopping spontaneous family conflicts. *Journal of Marriage and the Family, 49*, 591–601.

Vuchinich, S. (1990). The sequential organization of closing in verbal family conflict. In A. D. Grimshaw (Ed.), *Conflict talk: Sociolinguistic investigations of arguments in conversations* (pp. 118–138). Cambridge, UK: Cambridge University Press.

Waldron, V. R. (1990). Constrained rationality: Situational influences on information acquisition plans and tactics. *Communication Monographs, 57*, 184–201.

Waldron, V. R. (1997). Toward a theory of interactive conversational planning. In J. O. Greene (Ed.), *Message production: Advances in communication theory* (pp. 195–220). Mahwah, NJ: Lawrence Erlbaum.

Waldron, V. R. (2003). Relationship maintenance in organizational settings. In D. J. Canary & M. Dainton (Eds.), *Maintaining relationships through communication: Relational, contextual, and cultural variations*. Mahwah, NJ: Lawrence Erlbaum and Associates.

Waldron, V., & Kelley, D. (2005). Forgiveness as a response to relational transgression. *Journal of Social and Personal Relationships, 22*, 723–742.

Walker, V. & Brokaw, L. (1995). *Becoming aware*. Dubuque, IA: Kendall Hunt.

Wallace, H. M., Exline, J. J., & Baumeister, R. F. (2008). Interpersonal consequences of forgiveness: Does forgiving deter or encourage repeat offenses? *Journal of Experimental Social Psychology, 44*, 453–460.

Waller, M., & McLanahan, S. S. (2005). "His" and "her" marriage expectations: Determinants and consequences. *Journal of Marriage and Family, 67*, 53–67.

Watson, P. J., Trumpeter, N., O'Leary, B., Morris, R. J., & Culhane, S. E. (2006). Narcissism and self-esteem in the presence of imagined others: Supportive versus destructive object representations and the continuum hypothesis. *Imagination, Cognition and Personality, 25*, 253–268.

Watzlawick, P., Beavin, J. H., & Jackson, D. D. (1967). *Pragmatics of human communication*. New York: Norton.

Weiner, B. (1986). *An attributional theory of motivation and emotion*. New York: Springer-Verlag.

Weiss, R. L. (1984). Cognitive and behavioral measures of marital interaction. In K. Hahlweg & N. S. Jacobson (Eds.), *Marital interaction: Analysis and modification* (pp. 232–252). New York: Guilford.

West, P., & Merriam, L. C. Jr. (1970). Outdoor recreation and family cohesiveness: A research approach. *Journal of Leisure Research, 2*, 251–259.

White, L. K. (1983). Determinants of spousal interaction: Marital structure or marital happiness. *Journal of Marriage and the Family, 45*, 511–519.

Wiemann, J. M. (1977). Explication and test of a model of communicative competence. *Human Communication Research, 3*, 195–213.

Wiemann, J. M., & Backlund, P. (1980). Current theory and research in communicative competence. *Review of Educational Research, 50*, 185–199.

Wiemann, J.M., & Kelly, C.W. (1981). Pragmatics of interpersonal competence. In C. Wilder-Mott & J.H. Weakland (Eds.), *Rigor and imagination: Essays from the legacy of Gregory Bateson* (pp. 283–298). New York: Praeger.

Wieselquist, J. (2009). Interpersonal forgiveness, trust, and the investment model of commitment. *Journal of Social and Personal Relationships, 26*, 531–548.

Wilmot, W. W., & Hocker, J. L. (1991). *Interpersonal conflict*. New York: Brown.

Wilson, S. R. (1990). Development and test of a cognitive rules model of interaction goals. *Communication Monographs, 57*, 81–103.

Wilson, S. R. (2002). *Seeking and resisting compliance: Why people say what they do when trying to influence others*. Thousand Oaks, CA: Sage.

Wilson, S. R., & Putnam, L. L. (1990). Interaction goals in negotiation. *Communication Yearbook, 13*, 374–406.

Wilson, S. R., Aleman, C. G., & Leatham, G. B. (1998). Identity implications of influence: A revised analysis of face-threatening acts and application to seeking compliance with same sex friends. *Human Communication Research, 25*, 64–96.

Winstok, Z., Eisikovits, Z., & Gelles, R. (2002). Structure and dynamics of escalation from the batterers' perspective. *Families in Society, 83*, 129–141.

Witteman, H. (1992). Analyzing interpersonal conflict: Nature of awareness, type of initiation event, situation perceptions, and management styles. *Western Journal of Communication, 56,* 248–280.

Witvliet, C. V. O., Ludwig, T. E., & Vander Laan, K. L. (2001). Granting forgiveness or harboring grudges: Implications for emotion, physiology, and health. *Psychological Science, 121,* 117–123.

Wohl, M. J. A., & McGrath, A. L. (2007). The perception of time heals all wounds: Temporal distance affects willingness to forgive following an interpersonal transgression. *Personality and Social Psychology Bulletin, 33,* 1023–1035.

Worcel, S. D., Shields, S. A., & Paterson, C. A. (1999). "She looked at me crazy": Escalation of conflict through telegraphed emotion. *Adolescence, 34,* 689–697.

Worthington, E. L. (1998). *Dimensions of forgiveness: Psychological research and theological perspectives.* Philadelphia, PA: Templeton.

Worthington, E. L. (1998). The pyramid model of forgiveness: Some interdisciplinary speculations about forgiveness and the promotion of forgiveness. In E. L. Worthington (Ed.). *Dimensions of forgiveness: Psychological research and theological perspectives* (pp. 107–137). Philadelphia, PA: Templeton.

Worthington, E. L. (2005). *Handbook of forgiveness.* London: Brunner-Routledge.

Worthington, E. L., & Scherer, M. (2004). Forgiveness is an emotion-focused coping strategy that can reduce health risks and promote health resilience: Theory, review, and hypotheses. *Psychology and Health, 19,* 385–405.

Worthington, E. L., & Wade, N. G. (1999). The social psychology of unforgiveness and forgiveness and implications for clinical practice. *Journal of Social and Clinical Psychology, 18,* 385–418.

Wyer, R. S., Swan, S., & Gruenfeld, D. H. (1995). Impression formation in informal conversations. *Social Cognition, 13,* 243–272.

Young, M., Denny, G., Young, T., & Luquis, R. (2000). Sexual satisfaction among married women. *American Journal of Health Studies, 16,* 73–84.

Zillman, D. (1988). Congnition-excitation interdependence in aggressive behavior. *Aggressive Behavior, 14,* 51–64.

Zillman, D. (1990). The interplay of cognition and excitiation in aggrevated conflict. In D. D. Cahn (Ed.), *Intimates in conflict: A communication perspective* (pp. 187–208). Hillsdale, NJ: Erlbaum.

Zillman, D. (1993). Mental control of angry aggression. In D. M. Wegner & J. W. Pennebaker (Eds.), *Handbook of mental control* (pp. 370–392). Englewood Cliff, NJ: Prentice Hall.

INDEX